Straight Fro[m the] Horse's Ass

LEE HUGHES

Dedicated to Stan and Mad.

Random House New Zealand Ltd
(An imprint of the Random House Group)

18 Poland Road
Glenfield
Auckland 10
NEW ZEALAND

Sydney New York Toronto
London Auckland Johannesburg
and agencies throughout the world

First published 1996

Printed by Wright and Carman (NZ) Limited, Wellington
ISBN 1 86941 301 6

Contents

Key
>>> Continental Divide
----- My Path
British Colombia
Continental Divide
Water Valley
Calgary
Vancouver
Alberta
Washington
Sweetgrass
Cutbank
Maria's Pass
Great Falls
Helena
Montana
Oregon
Whitehall
West Yellowstone
Yellowstone Park
Idaho
Jackson Hole
Pinedale
Wyoming
Nevada
Salt Lake City
Scottsbluff
Feedlot
San Francisco
Craig
Steamboat Springs
Leadville
Denver
Utah
California
Montrose
Gunnison
Ouray
Las Vegas
Durango
Chama
Grand Canyon
Los Angeles
Santa Fe
Albuquerque
Belen
Arizona
New Mexico
T or C
Las Cruces
Scale
0 50 100 150 200 250
miles
El Paso
Juarez
Mexico
Texas

Introduction

Before you start, there are two things you ought to know.

First, you don't want to believe everything you read in this story. It's mainly true, but there's a couple of whoppers, a white lie or three, a fair amount of top spin, some bullshit and a little exaggeration. I didn't start out that way but I soon discovered that when you're writing your own story, it's easy to leave out all the bits that don't flatter. I've completely destroyed my faith in the accuracy of all autobiographies now that I've airbrushed this.

Secondly, if you're wondering whether it's worth the effort of reading it all, then you might usefully turn to the last page and read the last three words.

Chapter 1

Wherein I make known my discontent with England and fashion bold plans for an unusual journey

It was all Kevin Costner's fault. Him and that damn yellow horse he rode in the movie *Dances With Wolves*. On a dreary winter afternoon in Slough I watched as he and his loyal and intelligent horse pioneered their way into the heart of the magnificent wide-screen west. Confronted by Indians, wolves, evil cavalry and gorgeous orphans, he never hesitated. He and his staunch companion outwitted their opposition and generally were a credit to their old school tie. All in all, man and beast looked to be having a fine old time far from home on a Really Big Adventure.

I was even further from home when I decided to ride down the Rocky Mountains from the northern border of the United States to the southern. I was living and working in a pub outside London. I'd come to work there after visiting a girl in France. She received me with grace and charm. And a boyfriend. A decent enough chap, but what was he doing with the future Mrs Hughes?? There was clearly no need for a third wheel on that bicycle so I took myself off to London to get a job and put some money aside while I figured out what to do now that I was out of love, broke, and cast upon those cold foreign shores.

I did what every Kiwi does when he goes to Britain. I lived in squalor and poverty, drawing on the goodwill of friends until I arranged a loan from home and could live in comfort and debt, drawing on my Visa card (which, by the way, has saved me more times than organised religion. All praise, All praise). Anyway, the next step after bludging a place to stay off your friends for as long as they can stand it, is to get a place that not only pays but also feeds, clothes and houses you.

Prison does that. So do Ye Publick Howses of Olde England. Peopled with a captive audience of cheerful topers they are a perfect environment for loud, boring and penniless antipodeans. I fitted right in.

I arrived in November and by March I was sufficiently financial to slip off for a brief visit to the movies that rainy afternoon. I watched Mr Costner cavorting about the prairie with his loyal and cunning four-footed friend and that really was the cause of everything that followed. Summer was fast approaching and I was looking for something cheap to do for two or three months. I suppose if I'd seen *Braveheart* I'd have headed off to Scotland on vacation but *Dances With Wolves* was an advertisement for the wide open spaces that I couldn't resist. I don't even know how I came to fit it all together in my head, but without any second thoughts I had made up my mind to buy a horse and ride from Canada to Mexico through the Rocky Mountain states. I wanted to tie my spotted hankie on a stick and run away from pub life, pewter skies, red-brick houses and Aussie soaps. I decided I wouldn't object to stumbling across some winsome orphans too.

I'd seen the country at first hand on a six-month holiday the previous year, when I bought a car and drove around America. The land was still largely unfenced, the grass grew just like it had in the movie and it wasn't illegal to ride 2500 miles in your own time, on your own horse. It was damn stupid, of course, but fortunately there's no law against being a dickhead. If there is, then it ain't being enforced.

There was, of course, the small matter of money. Now before you start to draw conclusions about how a person can afford to travel around the world twice per annum on a barman's wages, and then go on holiday for six months a year, I must point out that *I no longer had a girlfriend*. That alone roughly doubled my disposable income. Add to that a pretty gullible Visa card credit manager and Hey Presto! LOADS-AMONEY!

I figured that by 1 July I could save £2000, which at that time was nearly $US3500. Also I would have $US2000 of credit left. Deducting $US1200 for a flight to the US I had roughly enough left to last 46 days at my normal rate of spending in

America if I travelled by car. I didn't think that a horse would cost more to buy or run than a car, so if I went on the cheap I could make it last perhaps 90 days. This sounded a lot better as I reckoned that in three months I could easily ride 2500 miles on a single horse.

Now you have to remember that at this point *I did not know how to ride*. The more horsey type of reader will spot about a thousand really, *really* dumb mistakes in all this, but then I never laid claim to being the smartest bloke to sit a saddle. No, I'm just an averagely dumb city slicker who figured that since he could walk all day at three and a half miles per hour with a 100-pound pack on two legs, then a horse should easily be able to crack along at five to seven miles per hour by virtue of having *twice as many legs!* So there.

These were elementary figurings, (actually 'elementary figurings' is not really the right term, the right term is more like 'wild-ass guesses'), but they led me to believe that 50 miles per day was quite the right speed to see the sights, get to Mexico and still allow a generous amount of time for rest, recreation, side trips, days off and perhaps a little shopping too. What a fuckwit!

I checked the cost of a horse in America with two Canadian girls who worked in the pub and discovered that I could buy a horse, saddle and basic tack for $CA1500 in Canada. Such a horse, I was assured, would get me to Mexico. No doubts at all. Another call to the BNZ Visa Centre, some quick lies and the deed was done.

I had a word with another girl who worked in the pub and she agreed to give me lessons on horse buying, maintenance, troubleshooting, minor repairs and, of course, the delicate art of equitation. Six lessons for £48 seemed fair. What else did I need? Ah, yes. A map. A quick trip to a superior map shop in Piccadilly gave me a pile of guide books (many with coloured pictures) and a sheaf of maps. These delighted me no end. For a start, the place names were both familiar and exotic. Everyone has heard of Denver and Santa Fe and Calgary so to see them on the map is to reassure yourself that you'll not be too far from civilisation and help. Especially when you see them on a 1:10,000,000 scale map. The whole lot are only a

Cruelly misleading cartography.

postage stamp apart which is, I feel, just a tad misleading to a potential explorer.

Surrounding these oases of the twentieth century are the exotic places, Helena, Montana; Truth or Consequences, New Mexico; Jackson Hole, Wyoming; Leadville, Colorado and Pincher Creek, Alberta. Wonderful names for tiny map dots in the thousands of square miles of wild places that separate the modern cities. So on paper it seemed that every few days I'd be able to pull into a town and take a break from the rigours of adventuring. On paper I was never going to be more than a postage stamp away from help. This was true, always assuming that the stamp was on a letter to International Rescue c/o Tracy Island.

By highlighting all the places in the guide books that seemed worth visiting and then plotting them on the map I was able to play a game of continental join-the-dots. Lewis and Clark couldn't have done it better.

That, however, was not the end of the fun with maps. Night after night and on my half Sunday off I would pore over them marking places with romantic and improbable names. I would delve into the books marking more and more things of interest. Most of the reading was from the *Let's Go USA* guide

The gentleman explorer's complete travel library, £19.95ish.

book. Undoubtedly it is the best book for that purpose as it is printed on cheaper newsprint paper which soaks up highlighter ink much better than the higher quality glossy pages of *National Geographic*'s book. Thus the interesting bits stand out from its 1000-odd pages clearly enough to impress the most sceptical of visitors with your diligent research into the minutiae of the area. *Let's Go* is pretty much the Bible of budget travellers and is rivalled only by the *Lonely Planet Guide* published on unfriendly non-absorbent shiny pages.

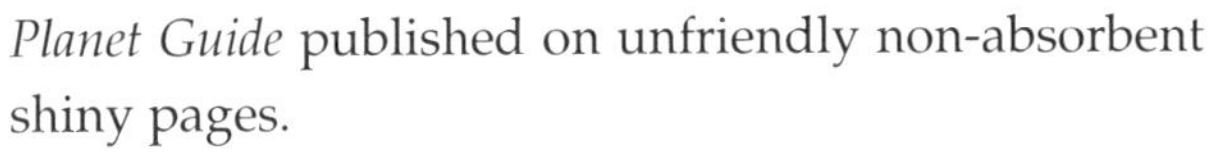

Next, a trip to the local library provided a book for beginners on how to ride. It didn't look that hard, especially from the photos of Angela Rippon on Red Rum. She was neatly dressed in a riding coat, jodphurs and boots and sitting on an English flat saddle. The book even had pictures of western rig saddles and tack. Definitely the biz. Big flashy engraved saddle, lots of silver and wide leather straps. It was a '57 Cadillac to the English Mini Minor saddle. One thing stood out from all the photos of western riders. The hat. Invariably it was big and impressive and reeked of testosterone. However, I am not a hat person in the way that I am not much of a cigar smoker. It's just too showy and stand-outish. I compromised with a visit to a hatter in Jermyn Street. He provided me with a greeny khaki hat similar to the Australian Army slouch hat but a little smaller. A cigarillo rather than a full Corona.

The only thing remarkable about it was its price. Seventy bloody pounds! Still, it was that or a Panama, as the selection of tiles in the capital has shrunk somewhat since the days of empire. No pith helmets, no lemon squeezers, not even a decent fedora in the style of Humphrey Bogart. Suitably equipped as far down as the neck, I set out on my days off to buy up boots, coat, pack, camping gear and other essential stores. Toys in other words.

I began with a mammoth list and pruned it down only when I realised that I couldn't afford it. What I actually began the trip with was about the same as I finished with, except that a lot of the gear was replaced on the way with newer or better quality kit. A few things stayed with me throughout and I treasured them accordingly. Some were valuable, like my Swiss Army knife and my Zippo lighter, others of only sentimental value such as my indestructible plastic one-pint Johnnie Walker Red whisky-cum-water-bottle, bought duty free in Amsterdam on the way to Canada, or my Navy-surplus blue jersey.

One of the best things about a holiday is going to the shops and places that deal with holidays. Certain shops are particularly dangerous for me. Tobacconists, camping equipment suppliers and luggage shops make a fortune off me with virtually no sales pitch at all. Lured into the places by their shamelessly provocative window displays, genuinely interested in the latest Goretex and Kevlar doohickey I am instantly transformed into SUPERSHOPPER. A harmless but expensive addiction to survival aids sees me equipped to survive every conceivable situation that might require the creation of a flame in high winds. (As long as the winds don't blow away the magnesium shavings.) Shop assistants wash their hands with invisible soap when I walk in. Smiles crease their faces. Heads bend to one side and shoulders hunch up. Of course they're obsequious and oily. They love me. Single handedly I am about to pay for *their* holiday.

Cancer? Ha! I cough in zee face of cancer!

Tobacco shops are worse. I don't smoke a whole lot but I only have to smell the aroma of pipe tobacco or cigars and I'm ready to lash out a week's wages on tobacco, cigars, lighters, papers, tins and pouches. The whole ball of wax. Drum tobacco and Camel cigarettes are the poisons of choice. Stationery shops take a similar thrashing too but I limited my choices to a two-colour highlighter and a travel diary.

I got off more lightly than usual in the luggage shop and bought only a small leather hip pouch for about £5. It turned out to be one of the more durable and practical buys. Better than the tin of Oxo cubes that I used about three of, or the half pint of tabasco sauce.

Most of the other bits and bobs weren't hard to get, but a decent pair of boots that would be suitable for both riding and walking just could not be found. I scoured every shoe shop in Oxford Street, Beaconsfield and High Wycombe. Nothing. It was a choice between bloated hiking boots that looked like Jiminy Cricket's shoes on steroids or else elastic-sided riding boots with soles the thickness of aerograms. Hopeless. In the end I stuck with my Swiss suede desert boots. (I know there are no deserts in Switzerland but Bally make a mean boot despite that.) Nice to look at, expensive and *almost* a perfect fit. (That last bit was to cause no end of problems much later on and eventually I was forced to buy some proper walking boots. I think they were made by the people who design mooring buoys for battleships. They were bulbous and ugly and looked like the Jolly Green Giant's fireside slippers.)

Good looking *boots, but at least the hip pouch was a bargain.*

I knew that it was pointless buying any tack as I was able to get it thrown in with the horse for a lot less than I'd pay in the UK. However, I checked my Swiss Army knife and discovered that for the only time in my pocket-knife-owning life *I did not have a thingy for getting the stones out of horses' hooves!* Since I didn't have a horse yet it wasn't an immediate problem. Not that I was short of immediate problems. Oh no.

The problem's name was Ashley and he worked in the pub restaurant as an apprentice chef. He was a nice enough young chap, aged 19, and he wanted to come with me on the ride. Which was OK by me since I figured he would give up the idea when he realised the cost or found he couldn't get time off. Unfortunately he had no trouble coming up with the money and decided he'd quit his job and take a three-month holiday. I said OK but I'll take you only if you get medical insurance, a credit card and riding lessons. He said that was fine and when were we leaving?

I did a few more calculations and decided that 30 June was a good day to begin. I told my boss I was leaving on that day and he said that was fine too, in fact I could leave now if I wanted. Then I said Ashley was coming too and he relented and said I could stay. Good chefs are rare and Ash was a mean hand with a skillet.

All I needed then was to learn how to ride. To be honest, I had been on a horse a few times before. When about 12 years old I had ridden on a dude ranch horse a couple of times and in the army I had ridden on two other pony club horses giving me a total saddle time of about four hours. I figured that since the first caveman had ridden the first cavehorse a lot of work had been done to convince horses that their role in life was to carry the likes of me around. Genetic imprinting should have done a big chunk of the work and if I got lessons then I should have no trouble. After all, I was smarter and I knew it could be done, which was more than Joe Caveman did. I never lacked confidence, that's for sure. What I lacked was wisdom. Specifically, I lacked that measure of wisdom that says that confidence is a poor substitute for experience.

Nevertheless, the first lesson was a roaring success. It didn't involve any actual getting on the horse until I'd learnt how to groom, check and saddle it. The beastie in question was called Panacha and she was a typical riding school hack. Fat, dumb and happy. I spent about half an hour walking around and then trying to get the hang of a rising trot. Not very easy but I didn't fall off and my legs didn't buckle when I got down. I felt quite chuffed after I'd brushed her down and fed her. Claire, who was teaching me, didn't express the least bit of surprise at what I was planning and in fact was envious that she couldn't come too. Until I got to the States, she was almost the only supportive voice I heard. Once I began the ride virtually every single person I met wanted to come with me or do it themselves, but at first all I heard was 'What if . . .?' and 'You won't be able to . . .'

Without knowing anything about me, the customers in the bar were unanimous in saying I wouldn't make it. *I* thought I was a rufty-tufty steely eyed killer trained by Her Majesty's militia to deal with all kinds of wars, riots and end-of-season sales so I was a bit offended by their casual dismissal of my ability. I felt I was *quite* the wild colonial boy. Needless to say, none of the customers (they being in full possession of the wisdom I lacked) had done anything remotely similar before and it seemed to me that their opinions were just about as ignorant as it was possible to be. After a while I ceased to discuss the subject for fear of ridicule.

The rest of the lessons went fairly smoothly. Each Wednesday evening I'd walk two miles down to the stables and bounce around on the back of whatever long-suffering ride they pulled out for me. By the end of my second lesson on the longe, I was able to stay in the rhythm of a rising trot for about ten steps. The longe is a long leading rein that allows the teacher to stand in the middle of a soft-surfaced arena while the horse runs in a large circle around her. By using a whip she can gently keep the horse at a constant speed while the rider concentrates on balancing, posture and so on. The horse, of course, is bored rigid the whole time. It's the equine equivalent of autopilot. Or maybe training wheels. Anyway, by the time the second lesson was over I could balance without stirrups and rise to a trot with them. *Righto then, now let's learn to jump.*

The first couple of hacks had involved galloping across a few fallen logs but all I contributed was to hang on. I wanted to learn how to stay on when jumping fences and streams. Eventually I was able to get over twigs and puddles but I would have needed lots more lessons to clear a five-bar gate. In the long run it didn't matter since even the least perceptive reader will know that the horse has to know how to jump as well as the rider. The horse I bought in Canada didn't, so that was that. We did get good at finding bridges and opening gates but as far as he was concerned jumping was for horses too dumb to find a way round.

By early June it was obvious that Ash was going to come with me no matter what. I tried to get him to read a bit more about the West but he wasn't interested. The James Michener book *Centennial* tells the story of the West better than any textbook but Ash wasn't interested. All he wanted to do was finish the ride and get back home to bullshit the locals about what a hero he was. I was pretty sure that he would be happier talking about it than doing it. That later proved to be true. I didn't much care. I knew I could do the trip without a partner and so I was ready to go it alone. Just like Kevin.

Ashley — utterly cool? — or utterly bewildered?

Since Ash had never travelled to America, I took him to see *Dances With Wolves* to give him an idea of what to expect. The land was easy to gauge but the people weren't. What he could never grasp was that he would be in a heartland of Republican conservatism, where being the son of a wealthy lawyer and having waist-length blond hair might not go down so well. I think he never really believed that there is a kind of person who would take his accent and physical appearance as an open invitation to whack the tar out of him. More than once I was accused of being a faggot with a toy-boy partner. To good ole boys in Alberta and Montana, Ash just had to be as queer as a three-dollar bill. Never having seen the weirdos, techno-trash and pond life that inhabit most big cities in the world they couldn't ever get a fix on Ash, who really was a decent guy who looked perfectly at home at a Metallica concert but who was just a trifle out of place in a ten-gallon hat. It was like Axl Rose walking on to the set of *Gunsmoke* and asking Sheriff Dillon where he could buy an ounce of blow and meet some teenage girls.

By 22 June I had finished my lessons, booked our flight and assembled all my gear. All that remained was to see if Ash could actually ride. We both went down to the stables and I saw the results of Ash's private lessons. It wasn't a pretty sight. He was scared of his horse and had no balance. He didn't control the horse at all, he was just a passenger and after about five minutes he fell off. He got back on right away (full marks for effort) but I could tell he was gritting his teeth and wishing it was over. Nevertheless he was determined to come and nothing I could do at that stage would change that. Months earlier he'd announced to his friends that he was going and had already quit his job. It was obvious he couldn't back out even though he must have known he was going to have a tough time on horseback until he got the hang of it.

Now some of you folks might think that it showed remarkable determination and self-confidence to set out on this kind of thing without really knowing how to ride, but what it really calls for is a degree of dumb equalled only as far as I can see by people who bet on professional wrestling. I guess it's heartwarming to know that there's still room in the world for blue-chip pillocks like me. Without us there'd be nothing in the human interest columns of the newspapers.

On the second sunny day in the summer month of June (which was also the last day of June), Ash and I boarded a flight to Amsterdam where we connected with a KLM flight to Vancouver. At duty free in Holland I bought the famous whisky/water bottle and Ash bought a camera the same as mine. An indestructible Olympus AF10 with only one button to push. Ideal. For the record, at the start of our search for something to do on our summer holidays we had about $US500 and $CA2000 each. Out of this we planned to buy horses, tack and saddlebags as well as feed, clothe, shoe, doctor and entertain ourselves and our horses for three months. As it turned out that wasn't a bad budget for three months. The only thing wrong was that the trip would take a year.

Chapter 2

I DISCOVER THAT ASH IS ALARMED BY ALL FORMS OF TRANSPORT FASTER THAN A WALKING FRAME

We landed in Vancouver in the early morning. It was a gorgeous summer day — warm breeze, blue sky, clean air. Everything the start of a vacation ought to be. The holiday feeling hit me like the first wave on a surf beach. I had no job, no wife and family, no appointments for the next three months and I had all the money I'd need. Bliss.

In the fifties and sixties in Alaska the US Air Force noticed that in the long sunless winters, many of their technicians were experiencing mood changes and suffering minor illnesses that seemed to have a psychosomatic basis. Eventually those symptoms graduated into depression, alcoholism, jazz music, etc. They cured it by issuing sun lamps. The results were great. The staff went from feeling miserable in winter and cheerful in summer to being happy to stare at radar screens all year round. Powerful stuff that northern sun.

Vancouver — blue skies for free, brown liquor $1.25 a shot.

They named the condition Seasonal Affective Disorder or SAD. And sad was what I was in England with not enough sunlight, so I turned my face up to the sun and let it soak in. I could feel all the frustrations of the previous nine months being burned away and I was standing there with a dopey self-satisfied grin on my face when Shannon appeared.

Shannon was a friend of ours

who had worked in the bar in England and who had returned home to Canada a few months before. Ash had written and asked her to meet us at the airport. We planned to stay a night at her apartment before catching a Greyhound to Calgary where we had arranged to look at some horses on a ranch nearby.

The rest of that day was terrific. Shannon took us to meet her family and we went to a barbecue that afternoon with her. Later that night we loafed around her favourite bars and got blitzed on shooters. Liquor was a dollar and a quarter a shot so the whole deal was pretty cheap and we all got thoroughly immunised against common sense in six separate bars. Ash and I crashed at Shannon's apartment but it took me hours to get to sleep. Too many things to think about. It was like the night before the start of a holiday when I was a kid. You lay awake half the night and then you just couldn't sit still when you got up.

We spent the first few hours of the day sightseeing around the city and shopping for a few little bits and pieces. While we were having a quiet beer in a shopping mall, Shannon slipped away and when she got back she had a present for me. It was my birthday in two days' time and even though she hardly knew me from a bar of soap she had gone and done this sweet thing. The present was a T-shirt and I kept it for the entire trip. It was just a taste of the generosity that was to come from virtually everyone I met.

By 5.30 pm Ash and I had collected all our gear and Shannon dropped us off at the Greyhound station for our trip across the Rockies to Calgary. The onboard movie was *Bill and Ted's Excellent Adventure* but it wasn't as interesting as our own, so we talked through it until we fell asleep. When I woke up later that night the window on which I was resting my face was freezing my cheek through the sweater I had bundled up for a pillow. I looked outside and saw that we were in the heart of the mountains. The steep sides of the valley rose up above us like a cliff and covering the slopes all the way to the top were firs, still standing knee deep in the snow. They were a greenish-black wall against the white snow. The sky was a deep purple-blue like the ceiling of the Civic Theatre in

Auckland where I used to stare at the roof more than the movie. With no clouds in the sky and no moon yet, I could just see the first winking stars if I craned my neck and looked right up to the top of the window. We were climbing steadily up a river valley on the Trans-Canada highway. The bus purred on and the only other sound was a tiny scratching from a walkman. I'm sure I was smiling when I dropped off to sleep again.

When we stopped at dawn at a café on the eastern edge of the high country I stretched and sucked in huge lungfuls of the coldest, cleanest air I'd breathed in months. The sun was just coming up over the great plains and we could see from the east an ocean of golden light. Black shadows on the near side of the valleys were all that broke the huge glistening sea that grew each minute and engulfed the prairies. The tops of the low hills were washed by a tide of molten gold that slipped around the sides of the mounds to form again, ready to bathe the next hill in golden syrup. The light seemed to gently push the cold air ahead of it, across the plains, over the foothills and upwards into the mountains until the breeze reached Ash and me standing 2000 feet above the prairie, faces into the sun, basking like two scarecrows.

Still tired and jetlagged, our bodies reluctantly woke up, and as we wound down out of the mountains, Ash and I discussed what we would do in Calgary. The plan was to check into a youth hostel, call the ranch that we had contacted in England and then go out and look at horses. We also had to see if it was still possible to buy saddlebags. If not we would have to find someone to make them for us. Then we would load up and ride off south to Mexico. As far as plans go, it had the cardinal virtue of simplicity. No one ever accused us of weighing it down with a mass of detail. Nevertheless, there were a few little bits that did concern us. For instance, what do you do with a horse at night? Could we find enough water for the horses to carry us across the deserts? What would we do if a horse got sick way out in the backblocks? What if they broke loose and ran away? Just little things like that. As it turned out, I was right to worry and right to plan for each eventuality. I don't recall Ash ever asking about anything like that. Either he trusted me completely or he assumed that a horse was like a car. Park up at night. Gas it up each day and get it serviced every 10,000 miles. If it breaks down call the AA. If it gets stolen, claim insurance. No problem.

By 11 am we were in Calgary, Alberta. Home of the 1988 Winter Olympics, the Calgary Stampede and oil capital of the prairies. A neat, clean, modern city laid out on a user-friendly grid of streets. Home also to one of the world's best youth hostels just a few blocks from downtown. We bought memberships in the YHA, checked in and rang the ranch. We spoke to Bill Nugent's wife and got directions to the ranch in Water Valley which was about 60 miles north-west. I had called Bill from England after being given his name by a friend of one of the Canadian girls in the bar. I had also called the local Quarter Horse Association and several outfitters, all through international directory enquiries, but the most helpful voice was Bill's so we picked him as the first choice to deal with. Not to mention the cheapest. The Quarter Horse Association recommended . . . a quarter-horse! A purebred one no less! Which wouldn't cost much over $5000! A snip! Of course it's not surprising that they would. If you call a Mercedes dealer he's hardly likely to recommend a Toyota.

Bill hadn't laughed at our ideas although he did say that we needed packhorses to carry our gear. I said we only wanted a saddle horse as we were going to travel light. What I really meant was that the budget wouldn't stretch to two horses, even if I knew how to lead a packhorse, which I didn't. Now, as I found out later, that is not like saying to a car dealer that you want a motorbike because you don't need the capacity of a car. It's more like setting out to walk the equator wearing only one shoe. It's possible, but it's also pretty stupid. Bill, to his enormous credit, never said just how stupid he thought we were. To this day I think he figured that we would give up before we got to the US border and so the horses wouldn't die of overwork. Well, he was nearly right.

The next step was to check the bus schedule to see how long we'd have to wait for a bus to Water Valley. We didn't have to wait long at all. There were none. However, a bus did run downtown to a Rent-a-Car place that gave us a nice little yellow five-litre Chevrolet Sunbird. Or something. It was definitely yellow and it definitely could scat. Mmmmmm mmmmm. I got behind the wheel and eased it out ever so gently on to the right side of the road. I pootled through traffic all the way to the Trans-Canada highway. Then I just turned up the radio and put my foot in the carburettor. Ash didn't speak at all for about 30 miles and then he just let go of the dash long enough to pull down the sun visor. I don't know why, as he'd had his eyes shut up till then. Ash has a kind of conservative attitude to speeding and it showed in the way he was braking in advance of me on the bends. He refused to tune the radio and leant into the corners.

We whizzed along Route 22 to Bill's ranch and eventually pulled up in front of the house. It was a typical family ranch. Big barn, big horse trailers, big pick-up trucks and a big arena. The last-mentioned was a large, dirt-floored hangar big enough to practise roping and suchlike. Bill's son was inside practising on a couple of tired-looking calves before he entered the Calgary Stampede in a few days' time. Other people were watching and all of them looked to be chewing tobacco. They all had hats, check shirts, jeans and cowboy boots or else some kind of footwear that looked like a cross between a high-heeled lace-up lady's boot from the 1890s and a pair of industrial safety golf shoes. They even had a tassel on the front. Weirdest things I'd ever seen. Never did find out what they were called but they only ever showed up on proper working ranches. Never saw a dude or a truck driver in them at all. I was staring at a pair when Marcie introduced herself. Marcie is Bill's daughter and he'd told her to show us the horses he'd got ready. Bill was busy when we arrived but he showed up soon after. He too was tall, lean, tanned and wore a hat. Even his hat was tall and tanned and lean. I liked him although I knew that we'd probably get fleeced by him. He was only too helpful as I guess I would be if I met a couple of pigeons like we were. We explained that we weren't very good riders and Marcie looked at us like we were lying, because it was obvious to her that only *real* experienced horsemen would ever consider riding to Mexico. She wouldn't dream of it, but she'd only been riding since she was three.

She showed us seven different horses and we liked the look of five of them. Two whites, two browns and a black one. The whites were actually greys of Arab ancestry and the browns were actually a bay and a chestnut but we didn't know that until later. The black was technically a brown and one of the two greys had two white hoofs. Or hooves. The other grey/white had one white hoof. Or hoove. The non-white horses were all quarter-horses and the whites were one quarter quarter-horse and one was half Arab and a quarter thoroughbred and the other was three-quarters Arab and full-blood stupid. There were three females, and two were geldings, and the man who drove the yellow car smoked Camels and lived next door to the man with the baseball cap who drank whisky. Now, who lived in the red house and how much should he pay for his horse?

Your basic horse — sticker price $1500. (Guess what I paid?)

The test rides were pretty straightforward in the sense that the horses did exactly that. None appeared to have mastered the concept of turning. Or slowing down. From the first moment it was obvious that we were not in charge. All the horses just took off if we so much as clicked our teeth. What saved us from looking complete idiots were the saddles.

The moment we sat in the saddles we began to understand the difference between English and western riding. The English flat saddle is a very small affair with no contours. It has no high thingy in front to stop you flying over the handlebars and it has no big seat-back to stop you going arse over tip if the horse pulls a wheelie. The cantle and pommel (for those, dear reader, are their names) are reduced to mere swells in the little seat. It's as well equipped with safety restraints as a bicycle seat and is about the size of a decent omelette.

The western saddle, however, is a different matter. At the front it has a pommel (or cantle, I still don't know which is which) that is shaped like a small bollard. This consists of the 'swells' which are like the shoulders. They support the 'horn' which is exactly like a bollard that you tie up ships with. In this instance you tie up cows with your lariat. At the other end you have a high-backed seat that is similar to the kind of shaped chair that Formula One racing drivers and astronauts have. The two ends are connected underneath to a chassis called a 'tree'. This is steel or fibreglass and is the backbone of the saddle. It is strong enough to stop a 1000-pound steer moving at 20 miles per hour. In spite of this, occasionally a tree gets broken. Probably when a cowboy has a few beers and rolls his horse or hits a real tree at high speed. The seat of the saddle is padded and contoured to suit a range of sizes. The saddle is measured in inches from the horn to the back of the seat. A large saddle is 16 inches or more. A small one is about 14 inches. Saddles also come in kids' sizes, as we were to discover later. Hanging off the sides of the saddle were the stirrups. These were big but light 'U'-shaped ones about two inches wide and made of fibreglass and rawhide. The stirrup leathers (which the stirrups hang off) were about four or five inches wide and were engraved like the rest of the saddle. The whole shebang weighed in at around 30 pounds as opposed to an English flat saddle at about half that. Sitting on a flat saddle is like perching on a pikelet secured to the horse with garters whereas a western rig saddle is as comfy as a Lazy-boy armchair lashed down with hawsers. And assuming that it didn't start bucking, who could fall out of an armchair?

Ash could, that's who. On the second ride Ash was atop a tall, rangy-looking brown who knew not the meaning of 'Whoa, motherfucker, whoa!' He took Ash straight at a low pile of hay at a full gallop and jumped it. When he came down, Ash was still on him but the damage was done. That critical trust between man and beast was breached. Ash was hauling back on the reins like he was pulling in two tons of fish and he lurched from side to side like a deranged metronome. The brown was pounding up the field towards the gate to the yards. The classic Hollywood-style low branch intervened and Ash ducked down to avoid it. While Ash's eyes were still closed the brown sidestepped an imaginary tackle and Alakazam! An empty saddle!

To be honest I was surprised he stayed on over the jump and he did well to hit the ground so hard and not injure himself. He bounced and rolled a fair distance though, and for a while he was ominously still. Only his hand moved. I think he was looking for a weapon. Whether to use it on me or the horse I don't know, but to be fair, who wouldn't laugh at something like that?

Ash deserves a lot of credit for walking back to the yards and gathering up the reins like nothing had happened. He rode the brown back out and kept it under control for the rest of the test ride which was basically what I do when I buy a car. Go, stop, left and right turns, a quick burst away from the lights and a good run with it fully wound out. The only thing I left out was a handbrake turn. The horses all wanted to run like hell, which was a bit alarming after being exposed to the riding-school blobs. It was all we could do to turn a corner or stop before a fence. They were probably all very good horses for experienced cowboys, but even a good English rider would have had trouble with them. As we found out later, ranch horses are trained to go as soon as you get a foot in the stirrup. To climb on board is not possible. You have to leap up and simultaneously poke your left foot in the stirrup, grab the horn with your left hand (which is already holding the reins) and fling your right leg over the saddle. By the time your bum has hit the seat, you're doing 20 miles an hour and your right foot is still poking the horse in the ribs while you feel for the other stirrup. All this happens in the time it takes to change gear in a car. After a while it's fun to take off in a Le Mans start, but at first it's a bit of a trial. If you want to try this trick, just run up a 'Down' escalator and you'll know what I mean.

There isn't much more to say about the test rides because there wasn't anything more to do. We figured that if we didn't like the way they rode, then there wasn't any point in examining them more closely. Of course we barely knew a fetlock from a footlocker so by the end of the day we'd done everything we could think of.

We returned the horses and thanked Marcie for helping. We said we'd be back the next day to check out the five we liked. On the way back to Calgary we listed again the items of tack that we'd need and tried to estimate whether our money would last until we reached Mexico. After dinner in the hostel, Ash and I gave a group of 11 backpackers a lift downtown where we had a couple of beers and practised bullshitting them about riding to Mexico. You can easily fit 13 in any rental car but getting in and out took longer than the drive to the bar. The rest of the evening was spent writing up diaries. At the start of any trip I begin a diary and spend at least half an hour per night keeping it up to date. This effort always decreases at a rate of knots, until by the tenth week I am able to update an entire action-packed week in just 30 seconds and three lines.

It was hard to sleep that night. Partly it was the strain of several weeks' preparation building to a head and resulting in my handing over about $2000 the next day for a horse that could have anything from whooping cough to leprosy. How the hell would I know? There's no AA checklist for buying a horse. The best I could do was get a vet to check him out. That was necessary anyway, as I'd checked with the Canadian and American embassies about taking a horse across the border when I was planning things back in March. The only restriction was that I had to have a valid Coggins test certificate for equine infectious anaemia to show to the vet at the border. A Coggins test requires blood to be drawn and analysed and the horse is then deemed free for three months. However, the certificate must be less than a month old when it is presented. Bill agreed to mail the certificate to us when we got to the border as the results would take a few days to be ready and we planned to buy the horses and shoe them the next day and then leave the day after.

There was a bit of jetlag to sleep off and a lot of worry as well. One worked against the other and eventually I flaked out at about 2 am. As I dropped off I remember I still had one nagging thought. What do I do with the horse at night? I checked my memory but I didn't recall Kevin Costner having that problem.

Chapter 3

In which we buy the horses and learn the importance of holding on to them at all times

July 3rd was a beauty. Blue sky and warm breeze. The kind of day I remember as clear as can be, even now. All the other details about where we bought the saddlebags and tack, the food, the postcards and so on, are pretty hazy, but I can remember the sun and the dust and The Great Trial Ride and Horse Chase that followed our shopping trip.

All up, we spent about $270 on two pairs of saddlebags (one large, one small: because they didn't have two the same size), two brushes (one big, one little, because . . .) two combs, two sponges, two hoof picks, one tub of hoof grease, two nosebags, one canvas water bag, two pairs of gloves, one poncho, a couple of maps and a whole bunch of food.

By noon we were headed for the ranch where we planned to ride the two greys. We picked them because they were the least crazed. And that's all that decided the matter. We had a very strong feeling that if we could get the others pointed in the right direction then we'd get to Mexico in three weeks instead of three months but there was just as much chance that we'd break our necks inside three minutes. The greys were just barely manageable but that was what sold me. We never planned to look too hard anywhere else as we knew we'd only get shown the dregs anyway. Plus, Bill promised to help kit us out in tack for next to nothing, as well as sort out the Coggins test and shoeing and all that stuff. All in all I figured that any horse was as good as the next one as far as we could tell, so it didn't matter which one we picked. If we were offered Bonecrusher and Phar Lap we wouldn't have known them from Pogy and Mr Ed. We were blind men in the land of the perfectly sighted and we knew it. So did Bill.

Marcie had the two greys tied up ready for us. We took them out on to the road and headed off at a walk. The gravel road was dusty and the air was heavy with pollen and drifting seeds and spider webs and little flying things. The saddles were hot in the sun and the horses' heads were drooping down. We set off to ride around a square mile and all went well as we turned the first corner. A dog trotted out of a drain by the road and sniffed around the horses' feet. They weren't the least bit bothered and continued to amble along. There didn't seem to be any urgency to the day after all the rushing around buying things in the morning. The horses seemed pretty relaxed so I took the opportunity to pull a cigarette out of my pack. All went well while I nervously held the reins in one hand and lit up with the other.

I mentioned earlier that I carried a Zippo lighter. Non-Zippo owners may not know that when you flip open the lid of a Zippo the wee metal spring hinge makes a tiny 'ting' noise. This is not the sort of noise that you ordinarily notice. It wouldn't stop all conversation in a crowded bar for instance but it nearly stopped me for good. That 'ting' about frightened the bejesus out of my horse and he took off like a scalded cat. Ash's beast followed at a dead run and we headed for the next corner with stones flying from under our horses' hooves while the dog did the duty of a cheerleader and egged the whole sorry procession on with joyful barks.

I slapped a hand to my hat and stood up in my stirrups. Ash did the same and we both got a death grip on the horns of our saddles. The speed was appalling in view of the gravel beneath us that flew from the hooves like shrapnel. We didn't dare turn the horses off the road for fear of hidden holes in the long grass and we couldn't slow them down. Without an anchor or a gun we had no choice but to hang on for certain death.

We cut the next half mile out in about a minute flat and by the time we turned the second corner the nags were stretched right out. The dog was still full of bounce and looked so happy that I figured it wouldn't expect me to choke it to death when we stopped. Horse first and then dog. Clearly they both deserved to die, since the whole terrible mess looked suspiciously like a double act. Fortunately, the next stretch of road was slightly uphill and Pegasus the turbo-horse started to slow a little. Ash got control first and we started to wind down a bit. I was so relieved to be back inside the speed limit, that I decided to hold off on killing the dog, but I did plan to get a gun at the first opportunity.

By the end of the next quarter mile we had them trotting along well enough to risk turning on to the verge. A gate led into a large field which would take us back to the ranch road. I opened it and held the horse while Ash rode through. We followed a stock track alongside the fence until we were halfway back to the ranch road. At the next dividing fence, I experimented with dropping the reins while I opened the gate and my horse ambled through after Ash and then stood grazing while I closed the gate and mounted up. That seemed pretty good, and so a short distance further on we decided to give them a thorough examination.

We began by adjusting the stirrup length on the saddles as my legs were too bent and my knees were starting to hurt. Then we went over them slowly checking for swelling and tenderness. We picked up their hooves with a bit of trepidation lest they drive out a leg and launch us into next week. (Until a horse or a cow has fired a hoof into your leg, you only *think* you know what pain is. Pain can be many shapes and sizes, but for me it came in a small hoof-shaped package and was always delivered by Fastpost.) The legs seemed OK and they had the right number of bones, so we judged that they would get us to Mexico. As added insurance, we counted them and between them they had eight legs which was essential if my calculations about the daily rate of travel were to be upheld.

We decided to buy the horses. I thought it would be cute to have a matched pair of names for them as they were so alike in appearance. I thought of Salt and Pepper as well as Sugar and Spice. Strangely, Grumpy and Dopey did not spring to mind at that time. Ash was on the mare and I had the gelding, so he picked Sugar and I was happy with Spice. And that was how he got his name. Later on he would learn to answer to 'Old Fool' and 'Goddamityousonavabitch' (which is an Indian word meaning 'beautiful horse-friend') as well as learn to come when I whistled (but only if he was going that way anyway).

Coming to a small swampy patch, we hesitated to ride the horses into it as we weren't sure what might happen. After a lot of fiddling about by standing on wobbly clumps of grass that poked up, we decided to ride across fairly quickly. Spice splashed in without too much bother but Sugar hung back and Ash had to kick her on to make her go through. They splashed plenty of mud up at us and, once on the other side, they wanted to run again. We managed to give them a good blast and then pulled them up to a walk before the last gate that led us on to the road.

It was a 'Taranaki' gate — just a menacing section of barbed-wire fence attached at one end by two or three loops of wire around the hinge post. The post at the other end is dragged across the gap to the fence post which has two loops of wire on it. The bottom of the gate post goes into one loop and the other loop is hooked over the top of the post. In theory. Getting the posts close enough to hook the top loop can be a real struggle and usually requires two hands and a couple of big herniating heaves. Frequently it falls on you and scratches you and the wire loop traps your fingers. Once it's top-looped, that holds the wobbly fence up fairly straight. An improved version has a rope instead of a top loop. That is much better as the loose rope is wrapped around the gate post and then it is pulled tight like a pulley and half-hitched off, which requires less effort and gives a tighter gate. However, when you build a gate, you might not have any spare rope handy but you've always got wire for loops, so a lot of Taranaki gates are the nasty aggressive types that are lacking only a large lump of cheese in the middle.

I had been lulled into a false sense of security by Spice and so, as I pulled the gate open, I dropped the reins and expected that he would stand still like they do in the movies. No such luck. Spice didn't know what ground-hitching was, so he stepped through the open gate and turned for home. I fumbled with the gate, it bit me, tore my shirt, caught my fingers and I cursed and heaved and generally bust a gut trying to close it. I told Ash to grab my horse. Spice stepped out just a fraction faster than Ash, in the way that people do when they think they're being followed. He kept just ahead of Ash until I finished closing the gate and then, when he saw I'd done that, he whickered and lit out for home like a blue streak. I knew it was hopeless trying to run after him so I yelled at Ash to ride like hell and head him off. Ash took off at a glacial pace and I watched with a sinking heart as Spice effortlessly evaded capture. Ash compounded the error by coming up on the wrong side of Spice and thus steering him back out into the middle of the road instead of into a fence where he could be turned back or stopped. This wouldn't have mattered much except for the bus.

A little yellow school bus crested the rise and seemed to pause in astonishment as the whole sorry parade thundered down the road towards it throwing up a steady stream of gravel, sweat and bad language. A riderless horse trailing his reins, followed by a brainless rider bouncing and swaying on top of a lunatic horse that crabbed sideways as it gasped its way up the road at evolutionary speed. In its wake, a panting and hysterical pedestrian watching the prelude to a lawsuit of biblical proportions. I could just imagine what would result from a high-speed meeting between a manic horse with a death wish and the 4th grade class of Water Valley. It was mid-summer and the vacation was in full swing. That bus *had no right to be there.*

Incredibly, the bus seemed to sidestep in perfect coordination with Spice, just as you do when you try to dodge past someone and keep moving to the same side as them. Ash was possibly unaware of the drama as by then he was fully preoccupied with staying in the saddle. It was the metronome thing again. The full horror was shared only by me, Spice and the bus, but especially the bus driver, who stood to collect 900 pounds of prime equine steak square in the face if she misread the next move. Spice dropped his head, the bus driver braced herself and I prayed. Fortunately, there was a meeting of the minds and, in the split second remaining, the bus swerved east, the horse swerved west and I began life as a Catholic.

The bus passed in a blur of open mouths and dust as I tried to pull my hat down over my head and into my boots. By the time I looked up again, Spice had turned into the ranch gate, Ash had caught up and I was winded and planning to renege on a certain pledge made under extreme duress.

With a 'cat that got the cream' smile, my horse was standing casually chewing on a blade of sweet grass as I lumbered up to him and grabbed the reins. I gave Ash a burst about the smart way to ride a horse down, but he forbore telling me about the smart way to lead a horse through a gate. Ash was always a gentleman. I hopped up on top of Spice and nonchalantly rode into the deserted yard. The testing was over. I couldn't fault the horses' wind and stamina, they were willing and would probably be biddable once they calmed down a bit, or perhaps broke a leg or two. All in all, I think we were getting about what we could afford, which was about 50% more than we could handle. The rest of the deal was pretty smooth.

We picked out some comfy saddles and Bill lined us up with all the other tack we needed. The saddles were a huge improvement over the English ones we had ridden, but mine had a small fault that would only become apparent much later on. The bridles were worn over one ear and were very light and well worn in, the bits were jointed in the middle and had small copper inserts to help the horse salivate. They looked a bit ferocious to me and seemed able to apply a fair bit of leverage, but I was assured that they were gentle on the mouth. The reins were split and the halter and lead rope were made of nylon. A split rein is one that is not joined together and running from one side of the horse's head to the other. Instead, it is two reins that are held together in the rider's hand. He drops the reins, they drag on the ground instead of lying across the horse's shoulders or neck. That is good for cowboys but I wasn't used to it so I tied them together with a granny knot.

We unloaded a lot of the food we had brought and took our packs and tried to fit them behind the saddles. As soon as we did it we realised that with or without a frame, the packs would never accommodate themselves to the shape of a horse's rear, so I decided to replace them with duffel bags that we'd seen in a shop in Calgary. Of course we tried the saddlebags as well but both horses were unused to such a load and showed their objections by starting and stamping and snorting in their stalls. After calming them down we decided that the full dress rehearsal would have to wait until we were ready to leave the next day.

I handed over the money for the horses and tack and we watched the horses being shod. After that, we loaded them up into an eight-horse trailer and took them to the vet for a check and a Coggins test. That all went very well and when I asked how old the horse was, the vet licked his lips with a forked tongue, glanced sideways at Bill and assured me the horse was 'seven or eight judging by his teeth'. Well, Spice must have been wearing dentures because the rest of him was at least 12. I remained ignorant of that black lie until many miles later when a vet from a neutral corner correctly picked him as a teenager. (Later on when people asked how old he was, I'd say that 'the journey's aged him because he was eight when I bought him but now he's twelve'.)

Privately I told Spice we were bound for Mexico over the next three months and his eyes narrowed. He looked at me with a face like a bulldog licking piss off a thistle. Not impressed.

That completed our chores so we left a pile of stuff at the ranch and set off back to the hostel. I offered Ash the chance to drive home but he turned it down. I couldn't understand how any normal 19-year-old male would turn down the chance to drive a V8 on the open road, especially a rental that you can really flog without a guilty conscience. That too would later be a problem for me. We sizzled back to town at record speed.

The following day, we bought the sausage-shaped duffel bags, returned the car, caught a bus to within 20 miles of the ranch and then shouldered our packs and prepared to hitch a ride. Half-way there it absolutely bucketed down and gave us a cold soaking before we could get our coats on.

It was 4 July and I was 30 years old. After several subtle hints like, 'Did you know it was my birthday?' and 'I'm a year older today,' Ash finally said, 'Oh, er, happy birthday' and promised me he'd make me some Oxo tea to celebrate. Good-oh. Shortly after that we got a ride. By 3 pm we had covered

D-Day, H-Hour, Ground Zero, whatever. 0 miles down, 3500 to go.

all but six miles of the distance so we phoned the ranch and Bill's son came and picked us up.

As was to be expected, everyone at the ranch turned out to see us off and were mightily surprised to see us easily climb aboard our overloaded mounts. The horses were nervous and uneasy as the saddlebags rubbed against their hindquarters and that made them think we were kicking them on. Bill took a photo of us just as we were leaving. I have it still and it is hugely different from the later shots of me riding the drift fence in Wyoming. For a start, I'd never put so much weight on a single horse now and I can't believe I didn't break my knees riding with such short stirrups. The saddle was a boy's saddle of about 13 inches and although it felt good after an English saddle, it was a bum-buster compared to the one I'd get later. It was also a single rig saddle and consequently had no ideal place to tie the load on to. We managed as best we could but it was a long way from perfect.

I also have a photo of Bill taken at the same time. His expression quite clearly says, 'I bin round the world twice, bin to three state fairs, two barn raisings, and a hanging, but I ain't never in my whole life seen nuthin' like this before.'

His son's cheery smile says, 'Wish I was going with you' (or perhaps 'This I gotta see') and their friend's look of surprised dismay just says, 'You jest cain't never tell what's gonna come down the pike next can ya?' Everyone I ever met after that registered all three expressions sooner or later and often simultaneously.

Horse dealers, all honest and upright men.

We waved goodbye and rode the horses slowly out the gate and turned south. By constantly checking them we prevented the unfamiliar saddlebags from causing a stampede as we walked slowly down the road. Our plan was to camp at about 6 pm at the first suitable place we saw. That turned out to be a camp ground about two miles away from the ranch. It took us an hour to get there which should have set alarm bells ringing in my head about my ETA in Mexico, but I put it down to the constant stopping to adjust the load. In particular, the duffel bags kept sliding from side to side and, when we went to a trot, everything thumped about so much that we pulled up short and settled for a walk.

The camp ground was half a mile from the road and included a river. As we rode up to the gate, a car containing the attendant who collected the fees was leaving. The driver looked slightly familiar but it wasn't till we had been talking for a couple of minutes that she revealed that the other job she

Happy Trails.

had was driving a little yellow school bus each day. I winced. She grinned at me and I weakly smiled back, while hoping for the earth to swallow me up. She told me the kids hadn't seen anything like it in their lives and looked forward to seeing more. 'It was better than the wild cow milking contest,' she said. We were embarrassed with a capital 'Cringe'.

Chapter 4

We learn more about holding on to horses and discover fresh things to worry about

'Worry' is the word to describe the first few days of that trip. It started the next morning when the horses wouldn't drink. It lasted all day and into the next night when they still wouldn't. All day it bugged me. Even when we stopped at noon at a little country store to buy rope for a high-line and the men on the porch said, 'Don't worry,' I couldn't stop stewing. Why wouldn't they drink? It was over 24 hours since they'd had a drop. Never again would they go so long without quenching their thirst. The answer, I still believe, was Intimidation.

Spice knew I'd be too ignorant to know that there was nothing to worry about. A horse can easily go 24 hours without a drink and the only effect is to scare the hell out of a tyro like me. Spice was just trying it on. He was in a pet because he didn't go back to the ranch for a nice feed and a roll in the dust after a hot afternoon's ride, so when I led him to water at night and in the morning and again at night, he was sulking. He could see I was worrying and so he refused to drink or do anything reasonably. Threats and Intimidation.

He wouldn't stand still while I saddled him, or while I climbed on. He wouldn't walk. He wanted to trot. When he trotted, he got scared of the saddlebags and galloped. When he galloped, I got scared and pulled him up. When I turned round in the saddle to straighten the gear, he'd get startled and trot again which would set the cycle once more. He couldn't keep to a walk and so all day we suffered from *gaitus interruptus*.

I didn't dare do anything as silly as light a cigarette on his back that day, let alone glance at a map or even remove my hat to wipe my brow without planning the whole operation with enormous care. At every movement, he'd start, and then I'd panic a bit and pull him up. No wonder he was uptight and cranky by the time we stopped to buy rope.

High-lined for a siesta.

The idea was that I'd tie a length of rope at ground level between two trees and then tie Spice's lead rope to it so he could walk up and down it and graze when we stopped for the day or at lunchtime. The little store had only thin nylon rope but, since I had no idea how easily a horse could snap a rope like that, I bought 100 feet of it for Ash and me. The men on the porch suggested that I tie it at head height so that the horses could walk under it safely and also not get their feet tangled up in it. That's what a high-line is and that's one thing you can do with horses at night.

Another thing is to hobble them. The hobbles are like soft-padded handcuffs and can be made from leather, rope, nylon webbing, or even metal. You put them around the horses' front legs and that allows them to take very small steps, or big bounding leaps. Using the leaping method, an experienced horse can get along at a fair old clip and can cover plenty of distance. I later heard of a dude ranch horse that covered 60 miles across rivers and streams that way and finally turned up at the owner's gate two weeks later.

Hobbles can look a bit cruel but they aren't at all painful and, after a while, a horse can get the hang of them pretty well. To begin with, though, they look like they're anchored to the ground. Sugar never got the measure of hobbles and finally she and we parted company because of it. It was to be several more days before we could find a place that sold hobbles, so meanwhile we were stuck with the high-line.

The third option is to put them on a picket rope. That requires a large open area and a 30 foot length of one-inch soft rope. A big stake is driven down to ground level and the rope is fixed to it. Usually a metal stake with a loop on the top is used. The other end goes to a single cuff that goes around one foreleg. That leaves the horse free to roam in a big circle. The only catch is that a horse like Spice would occasionally get the rope tangled into a big cat's cradle around his feet and would then bellow at you to untangle him. That was less than hilarious at 2 am on a frosty night.

Since neither of us could tie a single knot that was reliably safe, both Ash and I took ages to tie the high-line off to two convenient trees about 50 feet apart. I used to tie a bowline type of thing with a granny knot or six to back it up. Ash tied a bow and then double tied it for safety. Most mornings, Ash would forget to collect his high-line and there'd be another delay while he untangled the knot. Each horse had its own line so they wouldn't get twisted up with each other. By moving the line a couple of times each evening, it was possible to give the animals a fair amount of grass to graze, but still nowhere near enough to satisfy their needs or to provide the right variety.

'No photos while I'm eating, please.'

A horse will pick and choose the type of grass it wants to eat and, like humans, will change its diet as the mood takes it. It's best to let it just pick whatever it wants, but that usually wasn't possible for us. I had asked Bill how to ensure that the horses wouldn't eat poisonous plants and he had looked at me with a pitying expression and said, 'Don't worry. They know what to eat.' And they did.

Naturally, we worried whether we had loaded them up with too much gear, so each day when we groomed them, we'd rub them and check if they flinched. If the muscles twitched, we'd know that we'd have to alter the position, the shape or the weight of the load to eliminate the soreness. Fortunately, I knew a bit about carrying loads from my army days and I just figured that what worked for me would work for him too.

Now don't go laughing at that, because it turned out that I was right. Horses are people too. I knew that I didn't care at all about how much extra padding I had on my pack, the extra weight was easily worth the added comfort. I loaded things sensibly so that the frequently used things were at the top and on the outside, and so that nothing on the inside poked into the horse. All this takes is common sense, but on several occasions I saw other people who didn't have any, or else didn't care how the horse felt. To abuse a horse knowingly is bad but to injure it without even realising it is truly wicked for no other reason than the abuse will go on and on unchecked.

To give the horses a better go, we each had two saddle blankets or 'pads' as they call them in the west. These are big square fleece pads (either real or artificial) pretty much like sheepskin car-seat covers. Often they are made of felt or foam and they come in various thicknesses from half inch to one and a half inches thick. We had two one-inch-thick pads under the saddle.

The saddle bags sat behind the saddle, and to protect the horse's butt, we used saddle blankets (woollen blankets the size of a hearth rug), folded a couple of times and with a flap tucked in between the two pads to trap it in place. That worked well, although later I replaced that arrangement with a specially designed tailor-made fleece pad which covered the back, rear and flanks. Apart from common sense, there are only two things that you must know about horses to care for them.

First, treat horses like you would yourself. If you spend all day with them, doing the same things, then you'll get hungry, tired and thirsty at about the same times. If they get hurt, treat them as you would a human. Iodine for cuts, fly repellent if there's lots of flies and mozzies around, salve for galls, penicillin and bandages for wounds, and so on. Tired hot hooves like a good soak in a cold stream just like we do. Whatever afflicts a horse is generally best treated as if it was you who was hurting. Pay particular attention to their feet. A horse that can't walk is known as 'sausage'.

The second rule is that horses are social animals, which means that they like company and their behaviour is based around being in a group. For instance, at all times in a herd there is a lookout, watching for predators and other types of trouble. Without a lookout, a horse in the wild has a hard time eating or sleeping. The horse is stressed and nervous unless he can rely on someone to guard him. That is more true in areas where there are predators than on a semi-suburban ranchlet.

Horses also have a distinct pecking order, and if you don't recognise what's going on, your own horse usually gets a hard time whenever he meets up with an established herd. You have to make sure that he doesn't get bullied too much or else injuries will result. Spice was a big girl's blouse and every time we met other horses he'd always yield to the dominant one. Once, I was walking up to a ranch to buy some grain for him, and six or seven horses came trotting up the driveway to say hello. Spice didn't like the look of things so he actually stepped in behind me and kept me in between him and the horses all the way to the gate. This attempt by a 900-pound animal to 'shelter behind my skirts' was mildly embarrassing and I'm glad no one was watching. Trigger and Silver and Mr Costner's yellow horse never did such things. When I scolded him for it, he looked off into the middle distance intently and then glanced back at me with a look that said, 'Oh pardon me, were you saying something?'

Sometimes, he'd get picked on anyway so the best thing to do was to get him away right smartly. It's no fun for a strange horse to be trapped in a field with no escape from a herd of bullying brumbies. On one occasion, I was sleeping in my tent and woke to the sound of a whole herd of horses thundering around the field I was camped in. I turned on my torch as I

Cosy digs. My one-man tent. The 'House of Blue Light'.

heard them come galloping towards my tent in the darkness. I knew I was parked near the fence, and the herd, which hadn't seen the tent before, might either swerve into the fence to avoid me, or would jump the tent. Either way would be a wreck. Horses do foul up and run into fences at night when they are excited and ranch horses aren't trained to jump. In a bunch, one could easily be a bit late taking off, and then I'd simply be killed as the horse put a hoof on me and the rest of the bunch piled into the falling tent at 30 miles an hour.

The torch made the tent glow like a small blue UFO and the horses steered away safely. I knew better than to get up and explore what they were running from at night, but the next morning, I found Spice had burst through the fence and was a little cut up. Nearby were fresh bear tracks, so either the horses were chasing Spice around the field, or else the bear spooked them. In any event, Spice ran through the fence, either in fear or because the herd ran him through it. Of course it's possible that they were just tearing around the place having fun and Spice didn't know when to turn, but however it happened, it proved the point that meeting up with other horses was a risky business at times.

Horses outside a herd obviously have trouble sleeping without a guard. Although I saw Spice sleep on only three occasions in a whole year, each time lasted less than an hour, but appeared to be very deep. The sleep occurred when he was sitting down rather than dozing when upright which was common. The sitting sleep was so intense that I could walk right up to him and he would not even stir which was most unusual. In areas where there were bears and mountain lions, he'd stick close to the tent, perhaps trying to rely on me for lookout while he tried to get some sleep. He'd often poke his head inside the tent to tell me something, but I couldn't figure it out. I'm a bit slow that way.

There's one other thing that helps you to understand how horses work, and that's to have a detailed knowledge of their construction. They don't come with a blueprint, so the next best map of a horse is yourself. To figure out what does what, just get down on your hands and knees. All the parts of your body are now close enough to a horse for you to figure out what's going on. The one big difference is that your fingers and toes are welded together on a horse into a single finger called a hoof. The bit that you nail a horseshoe on to is the fingernail.

All the horsey-type people have fancy names for the parts of a horse, but the names aren't important. It's better to know where the shoulderblades are, and what they do, than to call them the hames or the withers or whatever the hell they are. It's better to know that the strong part of a horse's back is not the middle, but the shoulders. Likewise, the bum is strong, but it isn't a comfortable place to put a lot of weight. If you don't believe me, then give someone a few horsey rides and see where the weight feels most comfortable. High on the shoulders is where you want it. These things are important. Names are not. As regards the doctoring of horses, the golden rule applies: 'Do unto others as you would have highly trained medical specialists do unto you in a sterile environment accompanied by lashings of morphine.' If this is not possible then all vets agree that bacon grease is the best local remedy for all cuts and wounds and probably does no harm to them if licked off either. Chewing tobacco (if you can get your horse to eat it) is a sure cure for worms too.

So that's all you really need to know. Horses are social animals that rely on the herd for company and protection. Without company they don't eat or sleep as well. When in doubt (which I was always) horses should be cared for like humans. As far as their physiology goes, they are more similar to us than different. That's it.

Unfortunately, knowing all this didn't answer the question

of what would happen if we let go of the horses and stepped back. The answer we suspected was that they would go like hell for home. We were wrong, but not by much. It wasn't until three weeks later that we happened to stop for a short mid-morning break and we idly looped the reins over the saddle horns as we usually did. By that time, we were only 20 miles from the US-Canadian border and we figured the horses would have given up trying to run back to the ranch from there. Ever so slowly, first Sugar, then Spice started casually ambling south between bites of grass at the roadside. Just as Spice stepped past me, I reached out to catch hold of his reins to turn him back towards Ash and POW! — he was gone like a cat at Crufts. Sugar took off too and suddenly all four of us were sprinting down the road. The horses were shedding parts of their load at every step and small but valuable items were tracing graceful parabolas through the air and then splatting viciously on to the road. We'd never have caught them at all if they hadn't been restricted to the highway by the fences on either side and especially if a local rancher hadn't headed them off in his pick-up and stopped them for us. We repaired the gear with help from the rancher and bought a new latego from him for Sugar. The latego is the strap that hangs off the saddle on the left-hand side and is threaded through the end of the cinch. It is tightened up and buckled or knotted to hold the cinch on tightly. Ash's had burst and his saddle and pack had abandoned their positions over a distance of a mile or so. Spice had simply trodden on his reins and broken them for the umpteenth time. It took two hours to straighten things out and make repairs and that was the last time for a long while that I trusted a horse not to take off if I left it unhobbled or untied.

The only funny part was that they had taken off heading south towards the US! At least we didn't lose any ground. Much later, if we ever turned back toward Canada, Spice would always speed up and try to trot or gallop. Eventually though, I got to the point where he could be trusted to stand at the side of the road grazing without any fear that he would take off north or even that he would step out into traffic. It got to where I could cross the road to talk to passers-by and leave him to eat on the edge of a busy highway. If he wandered too

'You go on without me.'

far, I'd whistle at him. He'd stop and look back as if to say, 'What now for Chrissake?' I'd tell him to 'stand' and he'd drop his head and start eating again. Five minutes later he'd start to sneak off ever so casually and I'd have to do it again, but it beat having to tie him up.

Eventually, I developed a kind of sixth sense about when he was contemplating wandering off. In the evening, as soon as I'd selected a camp site, I'd unsaddle and remove his bridle. I'd put his lead rope on and let it trail on the ground. For the next few hours, he was free to wander around and eat. If he ever started to wander out of sight, I'd whistle at him and tell him to stand. He'd usually get the hint, although once or twice he'd give me a 'Who me?' look that was highly suspicious. Then I'd lead him back to an area where I could watch him. Each time I did that, my sixth sense never ever failed to tell me when he was leaving the camp. Occasionally, I'd catch him just as his tail was disappearing into the tall timber. Then the race was on. I'd run after him, and he'd start to trot. The problem for him was that the lead rope would drag along the ground between his legs and sooner or later, a hind leg would stand on it. That had the effect of jerking his head down as if I'd reined him in. Because he couldn't gallop like that without chin-butting his chest, his speed was cut to a fast walk. No sweat to catch the old fool then.

It worked the other way too. Once in a while, I'd leave the camp to get water or scout around, and pretty soon I'd hear a querying whinny. A 'Hey, where are you?' sort of thing. If I didn't front up quickly, he'd get a bit upset and he'd keep calling till I showed up. It was nice to know he cared.

Communication between us got better and better. It got so that as we were walking or riding along, I'd know that he'd want to take a bite of a particular bit of grass, and so I'd stop and look at the map or have a cigarette while he had a munch. I wasn't always right about which bit of grass he'd prefer, but I was pretty consistent. The feeling that he would like some of *this* plant but not *that* one, was like the intuitive mental images I used to get of the road ahead when I was driving at high speed.

In the past, I'd been a bit of a fan of fast cars and I used to drive them pretty quickly too. On a long run through winding, hilly, country roads I'd occasionally get very strong mental images of a colour and type of car that was to come around the next corner. That was very handy information since I regularly overtook cars on blind corners. I never overtook on a corner if I had an impression of what was coming towards me, and I don't recall ever having been wrong about what type of car came at me. I was concentrating very hard at getting that right one day when I had a passenger travelling with me. Colin had strong nerves and he was pretty intrigued by all that, so for a while I predicted the cars before they came around the corner at me. He was mightily impressed by this trick and had bags of confidence in it after that.

Sadly, I disappointed him severely after he settled down for a snooze. I was pretty tired too and eventually I was in that half-awake state where you nod off and wake up again a split second later with no idea how long you've been asleep. I got good at waking up for the corners and nodding off on the straights but after a bit, I got a tad too good at it. We both awoke to a rhythmic thumping. We were in the middle of the median strip of the motorway and the thumping came from the sound of small native trees disappearing under the grill of the car. When the leaves and branches stopped flying up in clouds, we saw in front of us a classically immovable object in the shape of a concrete bridge pylon. We both screamed and I charged back on to the road, trailing bits of vegetation. Of course now we were WIDE AWAKE and since there was no harm done, it only seemed proper to keep going. The really appalling thing was that after Colin swore he'd never drive with me again, just two weeks later, we were making the same run again and the same thing happened at exactly the same place! No thumping this time as the trees were all shaved off at about ground height, but something woke us and I nipped back into the fast lane just in time. Colin gave me the sickest look I've ever seen and asked if that was *déjà vu* or was I just a dickhead?

Sugar and Spice casually ambling out of sight, high up in the snowline, no doubt planning to bolt.

Horses can be counted on not to walk into trees almost all the time, but not entirely. Or perhaps I should say that they won't do it accidentally, but they will do it deliberately. I found that out when we were stopped for a few days on a ranch in Crows Nest Pass on the Canadian side of the border. We'd nearly finished a few days of hard riding, when Sugar went lame in the hind legs. We could see the swelling and feel the heat in her foot at the point that would be the Achilles tendon on a human. Because we didn't know what to do, Ash decided to head off to the nearest town on foot to seek a phone and then the advice of a vet. I stayed to look after the horses. Before lunchtime, he was back with a horse trailer. He'd hitched into town and called the vet who recommended that we get the horse to a ranch belonging to a local horse trainer, Marguerite Fraser, and her husband Barry.

The vet said she could treat that problem just fine and all it needed was rest and some ointment. Ash arranged for Barry to pick us up and we trailered the horses the 15 miles to their ranch. They diagnosed the problem as being 'scratches', a type of inflammation caused by too much standing around in wet conditions. That made sense, since the swelling looked like the tendonitis-cum-frostbite that I'd had a dose of a few years before on an army exercise. We'd just been through a cold wet patch for a few days when we'd climbed up to the snow level at about 10,000 feet to cross a couple of passes. Even in mid-summer, it can rain and hail and snow like hell at that altitude in the west. We'd had a bit of rain and even though the weather didn't seem too severe, the diagnosis fitted the symptoms and the treatment worked. Which proves what I said about treating them as humans.

Marguerite with Ash. She was a darling.

Anyway, there we were on the ranch with a few days to spare. Marguerite agreed to board the horses and treat them and let us camp next to them. There was an outdoor sauna house with a shower so we were able to have a proper wash in hot water. The river baths we'd had up till then were head-shrinkingly cold and therefore rather brief. After settling the horses down we washed and then we walked to town and did some laundry and had a few beers. Ash and I started taking on the locals on the pool table and Ash played like a demon. We never lost a game and hardly had to buy a jug all night. We wandered unsteadily home that night while huge gusts of warm wind rushing through the pass blew us up the road to the ranch. Next day we started to help Barry and his helper Robert to put on a new roof over their small barn. That took us three more days of very pleasant work in the hot sun and by then the horses were nearly fit. During that time, Marguerite and Barry and Robert were so friendly that it was hard to believe. Ash was kitted out with a sweater, hat and denim jacket. We were entertained to tea and our tack was improved with the use of their repair gear. We met friends and family and appointments were made for us at a vet and a horse shoer further down the road so that we would not have to waste time making enquiries. (Later on, the vet wouldn't charge us for his advice and the horse shoer refused payment as well.) When we left the ranch, Robert presented us with a parcel of gifts which included food, tobacco and two belt buckles. We picked one each and I put mine on. I have it still. That type of hospitality was typical of everyone that I met and was the thing that really made the trip.

Toasted marshmallows and beer — health food.

On the fifth day, Marguerite suggested we take the horses out for a gentle ride to see how Sugar's foot was. We rode quietly up to a big field above the ranchhouse and Sugar seemed OK. I was bouncing around on Spice who hadn't been ridden for four days and, without the saddlebags, he was full of beans. Ash had a turn on him while I held Sugar and, after a few hundred yards, he fell off as Spice turned. Spice always liked to gallop and hated slowing down or turning. With Ash riding him I think he got frustrated at being reined in all the time. Ash walked nonchalantly back to hold Sugar while I rode Spice. When I got on him he was raring to go and he didn't want to slow down for gopher holes. I wasn't keen on the idea of a broken leg so I checked him too. Soon he got annoyed and started to try to unload me. He did it by going full tilt towards a tree in the middle of the field. I couldn't pull him up and at the last instant, he swerved. I went flying out of the saddle and piled into the tree. However, I didn't let go of the reins and so Spice had to stop too. His whole body spun around to face where I was lying on the ground as if he was a whip I'd cracked. As soon as I realised I still had him, I leapt out of the branches and slugged him on his jaw. He jerked his head back and glared at me so I leaned back and really got my weight behind the next one. I punched him as hard as I could in the same place and then I grabbed his bridle and pulled his head down so I could yell in his ear. I called him all the names I could come up with and growled like a dog when I ran out of words. Spice rolled his eyes and stood perfectly still until I calmed down and released his head. When I got on him again he was as good as gold. Ash, however, was in bits at the sight of me flying into the tree and kept asking me things like, 'Did you aim for that tree or were you just lucky?' and 'Can you teach me that too?'

Except for the Pointless Battle of the Bridge, six weeks later, Spice never tried to hurt me again. (He did hurt me, but it was an accident, not because he was trying.) I never was afraid of falling off him after that and so that was one less thing to worry about, although it still left plenty of things to prey on my mind. All in all, I'd say that having a horse on my hands all day and night was about half as frustrating and worrying as having Ash to look after. The only bright spot was that we were in no danger of attack by hostile Indians. Hostile horseflies and mosquitoes kept them sensibly inside their pick-up trucks and houses. We were not so lucky and slathered ourselves and the horses in repellent goo and worried whether it was toxic as well as noxious.

Chapter 5

Things take a turn for the worse, time plays tricks on us, we are party to a tragedy and witness to a rodeo, we make friends with Indians and Spice meets Isaac

Ash and I had worked our way south through the state forests that run along the border between Alberta and British Columbia. Each day had a similar routine, with us rising at dawn and letting the horses off the high-line. We didn't hobble them much at night for fear that they would get to a road and get run over. At dawn we'd let one roam and we'd hobble the other or put it on a fresh high-line. After breakfast we'd pack the tent and load up. We'd be rolling by 9 am and then we'd walk and ride till about 1 or 2 pm. After a two-hour siesta when we hobbled or high-lined them, we'd ride again till about 7 pm. It got dark at about 10.30 pm so that left plenty of time for grooming horses, making camp, having dinner and rolling a cigarette. The grooming consisted of a thorough brush down, combing manes and tails, picking stones out of hooves, oiling hooves with lanolin cream to keep them soft and prevent them cracking, checking shoes, sponging noses and docks (which was exciting the first few times until they got used to it) and finally giving them their

Ash, snug as a bug in our two-man tent.

grain in feedbags. They ate about a gallon a day of COB — corn, oats and barley with a little molasses added for taste. We studied the maps a lot for clues as to where to go, but we also took the advice of people we met as to what was doable. There were a few ghost towns on the map that we nearly relied on for food and so it was always wise to check with the locals first. Those towns weren't the tumbleweed and boardwalk types, but were usually recently abandoned as economic circumstances changed and the people moved on to the next boom town. Old mining towns, cattle towns, oil wells, railroad towns and logging towns were scattered along our trail, some with a few old folk still hanging in there, surrounded by weedy back lots and boarded-up buildings with faded signs advertising Coca-Cola and gasoline.

About half-way to the border, I made the first of my two map-reading errors on the trip and I still wince when I think of it. Instead of getting lost, we were completely aware of where we were. The problem was that we weren't getting any closer to our planned stopping point for the night. What had happened was that we had been following a hand-drawn forestry map with a scale of about one inch to a mile (1:63,360). Part way through the day we came on to the edge of our store-bought metric map. The squares were the same size as the 1:50,000 maps I'd used for years in the army, so I estimated the time that it would take to get to a good place to stop and we set off for the afternoon. That morning we had climbed 1500 feet and dropped down 1500 feet and then climbed up 2200 feet again over Rikerts Pass (where a disbelieving mountain goat trotted past us just ten feet from our drooping horses) and down to the highway. At that point we joined the new map and set off for the last six or seven miles, having already completed about 16 or 17 miles.

Time wore on as we made our way along the edge of the road. We went through a canyon and the horses' hooves echoed off the walls. Spice couldn't figure out where the other ghost horse was. I started to whistle and that had him buggered as well. His ears were swivelling around like radar dishes trying to make sense of it all. Ash and I sang songs and smoked Drum roll-your-own smokes. We ate Bridge Mix

Half-way through a very strange day. Atop Rikerts Pass.

candy and slices of summer sausage, which is a cheap type of salami. Flies bothered the horses and we had no repellent. It was very hot and there was no breeze. The afternoon wore on and still we were only making the slowest possible progress. We never seemed to be getting to places on the map as fast as I thought we should. I assumed that the horses must be tired so we walked and jogged alongside them. Still we hadn't reached our destination and now it was looking as though we would have to find a place on the side of the road to camp. By six o'clock we had seen no good camp sites and no water. We were tired, since we'd walked up and down the two passes and at least half the distance on the flat as well. The horses were dogging it and clearly they'd had enough. All afternoon, we had been passing recognisable points, but progress was so slow it was almost like being in a time warp. Segments of the fourth dimension were being removed and added to the horizontal axis of the third. The tiny distance covered on the map didn't relate to the time taken. The sun was still high in the sky and the heat rose in shimmering waves from the melting tarmac road.

We drank water frequently from our tepid water bottles

and sweat soaked our hats and shirts. Finally, by 8.30 pm we reached a junction where we got advice from a shopkeeper. Our destination was only a couple of miles ahead so we pushed on to it. At nearly 9 pm we finally made camp in a meadow near a river. The horses were high-lined and we crashed after a  cold dinner.

Smoko.

The next day we declared a rest day as the horses had been doing around 20 miles a day for 11 days and were due for a break. We were tired too and it was a perfect spot for us to wash clothes and give the horses time to feed. Finally, I pulled out the map to try to discover how far we had gone and see if we could puzzle out why distances seemed to expand that afternoon. The answer jumped out at me as soon as I looked at the map. The second map was not a 1:50,000 scale, but was a 1:250,000! We had covered over 30 miles in the afternoon alone, after 16 or so over mountains and down valleys in the morning. That was why the afternoon had dragged on so much. We hadn't been going slowly at all. We had covered five times as much ground as we would have done normally!

As a point of comparison, an equestrian marathon is often around 60 miles, which involves vet checks every 10–15 miles. The horse is ridden by a lightweight jockey in triathlon clothes on a saddle of nylon and fibreglass that weighs about 5 pounds. We covered 46–50 miles with the horses carrying well over 100 pounds of saddles and saddlebags each, plus us for about half the time. That cock-up was solely my fault since Ash didn't map-read unless I made him. Even now I can't believe I made such a ridiculous mistake. After that, I always checked the scale.

Not long after we left Marguerite and Barry, we arrived at the border where we discovered that the horses had to enter the US at a customs post about 50 miles east. We decided to get them trailered there as it would serve no useful purpose to ride them there and would just add time to the trip. We entered Waterton-Glacier National Park which straddles the US-Canadian border and tried to find someone with a horse trailer and a spare day. Luckily, the village on the Canadian side had a horse and buggy ride concession and we found one of the drivers with a horse trailer who wanted to go to the town of Cutbank, in Montana, to do some shopping and didn't mind going the long way there. We said we'd pay the gas and so he loaded us up and took us through to the Sweetwater border post.

At the post, we called Bill and had him fax the Coggins papers down as they hadn't arrived and then we discovered that, as we were riding and not really trailering our horses around, we needn't have bothered to do anything. If we had ridden our horses over the border, then no one would have cared one little bit. The same would apply to stock. If we drove 1000 head of beef over the border on foot, no one would care, but if we trucked them over, then they'd all have to be inspected.

Better saddlebags and a lighter load.

Oh well. We got dropped off in Cutbank and popped into the western store there with Dave, our driver. I'm glad I did, as I saw for the first time a proper set of travellers' saddlebags. They did the job of our combined saddlebags and duffel bags and were just a little bit smaller than what I had at the time. I liked that idea as I had a feeling that I was carrying too much gear, and that it'd do me and Spice good to get rid of some of it. I bought them and set about getting rid of some excess clothes. By the time I finished, the load was about 10 pounds lighter and a whole lot tidier. Ash kept his arrangement and together we set off. Somehow, I managed to leave one of our horse brushes behind which later, at the time of the great divorce, resulted in me finally finding a use for the saw blade of my Swiss Army knife.

In case you're wondering what a man does with a horse in a busy modern town, then it really depends on the horse. If it's of a nervous disposition, then you securely tie him up on a vacant grassy lot or in a convenient park and hope he doesn't crap everywhere. If not, then by all means take him shopping with you. Eventually, I'd leave Spice in the car park outside a supermarket just as if he were a car. He'd stand and wait till I came out usually, but I'd watch him and if he wandered off to eat the gardens I'd whistle and tell him to stand. Often he was quite interested in the shops and would look in the windows. Reflections didn't bother him, but I know for a fact that you shouldn't try that with cattle.

Several months later, I was helping friends shift a herd of cows, calves and bulls through the main street of Pinedale, Wyoming, when a bull caught sight of his reflection in a shop window. He started pawing at the sidewalk and bellowing and we had to ride our horses up on to the pavement to turn him back in to the herd. He was probably saying to his reflection, 'You ugly sonovabitch, I can take you any day.'

We'd been through Pincher Creek and had the horses shod again at no cost by Jack Marr (one of Marguerite's friends) and were all ready to make some miles. Early the next morning, we set off heading west for Browning, Montana on US2. Amazingly, the horses took off like lightning. It wasn't till later that I realised that we were no longer heading south, and that for the horses, that meant we were going *home*. By lunchtime we had covered 18 miles and were just three miles from Browning. We decided to siesta till 2 pm and then push through town to find a good camp site near the Cut Bank Creek. Just before lunch we stopped at a roadside historical marker at a place called Camp Disappointment. It was where

Lewis and Clark discovered that the United States was not as big as they had hoped, as the area to the north did not drain into the Mississippi River as they had surmised, and therefore did not belong to the US under the terms of the Louisiana Purchase. It was an aptly named place for us.

The land in that part of the state is prairie and not mountain. Eastwards for hundreds of miles are the rolling plains and low hills and bluffs of the Midwest. Twenty miles to the west are the Rocky Mountains which we had left the day before. This land was dry and dusty and relatively treeless. It was classic ranch country and was also slap in the middle of the Blackfoot Indian reservation. Watercourses were low and hay needed irrigating in order to thrive. All this within sight of glaciers and tall mountain pine forests.

A few hundred yards further on was a small stream with some willow trees growing nearby. Not weeping willows with magnificent shade or even pussy willows with tall strong trunks, but puny little willows like tea tree and more use as a windbreak than as shade. In the boiling noon heat we swatted flies and prepared warm sandwiches of salami, cheese and jam. The horses were unsaddled and, since there were no willows suitable for high-lines, they were hobbled. Earlier in the month when we bought the hobbles I got an outfitter (a person who takes tourists and hunters on back country horseback adventures) to show us how they were correctly fitted. From then on, we each hobbled our own horse. Spice soon got used to it and would move around easily while grazing. Sugar would obstinately stand in one spot and sulk. We tried to encourage her to move but finally we decided that hunger would be the best teacher so we just left her to get on with it herself. On that occasion she did nothing until we sat down to eat.

We began spreading Cheez Whiz on crackers for dessert. Cheez Whiz is misnamed. It gives the impression of being a dairy-type sandwich spread of a generally cheesy flavour. It's not. It bears as much resemblance to cheese as the White Cliffs of Dover. I wouldn't be surprised if Cheez Whiz were 98% preservative, 1% MSG and 1% carcinogen. Its only redeeming quality is that it will never ever go off in hot weather and it will not freeze in cold weather. In these respects it is much like the antifreeze in cheap wine — only fatal in huge doses. Its contempt for the extremes of climate fated it to accompany me all the way to Mexico. Unlike Sugar.

Just as Ash and I started, Sugar decided to move. At the time she was wearing the bell which Spice normally wore when hobbled. It was to help us find them in thickly wooded country which we were planning to enter soon. To familiarise them with it, we used it in open country too. As Sugar moved, the bell hanging from her halter rang and she panicked. She reared and leaped forward and then crashed to her side on the ground. She didn't move.

We raced over to her and I saw that somehow she had got her hind legs in between her front legs and as a result, her back was arched like a bow. To get her feet between the forelegs meant that the hobbles were far too loose. I'd warned Ash about that before but I think he was opposed to properly fitted hobbles and thought that by putting them on loosely he was doing her a favour. I said nothing as I undid the hobbles, while Ash held her head down to stop her from moving. He needn't have bothered. As soon as she was freed, we stepped back, and she tried to rise. Her front legs worked but her hind ones were dead. She fell back on her side and we both knew she'd broken her back.

The next hour was not good. I sent Ash to find a rancher who was mowing hay nearby and ask for his help. He took an age and couldn't find him. Finally he returned with another Indian who agreed she had broken her back. I asked if he had a gun and he said no. He left to look for one and Ash and I waited for a while. Finally, I decided that it was cruel to wait any longer, so while I kept the flies from biting her I told Ash to go and stop a car on the highway and get a lift to town and borrow a gun or else have the sheriff come out and kill her. He was hopeless. His own horse was in great pain and Ash couldn't even get a car to stop.

I watched three cars drive past him as he futilely stood waving from the side of the road, before I walked out on to the highway and stood in front of a car. It stopped. It was full of women — Granny, Mom, Sis, three girls. I leant down to the driver's window and politely explained that I had a crippled horse nearby, and could I please either borrow a gun or have a lift to town to get one. The woman looked at me and freaked.

I was dirty, bearded, dark and sweaty. I was on a lonely road in an Indian reservation and the scene looked like a Pink Floyd album cover. She gabbled something about having an important appointment and put her foot down. I was cursing her for being a heartless suspicious bitch and . . . then a pick-up truck appeared.

It was also driven by a woman, but her husband was in the passenger seat. She stopped and I told her the same story. As I leant in the window I saw that her husband had a sweater on his lap. I said, 'I need a gun to shoot my horse — it's got a broken back.' I pointed out Sugar lying down 100 yards away and as I did so, the husband lifted the sweater and I saw the .38 aimed at my head. There was a looonnnng second's pause and then the man reversed the grip and handed it to me butt first. I thanked him and he followed me across to the horse. I asked Ash if he wanted to do it and he said no. No surprises there. I made him lead Spice away so he wouldn't be startled by the noise and then I shot Sugar once in the head, right between the eyes.

Out of respect, the man stood well back and waited. Sugar shuddered, let out a big breath and then lay still. I touched her eyeball and there was no reaction. As I turned away and gave the gun back to the man, he said it was hard to have to shoot a horse and that he was sorry. I thanked him and then he left.

Ash returned with Spice, and as he approached, Sugar gave a cough and started to breath audibly. I couldn't believe it. I yelled at Ash to stay away and said that she wasn't dead. Only then did I think that I should have shot her through the temple. I couldn't believe my luck. I knew that there was no chance of getting another gun as easily, especially without running a good risk of having my head blown off by the next driver I stopped. The first one *would have* and the second one *could have*. I wasn't game to go for *'did have'*.

I walked across to the saddlebags and took out a hatchet. The edge was fairly dull, but even a sharp axe is not the best tool for that type of job. A sword is better, but the longest blade

I had was a Swiss Army knife of two and a half inches. I pulled back her head and swung the hatchet at her throat. It bounced off. Not good. An axe is good for maiming, but it's not a clean killer at all. Not in my hands anyway. After two more swings I could see the terror in Sugar's eyes and I was ashamed, so I threw it aside and reluctantly pulled out my knife. I soothed Sugar and felt around a bit for the right pipe. Eventually I got it and there was a brief spray of blood. I cut everything back to the spine to be sure and then checked that it was done. This time I was right. That was the end of Sugar — a fairly lazy horse, but still she deserved a better end than that. Before Ash came back I closed up the wound and went to wash my knife.

I don't think Ash had ever seen anything dead before, either human or animal, but I was surprised how long it took him to decide to have a look at the carcass. Spice ambled over too and sniffed around before moving aside to graze. Ash and I debated what to do.

I asked Ash if he wanted to continue. He said he didn't think so, as he couldn't afford it. I said that if it was a question of money I'd be able to buy him a horse, and that he might regret it later if he gave up now. We talked along those lines for an hour or so and ate our lunch. The rancher hadn't returned, so I was glad we hadn't waited. Eventually we decided to find a ranch to put Spice on while we went to town so Ash could call home for some money. If he could get enough, and if a horse could be found that he liked, he'd go on.

First up, we had to find a place to stay while Ash called home. We loaded up my horse with Ash's saddlebags across my saddle and hid his remaining tack in the willows. We left Sugar where she was. With no shovel, there was no chance of burying her and the coyotes would pick her clean in a couple of days anyway. Walking alongside Spice we hadn't gone more than 200 yards when the bellowing started. Spice neighed and called for Sugar for three whole days almost without ceasing. Believe me, as they say in those parts, 'That gets old real quick.'

Luckily, within 15 minutes a rancher pulled up in a pick-up and explained that the guy who had gone to look for a gun had come to him as we were on the edge of his land. His name was

Larry Whitford and we were welcome to stay on his ranch if we wanted to. He was the first of three terrific Blackfoot Indians that we met on that reservation.

The Indians (no one out west calls them Native Americans except visiting sociologists) in those parts were all ranchers or else lived in town and did all the same things that people do in agricultural towns all over the world. One exception was that they ran a small casino which was a perennial local attraction to neighbouring townsfolk. Most Indians lead the same kind of life as their white neighbours and mix freely. They dress the same (although the young men often wear their hair in long braids), talk the same and are largely indistinguishable from the rest of the ranchers. Satellite dishes sit out in the back yard and houses look just the same as those outside the reservation. It is true that living standards are a little lower in many reservations but this is because of the poor land they were forced to settle a century ago as well as to the higher rate of alcoholism. Nowadays the most likely source of dispute between Indians and whites is the same as between whites and whites — development and water. We saw the Indians as no different from other folk. They were as friendly, generous and interested in our trip as all the others.

We put our gear in Larry's truck and I rode Spice the mile or so to his ranch. We got settled in next to the corrals and fed my horse. Spice kept on calling most of the night, but we weren't there to hear it. In the afternoon we started to walk to town so Ash could call home. On the way we were met by a little Toyota pick-up driven by a young Indian guy called Mike Bolan. He said he'd seen us the previous day with two horses and wondered why we were on foot now. As soon as we explained, he told us to hop in and he'd take us to town to look for horses.

Spice, Mike and Isaac.

Mike lived by himself in a shack on the edge of the park and worked as a welder. He was recently out of the Navy where he learned his trade after leaving high school. On his graduation day (in July) the ceremony was postponed because of heavy snowfalls! That's what they mean when they say the weather is changeable in the mountains. He said he had nothing going on and offered to drive us out to a few places he knew that had horses for sale. After Ash called home and arranged for his money to be wired to the bank in town, we headed for the bar to let people know that we were looking for a well-broken horse. But not as well broken as Sugar. For the rest of that day we drove from ranch to ranch looking at unbroken, half-broken and senile horses. Nothing was lively enough to make it to Mexico and quiet enough for Ash to handle. By dark we'd met up with Larry again and he offered to sell us one of his if we didn't find anything suitable.

The next day Mike drove us all over the county looking at horses and again, they were all wild as hell. Later on I realised that cowboys are used to getting on a frisky horse in one smooth bound, but I wasn't and I found just mounting up was a trial, let alone trying to turn or check them. Ash had no hope and hardly rode any of them.

On the third day, a Saturday, Larry took us to the local rodeo and Killer Horse Sale to see if we'd meet anyone there with a good ranch horse for sale. We had a fantastic time watching the rodeo. We sat on the fence by the loading chutes with the cowboys and smoked and talked and watched the headcases compete to break a record or a neck or both. Everyone who didn't compete had broken ribs, twisted knees, an arm in a sling or wore a neck brace. Those who did compete were usually either nursing an old injury or getting ready to host another. That day, all of the events were riding rather than roping ones and so the action was thick and fast. By sitting on the fence next to where the bareback and saddle broncs were released for their eight-second ride, we could see all the action at short range, as well as watch the cowboys load up in the chutes. That has its share of risk as just getting a saddle on a bronc is a difficult job at times. It takes three to do it and if you forget what you're about you can get your arm broken between the gates and the horse as you reach in to buckle the straps and so on.

Once the chute opens and the horse jumps out, anything can happen. Horses can unload their riders and go berserk on their own. One did the latter and ran head first into a gate. Dead before it hit the ground. Even after making a successful ride a cowboy needs a safe way of getting off the horse. A pick-up man on a fast horse rides alongside the bucking horse causing it to gallop. The cowboy leans out and grabs hold of the pick-up man's waist or arm and swings off his bronc and either on to the horse or down to the ground. But not always. One cowboy didn't get a pick-up in time and dismounted in the horizontal starfish position. He landed face first in the dust and twitched once. Silence. Then people started running out to him. Broken neck. He was rewarded with a ride in the ambulance but he'd probably be back on the circuit in a year's time.

Going, going . . .

If you ever go to a rodeo, pick a small one. You can sit with riders and ropers and smell the dust and chew tobacco and squint into the evening sun. Big hats and sweaty leather gloves, skinny teenagers with silver championship belt buckles, stained chaps with rosin on the knees, hard manila ropes and pigging strings held between the teeth. You get all that at a little rodeo but at the big ones all you get are tiny figures in the distance wearing costumes. It's like watching TV. There is no sport tougher than rodeo.

Gone.

The events each finished with the auctioning of a group of 'killer' horses. These were former rodeo horses that were past it and were to be sold to killer plants for conversion into Belgian sausage meat. There was high demand for horses at that time and prices were around 60 cents a pound. That was not a lot less than beef. We weren't interested in those animals, but we did meet a few ranchers that had horses for sale. One of them was Bill Fenner.

He said he had a horse that would be perfect for us. 'Raised him from a colt and used him all year round. Good cattle horse, good hunting horse. Why, last year I rode him into a thicket chasing a cow in the mountains and came out on top of a bear! Only 14 hands or so, but strong and willing. Raised him from a colt.'

That night, we met Mike and he agreed to take us up to Bill's to look at that horse. He said we could go in the afternoon and stay the night at his place, which was nearby. He knew Bill and said he was a good guy. We arranged to ride Larry's horses in the morning and then we caught a ride to town and set about some serious drinking. By midnight we had missed our ride back to Larry's and although Ash didn't know it, he nearly got beaten up for being a faggot. Ash wasn't, but he looked like it, so I convinced the guy that I'd hammer him if he moved from his seat and amazingly he believed me. I found out later that two huge Indians were standing behind me making signs I couldn't see to my opponent that suggested that they would back me up if push came to kick-in-the-crutch. They never said a word at the time and I only found out by chance when talking to Larry later. Discreet chaps. I figured that it was time to leave while we still could, so we took the short cut back to the ranch by jogging down the railway tracks that ran past Larry's house. By the time we got back, we were sober, but Ash was whining about how hard it was to run on railway sleepers (called 'ties' in the US).

The next day we tried Larry's horses, but they were just the same as all the rest, although rather better bred. Ash didn't even want to get on them and one of them dumped me when I was dismounting. I thanked Larry and offered to pay for our time on the ranch but he said no. We set off for Bill's at lunchtime and by 4 pm Ash owned another horse.

As soon as we tried Bill's horse, Isaac, we knew he was twice as good as Sugar or Spice. Isaac was nine years old (which we took to mean 12 or 13) and was a proper work horse. He neck-reined properly (that is to say, the touch of a rein on his right side of the neck would turn him to the left and vice versa, rather than having to put pressure on his mouth. This allows you to steer one-handed). He had no bad habits. He was a joy to ride and nothing seemed to faze him. Ash paid $1100 which was a good fair price. Bill agreed to get him shod and promised to collect Spice from Larry's and bring him up the 20 miles north to Mike's where we were staying. Mike's cabin had no power, water or light other than a candle and the headlights of his pick-up, so we cooked over a fire and slept outside. Some time that evening, he asked if he could come with us, and since he'd been so nice to us and because he was a decent chap we said yes.

It took all day to collect both horses together and for Mike to fetch his and to pack a few things, and it was too late to start into the park, so we spent another night at Mike's cabin. He said he would like to accompany us as far as Yellowstone Park in Wyoming and then he'd turn east and head for Ohio, where he had friends. That sounded OK, since it meant that if we didn't get on as a group of three, he would be carrying all he needed to go solo.

The next morning, Mike announced that he needed to take another day to make some travel arrangements, so we decided to head off to the Park Headquarters to get a permit to camp in the park and he could meet us there. Just as Ash and I were setting off, Mike's horse spooked and took off around the cabin towing the log she'd been tied to. We raced after her but she took off down the road and the log finally came free. Mike yelled at me to get in the pick-up and so I drove while he uncoiled his rope and leaped in the back. We chased his horse down the road with Mike in the back swinging the rope in a loop and getting ready to catch the crazy animal. Now at the time, I didn't realise how stupid that was, since if we'd roped her, there was nothing to tie the rope off to. She'd just have dragged Mike straight off the truck and down the highway. Fortunately she started to tire before we caught her and eventually we cornered her in a cutting. Mike led her back while I went to help Ash tidy up the camp.

In the confusion, my horse had thrown a paddy and caught his saddle on the tree he was tied to. As soon as I tried to get on it I realised something was broken. It turned out to be the tree. The frame that the whole saddle was built upon was wood and had been broken before and repaired. Now it had failed again and that was serious. Mike arrived and said that the only solution was to go to Browning or Cutbank looking for a new saddle to trade that one on. We set off within the hour and searched both towns. The only one that was affordable and in good condition was a secondhand one in the western wear store in Cutbank. It cost $700 and they gave me $100 for my old one.

That saddle was definitely in a different league from the one I'd been riding. For a start it had a 15½-inch seat instead of the 13-inch youths' saddle I'd been riding, which was exactly like wearing underpants three sizes too small. Morale improved instantly.

The seat was padded instead of just smooth leather and above all it was a double-rigged roping saddle. That meant that it was built to take thousands of pounds of strain and also had two straps running under the horse's belly to anchor it. The first strap was the cinch which, pulled tight around the chest, did all the work of keeping the saddle in place. The second strap was a plain leather belt that had about half an inch of air between it and the horse's lower belly or waist. It was there solely to prevent the saddle from tipping forward and spilling the rider at the moment that a cow starts pulling on the end of the cowboy's rope tied to the saddle horn. The good thing for me was that to hang that second strap off the saddle there was an additional set of D rings near the back. That allowed me to use the straps on my new saddlebags as they were intended to be used. Tied on to the D rings, the whole affair was completely stable and allowed me to get rid of several ugly straps and rubber bungees. Ash went green with envy when he saw it.

To thank Mike for all the running around for us, we had been buying him gas, but now we decided to shout a meal and a beer at the local pub and we even managed to buy a bag of groceries for him too. Without his help, we'd never have ended up so well equipped. Even if it had cost us nearly $2000, it was worth it. Things were looking up.

Chapter 6

Wherein I show off my skills as a rider and soon after make the acquaintance of a surgeon. Also another parting of the ways

The next day Ash and I set off for the Park Headquarters while Mike rounded up things that he needed. He said he'd meet us at the park the following night. On arriving there, we discovered that it was not possible to go over the route that we had planned as snow still blocked one of the passes. The alternative was much harder and longer so after Ash and I discussed it with the rangers, we decided to ask Mike's advice the following night. Since we had the next day free, and since the horses were well rested, we decided to go for a day trip without the saddlebags. We checked in to a camp ground that let us put our horses on the edge and left our tent up.

First, we rode down to the park to get a day-tripper's permit for our horses. Just outside the headquarters building was a big open area with calf-high grass. Perfect for us to try out our new horse and saddle. Ash was riding a lot better on Isaac and had quite a bit more confidence now that he had a properly trained horse under him. We started out trotting and neck-reining but quickly progressed to galloping, wheelies and handbrake turns.

We were racing around an imaginary figure-eight track when Spice saw Isaac in front of him. He was looking at the bay horse when a narrow shallow ditch appeared in front of us. I hoped he'd seen it but he hadn't and, unluckily, he stepped into the eight-inch depression and stumbled. It all happened quickly, but as he fell, I must have put my right arm out to break the fall. I hit the ground and rolled away from Spice. I had kicked my feet out of the stirrups because, although he had fallen on my left leg, when he jumped to his feet again, I wasn't entangled in anything. I'd lost the reins so I stepped up to grab them and anxiously looked at his legs to see if they were broken. I was terrified of the idea that I might have to kill another horse so soon and it was with great relief that I realised that there were only two broken bones and that they were both mine.

As soon as I went to lift his leg to check I saw that my right wrist was a very odd shape. Familiar, but odd. I'd broken the radius and ulna (that's the two bones that make your forearm) right at the wrist and they'd been displaced in a classic 'gooseneck', or Colley's fracture. I knew all about these things, as I had done the same thing to my left wrist when I was a kid riding my motorbike.

Ash saw it happen but didn't realise I was hurt and so it took a while before he came and collected my horse. I set off on foot to the ranger station to see if there was a first-aid post. I told the ranger on duty that I'd hurt my wrist and showed her my arm. She went white and called another guy. He called for an ambulance since I had no car to drive to hospital in, and put a cardboard splint on it to immobilise it while we waited. After that, it started to hurt.

Not the worst kind of pain, but the dull nagging pain that says, 'Boy, you screwed up and I'm here to remind you. All day and night for a week or two.' I had some experience of that in the army.

For entertainment, after boring formal dinners, young army officers often play some fairly simple and silly games, usually fuelled by a pre-dinner pint or three (just to take the edge off your thirst), a sherry or two (because it's traditional) and a dozen or so glasses of wine at dinner (because it's free) followed by a bottle or more of port (and by now who needs a reason?) and then, after dinner, the serious drinking begins.

One game we played was called 'aircraft carrier'. Three or four highly polished dinner tables were pushed end to end and cleared. These were then soaped and watered down to provide a nearly frictionless surface. The object of the game was to run at the tables and leap on to them belly first and slide the length of them at high speed. Originally, two chaps with a tablecloth stretched between them stood on opposite sides of the table to do the job of the arrester wire on a carrier. The jumper had to keep his knees bent so that the sheet would catch his legs and prevent him from ditching into the carpet, or, more commonly, given the restricted nature of the 'ocean', into the wall. Occasionally, the 'arrester wire' mysteriously failed to operate and the less well-liked members of the mess would be left to hurtle off the end of the deck to meet the cruel sea head-first. That was the English way of having a civilised bit of fun. Not in our army. We eliminated the sheet and simply slid as fast as we could down the entire length of the tables. The object was to *go for distance*. Everyone ditched on to the carpet belly first and with practice, you generally didn't break any ribs.

On one particular night, I was well lubricated internally and had the friction co-efficient of mercury. I also had the athletic ability of Eddie the Eagle. After several record runs, I had the number of tables increased to nine and was aiming at the tenth. I began the run-up from two rooms away and with teeth gritted I sprinted down the flight path towards the tables. I was utterly committed to breaking my record, and I was totally focused on gaining speed. By willpower alone I could have cleared at least four tables with a standing jump. What followed hurt more than you can imagine.

Beginning my run-up from further back, I made the fatal error of not checking my pacing first. I bowled a no-ball so to speak. I simply didn't take off in time and instead of a savage leap at the tables from three feet away and a touchdown at least 12 feet up the deck, I struck the edge of the table at peak force. I slammed face first into the table, striking the wood with the speed of a rake in the grass, and rocketed down the entire length of the soapy runway, spraying water and bubbles while clutching at the table top. I didn't scream until I fell off the edge of the eighth table and whacked the Axminster. I thought I'd better get the yelling done early, because later I knew I'd be in too much pain to bother, and I wanted someone to realise I was hurt and to wheel me off to the hospital.

The problem, of course, was that in slamming into the table, I had taken the impact across the tops of my thighs. And that, dear reader, is a euphemism for the NUTS. God it hurt.

Days, nay weeks later, the bruises were still coming up, yellow, purple, crimson, saffron, amber, aquamarine and ruby. Colours you should see only on drugs. The immediate horror was a nurse who solicitously enquired at the emergency room whether I'd been drinking. I said (enunciating with great care), 'Yeesssh, in fact I may have had a sherry.' She replied with spiteful joy that I couldn't have any pain killers then, but if I liked, she could apply ice packs to the injured region. I declined. That wouldn't have looked good on my medical records. I returned to the bar and applied ice to several glasses of rum and coke, and that seemed to do the trick.

So you see that if a man can stand being hit in the crutch by a dining table at 20 miles an hour, he can take care of a little thing like a busted wrist. All the same, when the ambulance came I was into the oxygen like a rat up a drainpipe. Good stuff oxygen. Gets you high and leaves no traces. Good for shock, pain and hangovers.

I left Ash with instructions to take care of the horses and to check for phone messages at the camp-ground office daily. The ambulance deposited me at the Browning Hospital where they X-rayed my wrist and said unwelcome things like, 'Hot damn! Hey Spike, Gina, Mel, look at this thing willya?' Those are not the things you want to hear when you're unemployed, and are travelling on horseback in a foreign country. They reek of things called 'complications' and 'surgery'. Sure enough, they recommended I go to Great Falls, Montana to get an expert to fix it up. Apparently there were bone chips floating around that needed pinning in place. Pushing all the chips back into place would be like playing one of those games where you have to tilt a board around to get 12 ball-bearings to line up on a grid. They put a temporary splint on it, gave me some Tylenol and one of the nurses gave me a lift to a little town on the south-east edge of the park called East Glacier, where there was a car rental place. I hired a car and drove the 20 miles north to the camp ground where Ash was waiting.

The next morning we set out to drive the 100 miles to Great Falls. As soon as we got on the highway I asked Ash to take over but he refused. I couldn't believe that he was scared of driving an automatic on the empty highway, but he was. I drove myself all the way and checked into the hospital in a silent rage. On the way I got stopped for speeding and had to pay a fine of $15 on the spot. The patrolman asked why Ash wasn't driving instead of me and there was an embarrassed silence. I was steaming when I drove off again.

I told Ash that since he didn't want to drive the car back to East Glacier, he might as well leave on the next bus or train and go and look after the horses while I found out how long I'd be in hospital. That meant an extra day's car rental but saved me having to return by train, bus and hitchhiking. Hard to believe that Ash wouldn't even drive his partner to hospital. He left, and soon after I was being examined by the doctor. He said that surgery was advised and I asked what that meant. He said I'd have a rod poking out of my arm for a month or two while it healed. I asked how I could ride a horse and camp like that and he just laughed and said to forget that idea. Now, since I was unemployed, and wasn't likely to get a job while I had a broken arm, it was clear that I had to stay on holiday until it healed. I couldn't afford to convalesce on my holiday money. That meant no surgery. I told Doc Jenkins that he was not to cut it open at all and if he couldn't fix it by wiggling it, then it would just have to heal as best it could. The next day he did just that and now that it's healed, I can only bend it to 50° instead of 90° and now and then the hand goes numb. Just like he said it would.

Two days later, after a very comfortable stay in a private room with TV, bathroom and phone, I was back in the car headed for East Glacier with a bill for $2500 in my pocket. I'd had enough of the park area and I was determined to get out before any more disasters happened.

When I got back to the camp ground I nearly lost it. I had a total sense of humour failure. If I hadn't had a broken wrist I'd have torn Ash apart. The camp ground was full of headlights, cars, loud music and people. During the day about 200 bike racers and their support crews had arrived and were busy cooking, drinking, singing and RIDING MY HORSE! Ash was showing off by letting people trot my nervous horse around while Isaac watched. Spice was not happy at all and it amazed me that Ash would take such a risk in such a place. All Spice needed to do was to throw a rider or kick out a headlight or crap on someone's dinner and there'd be an argument or a fight or even a lawsuit. I didn't have the money to settle disputes like that since I was facing several thousand dollars in medical bills that I wasn't sure how I'd pay. I went to bed very glad that in Great Falls I'd bought a tiny tent for $20, just in case Ash and I decided to split. His attitude about how far he'd go to help me if I was in trouble shook me a bit and along with all his usual weaknesses, I'd just about had enough of him.

After a bad night's sleep I spoke to Ash and explained that I wanted him to take a bit of responsibility for the trip from me. Specifically I said he would have to get up first to move the horses on their high-line in the morning for a change, he'd have to try to read the maps a bit and he'd have to care for his horse a lot better. That was just the start, but I knew it was pointless listing all his deficiencies. I said that if he didn't improve in three days, then I was not going to continue with him. Meanwhile, Mike had contacted us and said that he was going to be late starting, but that he'd catch us up. (Actually, he never did, but two years later he invited me to work on an Alaskan fishing boat with him.) Later that morning we packed and left the park heading down the edge of it towards Maria's Pass.

Not golfing weather at all. The 'once-in-a-lifetime' hailstorm that revisited two days later.

The only unusual thing that happened on the way was that in the middle of the afternoon we got hit by hailstones the size of golf balls. When the storm hit, it stung the horses so much that I thought they'd bolt. We sought shelter under a stumpy low tree and Spice tried to get his head under the brim of my hat. It was almost romantic there for a while. (Later that day I asked a local how often storms like that happened and he said he'd never seen one before: 'Once in a lifetime, son.' Two days later it happened again.)

By the time the storm passed it was obvious that nothing had changed with Ash. That night, the high-lines he tied came loose. (Larry

Tarn at 9000 feet. Just what the doctor ordered in 30°C heat.

Whitford showed me how to tie them properly, but Ash refused to practise the knot and got it wrong.) Spice got his legs tangled and in his struggles to get free he rope-burned his ankles. I finally sorted it out myself and stopped the bleeding. In the morning we set off to get a penicillin shot for him which we found at a ranch on the way to East Glacier.

By the time we got there I was fuming and Ash was still as useless as ever. In camp that night I told him that I wasn't enjoying the trip at all and he said the same. Without any bitterness we agreed to separate, with Ash heading west to Kalispell and me going south as planned through the Flathead Forest. We divided up the gear and I found myself with a much smaller load than I had before since I didn't have to carry the two-man tent. This was when I finally found a use for the pointless wood saw on my knife. I used it to cut our one curry brush in half. That made the divorce official.

The next day at noon, we said goodbye to each other at the summit of Maria's Pass and I turned south off the road again to really begin my adventure at last. I was free of the inconvenience of worrying about Ash and at last I was properly equipped with a minimum of top quality gear, and, as I now realised, that included Spice.

Somewhere in the preceding month of travel he and I had gradually got organised and found out how not to aggravate each other. He'd learnt to stand still while I got on (which was a huge advantage now that I had a broken wrist in a cast up to the shoulder with a bend at the elbow). He also stood still while I laboriously saddled him, and he always looked back at me when I whistled. Sometimes he even came when I called as well.

In return, I had lightened the load three times, for a total weight loss of about 30 pounds and about the same amount from off me. I had figured out that an early start and an early finish were what he preferred. (We never could quite agree on exactly how early to start. I preferred rising at first light and leaving an hour later and finishing at about 5 pm. He wanted to start an hour before and finish at 3 pm.) I also realised that he needed a lot more food than he was getting and so I upped his ration of grain and gave him more time to eat during the day. At the first chance I wormed him, got him some vitamin shots, some extra tonic for his grain and had him thoroughly checked by a vet who said he was 'awful thin, but so are you'. I figured that since the hospital said I had the vital signs of an athlete I was OK. We both did the same amount of work so I figured the old fool was probably as fit as a buck rat too.

By now, I was able to read a map while riding him, as long as I unfolded it carefully from the small saddlebags that I had hanging across the horn of my saddle. I would lean forward to show him the source of the crackling noise behind his head as he liked to know everything that went on around him. He got the idea eventually and allowed me to navigate properly but when it came to photography, no amount of showing and sniffing of the camera convinced him that it wasn't going to blow up in my hands and if I pulled it out to take a shot of him he invariably walked quickly out of range. I'm sure he thought that I'd press the wrong button and somehow kill us both. He never minded other people taking photos of us so I think he was just being unreasonable. I had bought the small horn bags in Great Falls too and they carried my:

whisky-water bottle

book of animal tracks

candy
maps
camera and spare film
sunglasses and binoculars
bandana
chapstick
mini-Maglite torch
gloves
diary and pen
spare tobacco.
It was like a glove compartment in a car.

More important gear was on my hip pouch, which had my:
passport
money
medical insurance papers
emergency fish hook
pocket knife
cigarettes and Zippo.

Everything else was in the saddlebags. The bags were in three sections: left side, right side, and top. The left side was mine and it contained:
five days' food and two pints of water in a day pack
walkman and six tapes
guidebook
medical box with Spice's bandages, ointment, tonic, etc
toiletries
cooking nails and firelighters
spoon and steel cup
trash
undeveloped films
electronic diary (knackered after the batteries froze and it dumped everything in its memory)

Good gear is worth the extra expense.

The complete gentleman explorer's travelling kitchen and five-day pantry.

sewing kit and plastic tape.

Spice had the right-side bag and he had:

six gallons of grain in two plastic-bag-lined canvas bags (one was a nosebag and the other was a canvas water bucket for use in camp grounds that only had taps but no creek)

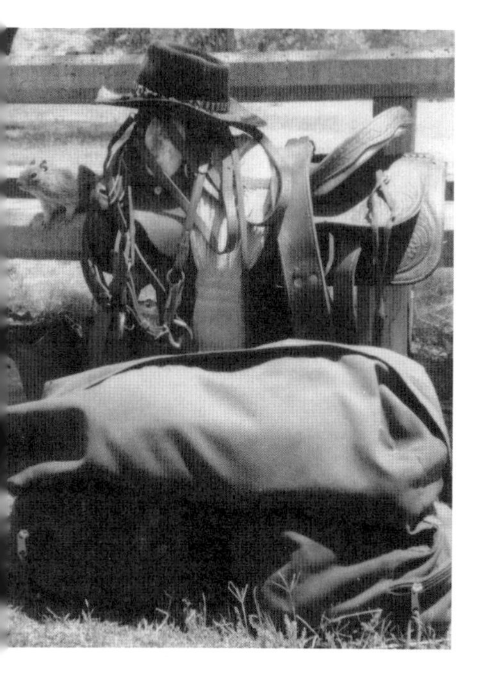

Everything I carried for a year is in this photo. (Squirrel not normally included.)

high-line rope
picket pin and cuff (hardly used because we usually camped in trees)
halter and lead rope (but often he wore it under the bridle and reins)
hobbles
breast strap (only used when going uphill all day)
hoof grease and brush and hoof pick
half brush and comb
fencing pliers (for sneaking through fences and repairing them afterwards)
spare poncho
spare rein
fly repellent and sponges.

I had all the top section and it contained a foam mat that lined the bottom and softened the load with:

sleeping bag
tent and poles
oilskin duster
sweater (later replaced by a quilted vest)
spare jeans, socks, T-shirt, shirt and underpants
hatchet and stone
fresh bread if possible
old maps and souvenirs.

From time to time I'd add or subtract certain things, mainly according to the climate, but generally, that was all I had. Eventually I was down to just the jeans and shirt that I wore and a single spare pair of socks and underpants.

With a better feeling than I'd had in weeks, I said goodbye to Ash and once again, as soon as we left him and Isaac, the neighing and whinnying began and continued for another day and a half, as did Spice's urgent efforts to turn north and find his friend. This time though, when he found he was not going to be travelling with another horse, he started to stick really close to me and it was from then on that we really relied on each other for company and advice.

I had a pretty strong feeling that Ash wouldn't finish the journey, and I was right. After I got settled that winter, I called his Mom in England. He was safely home after several adventures of his own. He made it nearly 40 miles to Kalispell before he sold Isaac to a rancher and bought a bike and then a rail pass. He spent a month travelling around the west coast and went back to Vancouver to see Shannon. Eventually, after being arrested and strip-searched by a sheriff for something petty, he flew home. Ash is a nice guy but he is not cut out for the west.

Chapter 7

A SYLVAN IDYLL, A BRIEF FAMINE, EXPLOSIVE CUISINE, AND A FISHING STORY THAT WILL NOT BE BELIEVED

The next few weeks were some of the best on the whole trip. Just a day after we separated, I felt sorry Ash had missed the easiest and most scenic section so far. Only a little bit sorry though, mainly I was rapt not to have to spend more time checking his work than doing my own. Day after day, we loafed along well-marked trails in river valleys, across mountain passes and through alpine meadows. We also went deep into thickets on game trails instead of horse trails, and had to back out again because there was no way to turn around. When that happened Spice would show his disgust by balking at every chance, stopping at every turn and generally malingering. I had to kick him on gently all the time until it seemed like I was peddling my way to Mexico. Mr Costner's wonderful buckskin horse never did that.

Rocky mountain high.

Show that damn prodigy an overgrown trail and it would have whipped out a machete and taken its turn as lead scout. Not Spice. Invariably my horse would give me a 'Yep yep yep' type of look, and I could tell he was saying 'I told you so' under his breath as we backed up or turned round and headed for the main trail. Most people don't think that horses have many facial expressions, but that's because they never do anything interesting around them that warrants a good look from a horse. I was always doing stupid things that Spice would see and have a good laugh at, like the time I blew up my dinner.

I used to cook my evening tin of beans by banging it on my knee a couple of times to put a dent or two in it. Then I'd put it directly over the flames of a firelighter and a few twigs resting on three of my cooking nails. I'd turn it around a few times using a gloved hand and wait for the two dents to pop out. It was like having a tender-timer on a turkey. The only problem was that if you weren't pretty quick at getting it off the heat, then the ends would bulge out under the pressure (it was a pressure cooker without a valve) and the next thing was DETONATION!! When I opened the can, I'd point it away from my face as it sprayed juice out in a little geyser, then I'd eat it out of the can. No dishes to wash, no firewood to gather, no water to boil and it was faster than any other way.

The gourmet's grenade.

I was used to cooking over my firelighters, but one night I built a little fire to cook up some water and to dry some wet clothes. The fire was apparently quite a bit hotter than the firelighters, because the dents went Pop! Pop! and before I could get my glove on, the ends bulged out, BUP! BUP! I had just a second to decide whether to risk trying to get it off the fire or whether to dive behind a tree. Well, he who hesitates is lost, and so is his dinner. With a thunderous BOOM! the can *and* the fire disappeared. The beans that weren't blasted into the trees were pattering down gently on to my tent before I could move. The can, when I found it, was perfectly clean and flat. The ends had disappeared into the weeds with my dinner and the fire. As I moved over to start wiping down my tent I realised that Spice hadn't moved despite the appalling explosion of my baked-bean bomb. When I looked closer in the fading light I could swear he was stifling a laugh. After a moment of immense internal struggle, he seemed to recover and with a gentle sigh he turned away, leaving me to my Cheez Whiz and crackers.

On scorching hot days we drank from icy streams on the edge of dark fairytale forests, and once, in a fit of stupidity, I lay down full length on the bank of the river just upstream of Spice to drink straight from the water. Just as I was finishing, Spice took a step sideways and planted a foot on the back of my calf. It ground my leg against the rocks and I let out a shriek. With piss-poor timing, a rock beneath my hand shifted, I slipped and my face went straight under the water. I surfaced squirting water like a squeegee mop and screamed at Spice to '*#%@ OFF!' He stepped back with a look that said, 'Well pardon me for living,' and moved downstream to get some peace and quiet while I rubbed my shin and shook the water out of my ears.

Wildlife and wildflowers thrive after the forest burns.

We picked our way through regenerating lodgepole pines with seas of wildflowers nodding in the warm breeze beneath the fire-blackened trunks. (I don't know a lodgepole from a telephone pole, but neither did anyone else I met, so anything that wasn't obviously a willow could safely be called a lodgepole. Or grass.) Woodpeckers drummed into the peeling bark looking for insects, which surprised me as I always had a feeling that the whole woodpecker deal was a fraud, like the lemmings leaping to their death. I'm not convinced about

All ribs and plaster.

woodchucks though. Why would they throw timber around? What would they get out of it? I saw chipmunks that were just as cute as Chip 'n Dale and after three days of that I was expecting to see Bambi, or Bugs Bunny being hunted by Elmer Fudd. The entire forest appeared to be a theme park.

Even when we got lost, we ended up seeing better things than we would have otherwise. I think. I mean I never saw the other things but what we saw was pretty good. Fawns playing around their mothers, dragonflies zooming over still green ponds, little birds flitting from branch to branch next to us, waiting for Spice to kick up a worm I guess. Amidst all nature's bounty, though, what we didn't see was a grocery store. That would have been perfect, since I was by then down to two handfuls of candy, one tin of beans and 40 rollies daily. Food like that was OK, but I've always tried to eat from the four basic food groups:

alcohol,
tobacco,
chocolate and
McDonald's.

Clearly I was missing three-fourths of a healthy diet and I began to notice a pleasing loss of weight. My trousers were now a bit baggy in the seat and I discovered that I could count my ribs. Spice too. His ribs, me counting that is.

Meanwhile, my left arm was becoming very capable at writing in my diary in a lop-sided, back-leaning, hieroglyphic sort of way. I no longer poked the toothbrush up my nose if I turned my head without thinking and I had even mastered the art of rolling a smoke lefthanded.

Whitetail deer, elk and moose ran before us or watched our quiet progress through their woods. I say quiet, not silent, because at every second step, Spice would fart or I would talk to him or just the regular creaking of all the leather bits would break the silence. To be honest, I surprised more game on the side of the highway than I did by clumping through the woods.

One day we followed the tracks of a mountain lion all day. It may just have been a big dog, but I couldn't see claw marks in the prints (which my tracking book said was a difference between cat and dog tracks), so I maintain it was a lion. I waited for the ambush, but Spice never scented it so I guess we got away with that. I tried hard to read other tracks of smaller animals, but unless I got a look at something I was never certain what it was. The only time I was sure, was following the tracks of a three-wheeler motorbike.

Something lurked in those woods that we didn't want to meet.

Once, when we were following a trail through a

huge meadow, Spice stopped dead and stared at a thicket of trees 200 yards ahead. For ten or more minutes he moved nothing except his nostrils, trying to scent something on the wind. Not even his ears moved, which was highly unusual. If I had carried a gun at that time, I'd have drawn it. This was a creepy moment. I was sure that something was watching us and that it wasn't the least bit worried that we might come closer. It almost felt like it was calling us in. 'Come closer, cowboy, and bring your tasty horse too.' I bet it had yellow eyes.

I was glad when Spice gave the all clear by twitching his ears and we walked on. He later did that on a couple of occasions and I never pressed the point with him. Since all I had as a handy weapon was a pocket knife, I wasn't ready to tangle with cougars. I'm convinced Spice thought I had some ability as a guard, since he never got uptight when I was next to him, but often got upset when I was away. Which goes to show that he was a very silly horse, because I wouldn't know where to start when it comes to fighting off wild animals. I'd probably begin by climbing a tree, which is not the type of defence that a horse should rely on.

Bears didn't bother him too much. The only time we ran into one on the trail was in Yellowstone Park. I was walking in front of him and all of a sudden he stopped. He didn't ever do that without reason, so I waited for him to take a leak and continue. He didn't, so I began to look around. Sure enough, about 60 yards to the left front was a momma black bear on a log with two cute babies, halfway up a tree, one little head peeping out from each side of the trunk. It looked like a perfect photo-op. I decided to get a picture, as I could see that the deep undergrowth would slow her down a

Bear seen from a safe distance.

lot if she charged me. Then I got smart and decided to GET ON THE HORSE FIRST and THEN TAKE THE PHOTO. Just in case. When I was aboard, Spice turned and looked back at me with his Homer Simpson 'Doh' look that he reserved for times when I was especially dense. After a while I walked Spice closer to the bear to get a better angle and he was not the least bit reluctant. He knew he could easily outrun dumb old Ma bear any day.

Moose were different. His hackles went up (actually horses don't have them but if they did, his would have), and he fidgeted and refused to approach a mother and calf that were blocking the trail. After they left he was jittery for quite a while. Once when we were in camp, he was tied to a high-line and a moose appeared on the other side of the stream about 50 yards away. Moose look so stupid that it's hard to take them seriously. They're pretty surreal for a deer — all lumpy with basketballers' legs and a Dr Seuss head, but they can sure eat your lunch if they corner you. I've heard of people trying to hand feed wild ones and getting seven shades of shit kicked out of them for their trouble. This time, Spice let out the loudest snort I've ever heard and started to pull the high-line down. I ran across and grabbed his lead rope and yelled, 'Go away moose!' and things like that. Spice was doing a war dance and I reckon if the moose had come any closer it would have been all on for young and old.

It was after about three days that I realised we were running out of food rather quickly. Well actually, only I was getting short since Spice was knee-deep in tucker every day. By the sixth day I was down to eating the rolled corn and oats out of Spice's grain (leaving just the barley which neither of us liked). For dessert, I ate the chapstick. By the seventh day I felt so hungry I thought I could eat the crutch out of a low-flying duck.

Alert readers may ask why I didn't trap something edible or else catch a fish, since I was surrounded by the entire woodsman's smorgasbord. The answer is simple. I haven't the faintest idea how to trap gophers or squirrels or elks and it is a matter of record that I don't eat fish. In fact, Spice caught the only fish on that trip.

Now I know I won't be believed when I tell this story, but I swear it's true, and I've almost got photographic evidence to prove it. Some months later we were camped in a private camp ground on the Yampa River and Spice was grazing with his lead rope dangling. I had my camera in my hands and I was trying to get a shot of him with the camp ground and my gear in the background. He walked over to the river to get a drink and I went across to lift the lead rope out of the water. As I did so, I looked down and bugger me if he didn't have his hoof on the tail of a trout!

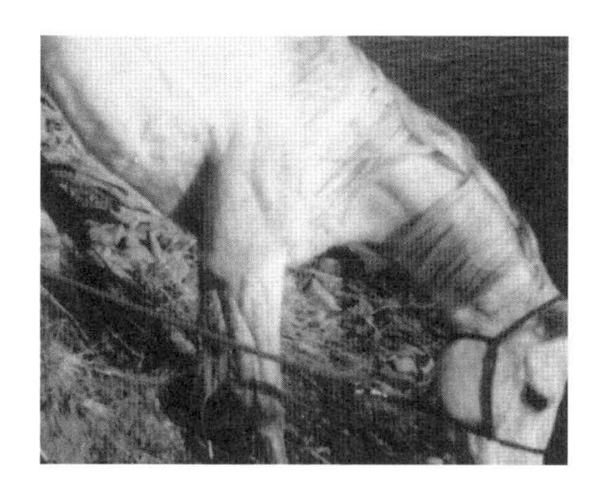

Spice is fishing off camera to the right. Honest!

It must have been basking in the shallows and now it was stuck between a rock and a hard place. I grabbed it and threw it on the grass. It flopped and gasped and I knew I couldn't eat it so I picked it up and threw it back in the water. As it was arching through the air I remembered the camera in my hand but it was too late. To compensate I took a photo of Spice who was still drinking. That's the almost proof I mean.

So there I was, with hardly any food, and not a lot of cosmetics left to eat either. (Toothpaste is strictly for seasoning. Mint dental floss, however, is a good substitute for chewing gum.) I had timed things pretty well though because I was finally within striking distance of a store. All I had to do was make it to the town at Gibson Dam. That required me to ride Spice along a narrow rocky path halfway down the cliff sides that bounded the lake behind the dam.

Huckleberrys, in case you don't know, are as real as woodpeckers, but much more rare. They don't grow in captivity very well so that is why huckleberry jam is more expensive than whisky. The bushes grow on rocky sunny slopes and are highly prized. Just before the end of the trail around the dam and just three hours from the little town was an enoooormous huckleberry bush. Usually, whenever we stopped for a break, I'd be ready to start again long before Spice had finished eating, but this was different. I got stuck in for a good hour and a half and Spice was bored in no time at all. When I'd eaten all the berries I could, I turned to look for Spice. He'd left me and headed on up the trail. There was nowhere else for him to go, since the trail fell away so steeply on each side, so I walked along happily after him.

After about 20 minutes I caught up to him at a patch of grass. He looked up haughtily and neighed reprovingly before grazing again. I think he was making the point that delays caused by being a guzzleguts were his job not mine. He always did think he was in charge.

After stocking up on grub, I bought a new saddle pad to replace an old one, which was looking a bit thin and ratty. I'd been given a lift by some folks I'd met at the stables where I put Spice up for the day. As long as I was in the mountains, there were often dude ranches and hunters' camps that could supply me with grain or lodging for Spice. If not, I would head out to a working ranch to get what I needed. No one ever charged me for grain for Spice as soon as they heard where we'd come from and where we were going. People were very friendly and helpful like that.

I also met plenty of people on the trail. As it was summer, many families were camping and some hunters were exploring their areas in anticipation of the hunting season. Fishermen and birdwatchers, hikers and rangers all stopped to talk to me and ask where I was going. After a while, the questions and answers were so predictable I thought of getting a T-shirt printed with the following answers to the commonest questions:

1. Canada
2. Mexico
3. Just one horse all the way
4. 25 miles a day
5. I have a map
6. No, I don't plan to write a book
7. Actually, I'm a Kiwi
8. That's a person from New Zealand

The 100-odd miles from the bottom of Glacier Park to the outskirts of the town of Lincoln took only nine days compared to the 29 days it took with Ash to go 140 miles in a straight line. The fly in the ointment was that I was getting short of money, as well as the fact that in six weeks I had only covered one tenth of the distance that I planned to. I decided to arrange for some more money and then crack on the pace and try to make it at least halfway to Mexico in the remaining six weeks. By the time I reached the tiny but perfectly formed town of Lincoln, I was down to $110 with no more credit on my Visa card.

Lincoln is a great little town. It has two bars, a motel, a grocery shop, a sporting goods store, a meat locker, a feed store and a hardware shop and, best of all, a Mountain Phone Company and the First National Bank of Lincoln. As soon as I arrived, I went to the feed store and bought a 50-pound bag of grain for Spice and got permission to stay in the camp ground next to the river for a couple of days. There was ample grass there as well as toilets, barbecues and running water. Since it was a Thursday, I had to move fast to call New Zealand and arrange for an extension to my credit limit on my Visa card. Because of the time differences and the approaching weekend, I knew that if I didn't get the loan approved quickly, I'd be stranded here for several days. When it was Friday in Lincoln, it was Saturday in NZ, so I tried to get it all arranged before the start of the Kiwi weekend. If I failed, then I'd have to wait until Monday in Lincoln (Tuesday in NZ) before I could try again. This was because the only suitable phone in town was in the phone company office, which wasn't open on weekends, and I couldn't afford to check in to a motel and call from my room. Pay phones weren't an option as it takes 52 quarters for a three-minute call to NZ and if the coinbox fills up and jams while you're putting them in, then you're stuffed.

'Canada.'
'Really, and where to?'
'Mexico.'
'Really . . .'

I had already dealt with that once before in Chicago, where I couldn't even get a bank to change $10 into quarters. They insisted I have an account. I insisted they would have to Swim the Seven Seas and Cross the Burning Deserts just to Drink My Bathwater, before I opened an account with them. They said they had a department that did all of that and that he was holding the door open for me now. He was a very large guard who could have squeezed my head between his finger and thumb, and he showed me out on to the street. When I finally got the money and called NZ, the receptionist put me on hold before I could explain that I was in a phone box, and my three minutes ran out listening to *Home on the Range* in dial tones. (When I find that woman, I will kill her. That will be doing God's work.) Naturally the bank wouldn't take a collect call from a customer. That would have been waaay too hard.

In Lincoln, I was determined to call from a phone that I could pay for *after* the call, and that meant the phone company offices. I still had the problem of time zones, so when the nice people at the little phone company saw my problem, they said that they'd leave the door key under the mat, and I could let myself in and make the call on one of their office phones after hours. Then all I had to do was call in and pay them the next day. I went to make my call at about 8 pm that night and finally got through to the man at the Visa card desk. He asked me how much I needed and I said $US1000. He said that that was probably OK, and that he would fax me the forms. I explained that I couldn't wait for that as I was nearly out of money, which was true. By the time I'd paid for our food, camping fees and phone calls, I was down to about $20. Not much to fall back on if the money was delayed, not even enough for another phone call to NZ.

I offered to give him all the details he needed over the phone. He said OK, but he still needed a signature on the application for a temporary increase in my credit limit. Then I played my trump. I reminded him that the reason I needed the money was because I had to pay a bunch of medical bills after I broke my arm. Pause. My right arm. Pause. My *writing* arm actually. Finally he agreed that a lefthanded signature was meaningless and instead he asked me a bunch of 'Who won the

Ranfurly Shield in 1985?' type questions until he was convinced that I was the legitimate cardholder. At last he said that it would take a day to process and that I could draw on the money in about 24 hours time. It couldn't happen any faster.

Disaster! That meant 8 pm Friday night, and the bank would be shut. I thanked the Visa chap and hung up. The next day I paid the bill at the phone company and when they asked how it all went, I sheepishly told them the problem. 'Why that's nothing,' the lady said. 'Go on over to the bank and ask Marjorie if she'll stay open for you tomorrow night, until the money arrives.' Yeah sure, I thought, banks always open up at night so tramps can get cash advances before the weekend.

Turned out they did too! The bank manager was only too happy to come in especially for me and give me my money. Yahoo! Do you get service like that from your bank and your phone company? Way to go Lincoln.

That night I went to the bar with some folks who were staying at the camp ground and celebrated. Later that night they offered me a job driving a combine harvester, and I said I'd think about it. There was live music from a real good C and W band and there were pretty women in little white cowboy boots and purple Stetsons twirling around tall skinny cowboys with two-tone boots and big moustaches. Middle-aged married couples strutted their stuff and drunken truck drivers fought in the parking lot. A great night in a great little town.

After drawing $750 the next night, I set out two days later with Spice rested and bloated on half a bag of grain. I filled my bags and left the rest for another cowboy who was passing through with a horse trailer and two horses. I was sorry to leave Lincoln. It was chockablock with the friendliest most helpful people I'd met so far and everyone wanted me to visit them or go work for them when I finished riding. Plenty wanted to adopt Spice and he flannelled them shamelessly by following them around and nuzzling the women and children. Disgusting if you ask me. Some folks wanted to come with me and abandon their jobs and families, but I managed to convince them that it wasn't all a bed of roses. Even though it was.

Chapter 8

In which Spice suffers from my singing, I acquire a new vice, and a small case of equine hydrophobia causes me to behave despicably (though I am severely provoked)

The next order of business after leaving Lincoln was to head south-east towards Helena, Montana, so that by the time I got there, one month would have passed since I broke my wrist and then I'd be able to get a smaller cast put on my arm. The doctor in Great Falls said I could have a forearm cast and gave me some X-rays and a letter to show to the clinic. I actually got to Helena a bit too soon, but it was the only city I'd get to before I went into Yellowstone and that was weeks ahead.

I put Spice in the barn of a friendly rancher's wife and hitched into town. It didn't take long to get my cast swapped for a smaller one and that time they let me pick the colour. I went for a nifty dark blue that matched my only T-shirt. The other choices were neon yellow, fluorescent pink or toxic-waste green. Just-plain-white was showing the dirt too much, so I was pleased to have a respectably dressed arm again. Later that day I pulled out and set off for the Deerlodge Forest. By now, I was halfway through Montana and had covered 300 miles as the crow flies but nearer to 450 in real terms. Only 2500 more to Mexico.

It was around this time that I tried to compose a song. I stole the opening bars of Arlo Guthrie's *(I'm a Train They Call The) 'City of New Orleans'*. I was in very high spirits, had plenty of money, no worries and the weather was ideal so I composed a number of happy verses about the joys of Riding Through Montana in the Summer. I can't sing and even my speaking voice sounds flat so it was a bit of a trial for Spice, and after two days of very theatrical ear-twitching by the old fool whenever

I started to sing, I reluctantly quit. All the world's a critic. Instead I began chewing tobacco.

I'd seen it in all the stores for weeks but I didn't know how to do it. Since I was all by myself now, I figured that this was the time to try. I bought a plug of Red Man tobacco for $1.35 and opened the pack. Chewing tobacco is nothing like pipe or cigarette tobacco and is totally different from snuff which is nothing at all like 'Snuff'.

Sporting a colour-coordinated half-cast, I park Spice at an information centre.

Chewing tobacco is coarse cut and you can still see the shapes of leaves. It is moist and sweet. It comes in various flavours, like regular, beechnut and mint. It isn't as finely cut or dry or as bitter as smoking tobacco and it hasn't the strong smell of unsmoked pipe weed.

What people think of as chewing tobacco is not the stuff that comes in little round tins, which cowboys put a pinch of next to their gums. That is called snuff and, although it is based on tobacco, it is more like a powder, and tastes like cough lollies. It's rumoured that it has ground glass in it, but that is untrue. It is as addictive as all the tobacco products and, like all the rest, it'll give you cancer. Actual 'Snuff' is a tobacco powder that used to be inhaled to induce sneezing. No one uses it so if you ask for snuff in the west you'll get offered a can of Skoal or Copenhagen, which are the two biggest brands.

Real chew isn't as popular as snuff because it's a messier habit. You spit a lot with chew, so it's an outdoorsman's habit. I was outdoors, so I opened my packet and discovered a tightly compressed block slightly larger than two matchboxes. I'd seen old miners in movies cut a piece of chew with a knife or else take a big solid bite of something that looked like tough liquorice. 'Fine,' I thought, 'if that's how it's done, here goes.'

I took a big bite off the corner of the block and started chewing it like gum. In seconds I was gobbing gallons and hiccuping violently. I spat it out and tried again with a smaller bit. Same again. I kept trying and eventually managed to control the hiccuping and expectorating by taking a piece the size of a pea and not chewing it. Maybe the stuff in the movies *was* liquorice.

After a while, I progressed to spitting a bit. I went for distance first, as the immediate objective was to spit beyond the horse. Like everything worth doing, there's a trick to it, and it took me a while to get it. By the time I could spit past Spice's shoulder, he was looking like a streaky piebald, with big brown stains on his side. I aspired to be able to drown a bug at 20 paces or to stun a dog at five, just like Clint Eastwood in *The Outlaw Josie Wales*, every boy's hero. Alas, I still struggled to hit the ground, let alone a barn door, but it gave me something to do when it was too wet to roll a smoke.

Around that time I became aware of a problem with my boots. They looked great but I was nearly crippled by them. At the end of the day when my feet started to swell, there was no room left in them and they pinched like hell. Exposed to the air they looked like two Sally Lunn loaves. It got to where it even hurt me to put on socks in the morning. I hadn't seen anything to replace them with so I persevered with them and in due course I found something better just after the Pointless Battle of the Bridge.

One boiling hot afternoon just after I'd stocked up on food and grain in the town of Boulder, Montana I stopped by a culvert on the roadside to let Spice get a drink. The culvert went under the road and on either side clean water flowed through it and out through a field. At the edge, I walked him down into the little stream and waited for him to drink. He didn't want to drink, so I stepped across the water and started to climb the other bank. Just as I was mid-stride, instead of following me across, Spice pulled back and since the lead rope I was holding was now tight, he pulled me off balance and I fell arse-first into the trickle of water. To understand what happened next, you have to know about Spice and water.

He loathed getting wet. Hated it. At first, he wouldn't even step in puddles, but would walk round them. On a rainy day that was like riding a drunk as he weaved from side to side. It was ridiculous. It made Cat Ballou's horse look like a Lippizaner. Our first stream crossing took 20 minutes and in the end I led him across and got wet ALL THE WAY UP TO MY ANKLES! Yes, gentle reader, it was as bad as that. Once, in Yellowstone, we were walking along a trail that had lots of little wooden footbridges so that tourists wouldn't get their sneakers wet. Each bridge had planks laid crossways with a rail nailed along the edge to hold them down on each side. The rail was three or four inches in from the edge and formed a sort of curb. One of the bridges had subsided on one side and the bridge had a 40° lean to the right. I had been leading Spice happily along behind me all morning, but when we came to that one, I knew he wouldn't be able to get a footing on the slippery slope so, while I balanced on the edge of the uphill curb, I expected that he'd splash into the foot-deep water alongside me. Wrong. He was such a pussy about getting his feet wet that when I heard 'clip clop' instead of 'splish splash' I turned around and stared at him in disbelief. He was following me by balancing on the edge of the bridge, putting one foot in front of the other in the vee formed by the outside edge of the curb! All that highwire work just to avoid getting wet to the knees. That's the kind of wuss that he was. Every river or stream deeper than his knees was a battle that I always won, but not without a struggle.

The Great Wallenda practises his high-wire act on a normal bridge.

By then I thought he'd accepted little events like that rivulet as routine and splashed along without a fuss. Not that time. I got out of the water and stepped across again, giving a sharp tug on the lead rope. He pulled back again more sharply and I stumbled into the water. I looked up and down to check that there was nothing dead there that could scare him and I stamped the banks on both sides to show that there was no quicksand or alligators. But I already knew the reason. With a perfectly dry crossing just four feet to our right, he didn't want to step over a nine-inch-wide water gap and then scramble up a three-foot bank. He'd rather turn around, go back up the bank he was on, turn again and cross the water via the road culvert.

He often made this sort of unilateral policy decision and it frequently didn't bother me. Occasionally I got a kick out of seeing him screw up, like the time he decided to cross a very wide river, not by following the line of the white water where it was shallow as it tumbled over a natural weir, but instead, he preferred the calmer water a few feet back from the edge, which I could tell was a lot deeper. As I was safely seated on his back, I was happy to indulge that idea and in fact I confess to knowing what would happen, so I lifted my legs up and relaxed the tension in the reins. He immediately turned away from the gravel weir edge and stepped into the quiet water. Two steps later he slipped off a boulder and plunged head-first under the water. His head was pointed down as he was looking for footholds and so it went about six feet under the surface. The water must have shot up his nose and he leapt back on to the rock again, like a movie run backwards, snorting and coughing with surprise. I got soaked in the splash and so did the bags, but I was laughing like hell at the way he blew all main

The Bechler River where Mr Clever-Clogs learned it's true what they say about still waters.

ballast and bounced back on to the rock. He hated to be laughed at and sulked for the rest of the day.

On the day at the culvert, though, I was hot and wet, my feet ached and I was in no mood for fooling around. There was no reason for him not to follow me as he wouldn't even get his feet wet. Since we were halfway there, it was also shorter by five or six yards. Now five or six yards isn't much when taken over a 2500-mile trip, so you can see that it was a matter of principle, which translated as meaning that there was no logical reason for either of us to squabble over his refusal to go across rather than around the stream.

I pulled on his lead rope more sharply and he backed up again. Then I gave a mighty yank that rattled his eyeballs and I stepped across the water. He dug his heels in and pulled back again. I swung the end of the rope at his hindquarters to drive him on and he reared up. I yanked again and he reared, I pulled and yelled and cursed and hit and he snorted and reared and yanked and glared at me. After ten minutes of that I paused for breath and decided to ride him over. As soon as I pointed him at the stream, he walked right up to the edge and stopped. I kicked him on. He balked. I backed him up and ran him at it. He slid to a stop on the edge again. I tried it another dozen times, and each was the same. He'd run right up to it and then skid to a halt in the bottom of the ditch. I tried the other side of the road. Same thing. I kicked him on and he reared. That wasn't funny, so I whacked him on the head with my plaster cast and kicked him on again. Rear, whack, kick, rear, whack, kick . . .

I spun him round and galloped him over the culvert and up the road for a half mile. He loved that and I let him think he'd won before I turned and raced back over the culvert and down and around to the water. He stopped so fast I would have pitched over the handlebars if I hadn't been expecting it.

'Youcocksuckingboxbitingarselickingshitheadedsonova-bitch.' I did it all again and it was the same. He'd go like hell across the culvert and up the road and back across the culvert and turn like a figure skater, and plunge down the bank and STOP! We were both pouring sweat and an hour and a half had gone by. Each time I put him at the stream he'd turn away and I'd wrench his head around and kick him on. The water was muddy now and the grass down the slope to the water was worn away by the constant traffic of his hooves.

I dismounted and tried to lead him across. I deliberately splashed through the water so he could see that it wasn't a trick. I was already wet, which was usually the sole precondition for him to cross water. Normally he just liked to see the misery shared but not that day. I paused for a moment to wipe my head and, as I only had one good arm, I held his lead rope in my teeth while I took off my hat. Spice jerked his head back and nearly tore two teeth out of my head. I checked them, and they wiggled. I was so furious that I completely lost all control and punched him in the nose. He reared and tried to back away. I ran to his side and kicked him in the guts as hard as I could. As tall as he was and with me standing on a lower slope and wearing tight jeans I was only barely able to reach his stomach with the toe of my boot, so it wouldn't have hurt as much as it sounds like, but it's the thought that counts at those times and the thought was murderous. I sprang up on his back and charged him at the crossing. He reared and I clubbed him with my cast so hard that my arm started throbbing as badly as when I broke it. After another ten minutes of kicking, clubbing, rearing, and trying to pitch me off I finally quit. If we'd kept going one or other of us would have been killed, since by then we were both trying to hurt each other as much as we could. I threw the lead rope at him and chased him away from me. He stood on the other side of the road glaring at me. He'd beaten me.

Never before or since has an animal or a child made me lose my temper so completely and never have I been so thoroughly whipped by stubborn insubordination. You might be asking why it was so important that he be made to cross a creek when there was a simpler but longer route around. The answer was part principle, that I was the boss, and part safety. If he refused to do something out of pure cussedness, then I couldn't rely on him not to do it when it really mattered, such as when the alternative might mean backtracking for days. Days when I might have no food or I might be injured and in need of attention. Mainly it was the principle, though, and he knew it too. Don't be in any doubt that it was a fight for dominance, and he knew he'd won. The look in his eye when we were going at each other was enough for me. If I'd had a rope strong enough, I'd have roped him down and tied him and dragged him across by force. If he'd known how to buck properly he'd have hurt me too. He was sure trying.

When I finally gave in and rode him up the road, it was two hours later and the start of a week-long silence between us. He wouldn't neigh or whicker or whinny, and he wouldn't come near the tent. He'd stand still while I saddled and mounted, he'd behave perfectly when I rode him and he followed me into quicksand on the very next river crossing, but we still didn't speak. The quicksand was plenty deep enough to drown us both but it wasn't too wide and with frantic lunges for the bank we managed to reach some firmer footing before we sank under the porridgey green surface. There was a brief moment after we got out when we were both so scared that we were shivering with fear and I hugged him and said I was sorry for hitting him before. He looked so unhappy, all covered in mud and weed and sand that I think he was glad I'd apologised, but after we got cleaned and dried up, the silence returned.

In the race to get out of the sand, he'd run over me and put his foot down the back of my leg. It slid down my boot and tore the back of the sole off. Within an hour I was limping and I could see I'd never fix the boot. I rode him instead and spat tobacco juice at his head.

Of course all that doesn't make a pretty tale and it shows I have less class than a horse. He never had a mean bone in his body but he had some damn stubborn ones. I got him to an empty corral three days later and was brushing him down as usual. He had a tender spot on his head where I'd thumped him with my plaster cast and it hurt when I touched it. His flank was sore where I'd kicked him and he wouldn't let me check him for cinch sores. He reared and snorted and it looked like another fight was developing. That time, though, I was equipped to win. I hobbled him and tied him to the corral fence. He reared again as soon as I touched him so I shortened the lead rope so he couldn't toss his head and then I looped his hind legs and tied them to the fence too. Now he was furious that he couldn't do anything and was forced to let me check him gently. I'd won through superior technology just as he'd won through strength and patience at the Bridge. One all.

The score reached two all before we patched up our differences. I got ahead when he plunged under the water at the wide crossing of the Bechler River. He got even when he refused to cross a murky creek in Yellowstone. I made him do it anyway and he proved me wrong. It was a victory for him as when we stepped in, it was a mud bottom that trapped him fast. I leapt off his back into the chest-deep water and grabbed his lead rope while he thrashed vainly in the sucking mud. His head was only an inch or two above water so at first I struggled to hold that while he floundered for a better footing. When he rested for a moment I struggled frantically to get the saddlebags off and then dived down to release the cinch. Just then he made a convulsive lunge and managed to get a foot on something solid. The next instant he was up and out of the water and I followed him a moment later with all the gear. He stood waiting while I cleaned the worst of the mess off him and loaded up again. At any point, he could have taken off, but strangely, I think he was more keen to hear me admit I was wrong than to leave for a safer career. At the next clear stream we both got in and I washed him down from top to bottom. He didn't object as he usually did, and even waited while I cleaned myself and the gear. That was the end of our fight and I call it a draw.

But back to the boots. After the Battle and the quicksand river crossing, I stopped for the night at a ranch. Nicky Shriver let me camp in her horse pasture down by the river, even though she was alone on the ranch with her kids away at school and her husband away working. She was an attractive woman in her late thirties or early forties and looked after their sheep and horses and dogs while her husband was away. The trust that people had for a dirty, dangerous-looking man on a horse was amazing. I could have been an axe-murdering rapist, but out west folks haven't got such a bunker mentality and they welcomed me into their homes again and again.

That night it stormed and rained and my $20 tent leaked.

By morning my eiderdown sleeping bag was wetter than a duck's nuts. I froze and things weren't very bright the next day when I found I'd misplaced my knife. That was the place where the herd chased Spice through the fence and I found the bear tracks the next morning when I was looking for Spice and discovered him forlornly looking over the fence, wondering how he'd get back in. The only gates were miles away, so I pulled a couple of staples out and held the wires down while he stepped over them. He was always pretty good about stepping over wire fences and that saved me a long walk. After replacing the staples and tightening the fence, I returned to the tent to find Nicky asking me what was wrong with my foot. I explained about my boot and she insisted on driving me the 20 miles or so back to town so I could buy another pair.

I took my sodden sleeping bag to dry in the laundromat as I wasn't looking forward to a week of sleeping in something that had all the insulating properties of a sack of seaweed. When down gets wet it turns into a sodden ball of feathers that need 50 or 60 hours of normal sunshine to dry out. An industrial tumble drier would do at least half the job in an hour or two. I left Spice to graze in another field and headed off to town with Nicky.

This phenomenally sweet lady had already cooked me a chicken dinner and left it outside my tent the night before while I was washing in the river and now was taking a day off work to run me around shopping. After I bought the boots she insisted we wait for the sleeping bag to dry and bought me lunch as well. I tried to pay but she knew the waitress, who wouldn't take my money. I bought some waterproofing compound for the tent and started to try on boots. Cowboy boots were out of the question for walking, so the boots I selected were hikers' boots. They were green and red and looked as if I'd brutally kicked two large green moles up the arse. They were, however, the most comfortable things I'd ever worn. As soon as I put them on I said to the salesman, 'I could walk around the world in these,' and he showed me that exact quote on the pamphlet from a guy who had. That did it. I was sick of boots that looked good but fitted like waffle irons. Recently, Spice had trod on my foot and broken my little toe and it didn't seem to be getting better. I figured that these boots would help it to heal faster as well so I plonked down $100-odd dollars and jumped into them with real pleasure.

After we got back to the ranch, I began to saddle up Spice when I saw he was cinch sore. Nicky called a vet who advised that a fleece cinch was the best solution, and that if I didn't cinch him as tight, then all would be well. Spice had high bony shoulder-blades that held a saddle in place without the need for a tight cinch. This is a big advantage over a barrel-backed quarter horse that needs a tight cinch to prevent the saddle from slipping day after day. There was no town within 20 miles that sold cinches so Nicky called around and found one in Whitehall, 30 miles away. She was ready to drive there immediately to get one but I said that it could wait till Spice and I got there in two days' time. I planned to walk until then anyway. She wouldn't settle for that and started digging around in the back of the house and came out with a brand-new one that belonged to her daughter. She refused to take more than $8 for it even though we both knew they cost $30 or more. There was no way she'd let me pay for gas or phone calls.

Don and Nicky Shriver. Waaay beyond mere hospitality. Typical of so many we met.

That night, after I finally found my knife, her husband Don returned from some contracting work and the following morning he looked Spice over and pronounced him fit for work. He used to be an outfitter and their barn was full of tack and pack saddles and the house was full of hunting trophies. They were a great couple and I wished I could have stayed longer. Later that day, I met them driving towards me along the road, Nicky snuggled up to Don in their pick-up, with his arm around her like a teenager. They stopped and Don offered me an ice-cold beer. Helluva nice folks.

Chapter 9

In which I contemplate the wonders of Yellowstone Park, Spice mugs for the cameras and we rescue a lost soul. Also, the tale of the bear and the preacher

Having come down out of the mountains into the ranch country of the Ruby Valley, I was now headed east towards Yellowstone Park. I hoped that this would be the highlight of my journey and in one respect it was. It's hard to judge the best part of that trip. Scenically, it was a toss-up between Yellowstone, the Gros Ventre river area and the forests just south of Glacier Park, but that was just the scenery. I met people like Don and Nicky Shriver whose hospitality was overwhelming. I got the greatest satisfaction from getting un-lost in an ordinary patch of forest, simply by puzzling things out correctly. Spice gave me some of the best moments too, just by doing something as simple as going to sleep in front of me, or poking his nose in the tent to wake me up in the morning. I won't forget the woman who stopped on the road and passed me two cold cans of coke because she thought I looked hot. I was too, but wasn't that a sweet thing to do? For going above and beyond the call of duty, though, the rangers at the west gate of Yellowstone took some beating.

Lee Lofgren (right) and friends outside his Pullman house.

When I got to the town of West Yellowstone, I met Lee Lofgren, who saw me with my horse in the parking lot of a motel asking directions to any camp ground that took horses. There weren't any. He ambled over from the porch in front of his chiropractic office to see what I was up to. After I explained what I was doing, he called a friend who called a friend who said I could stay in the rodeo showground corrals. I got Spice settled and fed and Lee invited me to have a beer after dinner. Turned out that he used to be a cowboy but decided that, although he liked it, there was no future in it, so he trained as a chiropractor and had recently hung up a shingle. Having done all the training and got himself into debt to do it, it seemed that there wasn't a hell of a lot of future in chiropractic either. I think he missed the cowboy life. He asked me whether I had a permit arranged to enter the park and I said no. He wasn't optimistic I'd get in and said that if it took more than a day to arrange, then I might like to come into the park the next night with some friends of his who were going to watch the elk bugle.

A bull elk looks like a shaggy red deer and produces the most amazing whistling sound in the breeding season to attract females and warn males off. This is called bugling and it's fun to watch so I agreed to meet him the next evening at his house, a converted railway carriage decked out like a Pullman coach near the park entrance.

For a while I thought this was all I'd see of it.

I spent the whole next day explaining to the park rangers what I was doing and getting permission to ride through the park. Fortunately, the busiest part of the tourist season had just finished so they were in a tolerant mood. There were a number of problems.

First, 'This is a gate that doesn't accept horses. Everyone who rides in the park goes in another area on the far side of the park.' Since the park is half the size of Belgium, that was more of a problem than it might appear.

Secondly, 'This side is all burnt out since the big fire.' To go where I wanted meant traversing part of the area that had been burnt in the big fire of 1989, which left thousands of acres of deadfall that closed hundreds of miles of trails. Fallen trees with fire-hardened branches like concertina wire are bigger obstacles to travel than nationalised railways.

Fire-hardened deadfall (left) makes burnt forests impassable even though they appear open.

Thirdly, 'You can't ride on the roads with your horse, sir — you'll get in a wreck.' To get anywhere, meant initially riding alongside the road, which was banned because of the risk of colliding with Winnebago camper vans the size of the other half of Belgium.

Fourthly, 'Where are you gonna camp?' Horses weren't allowed to camp just anywhere at night. There were already enough camp sites to accommodate the entire annual crop of wetbacks, and the approved sites were full.

Fifthly, 'What feed are you carrying?' I didn't carry enough feed to detour around those areas and horses weren't supposed to eat the grass in Yellowstone as it was for the wild animals.

Sixthly . . . All those rules were made to minimise the impact of horses on the ecosystem, and even included rules preventing the feeding of uncertified hay in the park lest weeds be introduced. Compressed hay cubes from commercial suppliers were OK, as was grain, so I was in the clear, but even after all the food had gone through the horse, there was a rule about poo as well. If your horse left a 'meadow muffin' you had to scatter it so that it would break down faster and not harbour worms and parasites. Thank God they didn't ask for pooper-scoopers.

After explaining where I'd come from, and where I was going, and generally giving the standard eight answers, the ranger called her supervisor. He called someone else and I had the feeling it was headed all the way up the food-chain for Congressional approval when a miracle happened. For the first time in my entire life, I heard a civil servant take a decision. He didn't consult any rules or regulations, he just said, 'All right, if there's only one person, I guess it's OK.' And that was that. After the rangers brought me water and quit fanning my face, they gave me a permit to enter the following day, and told me where I could camp. The route took me alongside the road, round the deadfall and right past Old Faithful, through hordes of tourists and, finally, into an area where horses weren't allowed, before exiting at the south gate. Perfect. I wish I knew that ranger's name as he deserves a medal for that. I repaid him by following his instructions faithfully, which was just as well as I was watched from a distance by armed rangers in radio communication with the headquarters for the first two days. All that sounds silly, but it is necessary to protect the park from the chaos and destruction that 5,000,000 tourists would create each year if they were let alone. I was happy just to be in the park and so I paid the fee for a man and a horse and walked back to find Lee and go elk bugling.

Early morning geysers made an eerie mist.

We headed into the park two hours before dusk with two of his friends and their car. We each contributed part of a picnic supper and before we even had time to make a sandwich, an elk that was knee-deep in reeds only a couple of hundred yards away started calling. Cars started to stop and people got out to look. That tends to happen a lot in Yellowstone as it's a cross between a safari park and Disneyland. You only have to stop and point and two tour buses, 60 cars and 25 Winnebagos disgorge about $2,000,000 worth of Japanese 'cameratry', all pointed at anything from a bear to a bunny rabbit. (Never ever get out of your car and go behind the bushes for a leak in Yellowstone unless you don't mind starring in several hundred home movies. I have seen people filming rangers collecting trash. What is wrong with these people?) The elk kept calling and eventually was answered by another one right next to me. It was Lee, who was lying on his back with his hat over his face so no one could tell that it was him whistling. He did a good enough impression to fool the elk who rounded up his females and started to get ready for a scrap. Before matters could progress, another call came from across the river, presumably a real one, as the elk then turned to face the new challenge. Nothing appeared, but the bugling went on for quite a while. As the cars dispersed and things got quieter the frogs broke out and birds reappeared and finally, as the sun went down behind the mountains casting shadows a half mile long, the elk and all of us packed up and headed for our homes. A great evening.

If you've been to Yellowstone then you know how magnificent the valleys and rivers are. If not, go there. For concentrated wildlife viewing, only an African safari park will beat it, but you can't ride on horseback through many safari parks for fear of lions. If Yellowstone is getting a bit Disneyfied, then it's understandable. People who could never ordinarily get close enough to see a wild bear, a moose or a buffalo can see all of them from the comfort of their car. This may sound a bit corny, but there are millions of people who can't afford the time to go walking through the forests in search of those animals in other parks. The US has a great selection of national parks, state parks and forests of all kinds, that range from heavily developed ones like Yellowstone where you can see everything from your car, to ones where you have to ride or walk or boat. Some parks are so remote that hardly anyone goes to them and a fit tramper can not only get close to nature, but more importantly, can get away from humanity, which is much better. They cater for everyone's abilities which is good. Without Yellowstone to satisfy hordes of casual nature lovers, it's doubtful whether the public would support the spending of millions of dollars on a host of smaller less-accessible parks.

As I rode through the park, I was stopped a number of times and asked to pose for photos by people who thought I was a real cowboy. That was downright embarrassing as I knew I wasn't even dressed for the part, let alone acting it. I

did it anyway, but only because Spice was mugging for the camera.

It was incredible how well behaved he was around strangers. I'd let him loose to graze while I talked to folks and he'd not even eat. He'd stand around being perfectly sociable and polite and letting little kids pet him. He had huge brown eyes and he used them to good effect on any passing girl who would invariably gush and gurgle at him. He perfected a George Clooney look that involved tilting his head to one side and looking meltingly at the woman as if she was a five-gallon bucket of grain. Sickening really. As soon as they left, he'd drop his head and start to eat and if I insisted on moving on he'd refuse and I'd have to wait until he was ready. If a camera was produced, he'd stand perfectly still with me but if I stepped away to get my own, he'd walk off to eat immediately. He had plenty of time for the paparazzi to click and flash, but not for me. If he could have held a pen I'm sure he'd have given autographs. He was a ham all right.

Posing for tourists.

Dances with buffaloes.

The herd of buffalo we met on the first day was about 50 strong and was right next to the road. Buffalo are quick and aggressive if you get inside the herd and they'll kill you as efficiently as any carnivore. To be safe I got on Spice and rode around the edges of the herd towards the start of the track I was required to take. As I passed a row of cars full of camera-clicking tourists I heard one say, 'Just like *Dances with Wolves*.' So there I was, in the wild west, on a trusty horse face to face with buffalo just five months after seeing it on the big screen in England. Neat.

As I left the herd and rode up a small ridge, I looked back at the cars and saw them crawling along the winding road and thought how lucky that I wasn't stuck in nose-to-tail traffic jams. No one was overtaking on blind corners either.

The park allowed me to see certain animals I hadn't seen at close range before such as buffalo, porcupine, elk and moose. Occasionally I saw something more rare like a pine marten and all day I was scolded by small birds. I may have seen a bald eagle but I'm not sure. It looked a bit small. Maybe it was a bald jay. I certainly saw plenty of fish eagles, which look similar to me. I saw no rattlesnakes or scorpions or poisonous spiders at any time. Up high in the northern states the winters are too severe and even racoons aren't comfortable there. That meant it was pretty safe to stick a boot on without shaking it in the morning.

Bull hat-rack about to bugle.

I made a small detour to have a look at Old Faithful. I'd already seen it on a previous trip in 1989 so I'm not sure why I bothered again. A geyser is no more than a fountain that knows how to work a crowd. Like a Hollywood star it threatens not to appear, even while sending teasing spouts and gushes up to draw in the punters. Finally, a chic half hour late, it burst forth to cheers and applause. A lot of pictures are taken of a militantly vertical column of water, its remarkable appeal being based on the fact that it happens so regularly. When it finally roars out of the ground it seems angry and anti-climactic at the same time; imagine a cuckoo clock with a 400-pound bird on steroids bursting out of its little doors to growl at you. That's Old Faceful.

Soon after this I helped a lost visitor who had been deserted by his friends. A party had gone into the park to search for the remains of a World War II bomber that had crashed many years before and was recently rediscovered. One of the group got separated and, after a lot of wandering around, returned to the camp site to find that his friends had pulled out! They left no note about where they were going and so the man decided to walk out. With no food, water, knife, matches, map or warm clothes he set off to follow a trail to the edge of the park. On the way he came across me sheltering from the rain by my camp fire. It was just getting dark so he stopped for a couple of hours while I fed him his first meal since a small breakfast and dried his clothes over the fire. I fitted him out with a torch, knife, map and food and offered to take him out with me the next day, but he insisted on leaving and trying to locate his friends. From his description of them I realised that they had also passed through my camp earlier in the afternoon. They had not mentioned a word about having lost a member of their party. Instead they planned to just leave and presumably tell the rangers the next day. Madness. My advice to the man was to find his friends and whack the shit out of them. It's easy enough to get in trouble in the mountains without being abandoned by your mates like that.

One afternoon I made plans to leave very early the following day as I wanted to ride in the dark for a while to see if I saw any different animals, so I finished early and got ready to leave at 3 am that night. At the right time my internal alarm clock woke me up and I started to pack up my tent very quietly. It had rained lightly during the night and I was glad I hadn't slept outside.

I never use lights at night as I can easily find everything I need in the dark, I hate wasting batteries or candles, and it's a more peaceful start to the day with no lights flashing around. If I'm with anyone, I always whisper at night; it seems wrong to disturb all the quiet. On that night, I silently collapsed the tent and packed it away with my sleeping bag. I dressed and got my saddlebags and saddle ready for Spice. I checked the saddle pads for twigs and burrs (these were my mattress each night) and gathered my water bag and hatchet. Spice was fast asleep on his high-line only ten feet away and amazingly he slept through all the rustling and small noises.

Finally, I couldn't wait any longer and so I walked over to him and gently patted his neck. He woke up instantly and looked at me with the same blinking confusion that anyone has if their deep sleep is interrupted. I asked him to get up and he did so wearily. I told him we'd finish early that day, maybe just after lunch, and he perked up a bit.

As soon as we rode off, it became apparent that he'd never seen a flashlight before and if I shone the light on the ground, he thought the beam was an object and stepped around it. I turned it off and left him to navigate along the track hoping that there weren't any low-hanging branches. The moon hadn't risen and with the clouds covering the stars, it was as black as the inside of a cow. I never did see any creatures, but I liked the feeling of riding at night. I didn't do it again though because it was so hard to stay on the right trail without using the torch a lot. Tree shadows and no moon kept things pretty dark. It worked in Yellowstone but only because the tracks are very well maintained.

The next port of call was Lake Jackson. It took a few pleasant days' riding down roads and through the Grand Teton National Park before I came to the shores of the lake.

Spice was thirsty so I took him to the water. I happened to be riding him rather than walking him and as soon as he saw the huge expanse of water he spat the dummy. He thought that I wanted him to swim across it and so I screwed with his mind a bit by trying to ride him up to the edge. You have to do it once in a while, because animals will sure do it to you, just for shits and giggles. Spice used to play with my mind by rubbing his head on my arm while I read the map. This scratching would knock me off balance so I'd brace myself so he could do it properly. Then he'd smile and start eating again.

Finally I got off and walked him across the sandy beach to the edge telling him that maybe he was right and it was a big lake and so OK, we'd go round it instead. This mollified him and he went to drink feeling as if he'd won a round. The lake hadn't finished with him though, and when he tried to drink, the waves went up his nose. That was entirely new to him and he got pretty annoyed. He tried to get his head down but each time he'd have to jump back as the water leapt up at him. Finally I led him to a little sheltered bay where he got a drink. Later, when I was on a feedlot, I saw horses so hot that they'd hold their breath and plunge half their head under the water of the trough to get a drink. Spice was 'too refained' for that. If ever a horse drank with a pinky finger extended, it was him.

The next night I spent near the town of Colter Bay on the

lake. After I got Spice settled, I slipped into the camp ground for a shower and to do some laundry at a coin wash. Being so unusually spruce, I decided to stop in the bar for a quick beer or two to celebrate being clean. Any excuse eh! After two weak beers, I switched to a Scotch and 7-Up. Ten minutes later I felt faint and went to the washroom and woke up slumped on the floor. I didn't feel sick at all, just dizzy and when I got home half an hour later, I was right as rain. I think it was the alcohol that did it, as I hadn't drunk for weeks and in that time I'd lost a lot of weight.

I had started the trip at 12½ stone and by then I was down to the weight I finished it at — 9½ stone. My resting pulse was about 40 beats per minute and I felt great. Walking 20 miles a day for a couple of months will do that to you. I was looking forward to eating my weight in chicken McNuggets when I got to a town, safe in the knowledge that putting on 40 or 50 pounds was the best thing for me to do.

I remember when friends of mine who were in the SAS and were therefore ultra-fit, went on a bender. It took only about three pints to put them away for the night. They had no body fat and their digestive systems were used to processing things at top speed. It made for a cheap night, as by 8.30 they were usually eating glassware and assaulting guests.

The rest of the trip south towards Pinedale, Wyoming was a replay of the glorious days after I separated from Ash. The forests were still lush with summer grass and the weather was warm with nights just cool enough to sleep without sweating. My route took me through an area that was heavily hunted and since the season had opened the day I left Yellowstone, I took the precaution of buying a day-glo orange plastic poncho to wear.

Tattered orange poncho displays a safe amount of unnatural colour.

By law all hunters have to wear a certain square footage of orange on themselves in the form of hats, gloves, shirts or whatever. It only makes sense that if you take such care to protect yourself, then you should do the same for your horse, so I bought him some orange ribbons and tied them in his mane and tail. He gave a few shakes and actually looked pleased with the result. I started to wonder about that as it seemed to present a new side to his personality. Was he really that vain? I took the view that it just helped him to flick the flies off.

We met plenty of other horses with orange ribbons and blankets and things and quite a few were packing out meat. Spice wasn't the least bit bothered by all the dead flesh and blood and I began to think that he'd been used as a packhorse or hunting horse. I never really found out for sure but he wasn't ever bothered by dead animals or gunshots.

It was at that time that I screwed up my map reading again. I was following a trail and didn't notice when it veered off to the left, because there was a thick trail with fresh hunters' tracks leading straight on, which I took. By the time I realised something was wrong with the map, I was halfway up a mountain with no time to turn back and catch up ground before dark. I hate giving up ground and like a good Hash House Harrier I hate losing height even more. I pushed on and, after resorting to using my compass for the first and last time to get my bearings, I realised I was aimed unavoidably at a 10,500-foot peak. I finally got around the side of it a couple of hundred feet below the top. I stopped and took photos in all directions of the fabulous view. I could see the purple mountains majesty all right, not to mention a fruity horse with bows in his tail.

From there it was all downhill to the Gros Ventre River which I swam in the company of three devout Christian hunters. One was about 80 and had hunted the area for over 50 years. His younger companions helped him on to his horse after breakfast and there he stayed until he got back to camp at night. They shared their dinner with me and gave me some hay for Spice before beginning to tell me outrageous hunting tales.

The old man's best yarn told how, back in the '50s, he was trapped in a cabin with his family by a bear that was after

Preachers three.

some trash they had inside. Finally, long after nightfall, he snuck out of the hut to put the trash in a bin nearby where the bear could get at it and then go away. It was pitch black and it seemed as if the bear had left. He cautiously stole out the door and tippy-toed to the bin a few yards away. Keeping a wary eye out for the bear, he felt with his hand for the lid to the bin. Looking nervously in one direction and groping in the other with his free hand, he suddenly stiffened. His hand was resting not on the hard lid of a trash bin, but on something soft and furry. Worse yet, it was *under* something soft and furry and short. Something like a tail!

Rangers cabin. Not your typical state house.

There was a split second while both parties considered the implications of that fact, and then with a roar that split the night and loosened bowels for miles around, the bear, who was bending over with his head deep in the bottom of the bin, spun around to face the hunter who, by then, was back inside the cabin with a pulse you could measure on the Richter scale pumping 30 or 40 gallons of pure adrenalin thereby making his vision so acute that he could see *through* the walls of the cabin. Outside was a bear that was both angry and nervous.

If you can imagine how the hunter felt, put yourself in the bear's shoes. You're the meanest mother in the valley and *nobody* fools with you. Middle of the night and you've gone to the refrigerator to get a snack. Just as you reach down for the pickles and milk, someone takes your temperature. Manually. Well of course, you'd huff and puff and think about tearing the walls down until it occurred to you that whoever had the vinegar to perform such an act was very likely ten feet tall and bulletproof, and ready to dance with Eskimos, at which point you might just decide to leave quietly. And that's what the bear did, followed soon after by the hunter.

Chapter 10

In which I acquire a bear story of my own, stand guard on an elk, and discover the dangers of life above the snow line

After crossing the Gros Ventre, I was heading along the edge of Crystal Creek, up towards the ridge and then on to Jagg Creek. Hunters continued to pass me in each direction, their packhorses carrying in supplies or taking out game. The season in the US varies from state to state, animal to animal and forest to forest. Permits are issued for a fee to local hunters first and for a larger fee to out-of-state hunters. If there is a shortage of game to hunt, then a ballot is drawn. Fees are low, but when incidental costs are added, such as guides, which are usually compulsory for hunters to hire if they are out of state, as well as guns, vehicles and horses, then the total cost rises considerably.

Climbing Crystal Creek.

Certain animals are heavily protected, such as grizzly bears, but others, like antelope, are so numerous that almost all hunters can get a permit to shoot one. Black bears are now being shot in increasing numbers as they move down from the mountains into ranch land and towns because of population pressure.

Generally, game is well protected, is hunted responsibly and fluctuates in numbers more from natural factors, such as a harsh winter, than from being slaughtered by sportsmen. Punitive laws prevent hunters from wasting meat, poaching or endangering protected species. Nevertheless, on the first day of the season, the steady roll of gunfire promotes a strong feeling of unease amongst game and passing tourists alike, the differences between the two not always being readily apparent to some hunters.

On that day, fairly near the first weekend, traffic was heavy, as hi-tech riflemen with camouflage clothing, customised rifles, scopes and binoculars, horses, dogs, mules and motorbikes, all stopped to ask me what sign I had seen. It's a far cry from Barry Crump slaying red deer by the score equipped only with an army surplus .303, a swandri and a packet of tobacco.

They seemed surprised when I explained that for the money they spent on their hobby in the US, they could have flown to NZ, blown up every deer they saw and flown home again with money left over. Killing deer in NZ is doing God's work, since they are noxious animals with no natural predators or competitors and they live in a benign climate, but in the States things are different and deer are more highly valued.

When you add up all the claggage, crap and corruption that they took to make camp, I could see why they would arrive three days before the season opened just to get ready. (Actually, that's not strictly true, most got there early to scout out the best areas to hunt in.) The camps, however, were very comfortable and the food was infinitely superior to any I've eaten in NZ bush. The blue enamel coffee pots always delivered fabulously strong, black, unsweetened coffee with gravel in the bottom of the cup. That coffee compares to instant decaf like crude oil does to olive oil. They'd pour any amount of rum in it if you asked but never milk. Black, unsweetened and heavily spiked is how coffee is supposed to be drunk. It's in the Bible. Go look it up.

At night they'd toast marshmallows for dessert and wash them down with whisky or beer. Flapjacks and syrup for

Porgy, Mrs Porgy and luggage goats. (Spice refusing to pose for me.)

breakfast, eggs, bacon, jerky and fresh bread at any time, it was a rare day when I didn't take advantage of an offer to dine with outfitters and hunters. Asked about deer sign, I said nothing, not out of respect for the game, since I've offed any number of small furry animals, but because the only creatures in that neck of the woods were well hunkered down and must have decided to wait it out.

I was getting fairly used to seeing strings of up to a dozen packhorses or mules led by hunters or rangers, and I was prepared for pack llamas, which are a dilettante westerner's version of a Manhattan stockbroker's Harley-Davidson, but I wasn't ready for *pack goats*. Four fairly small goats with saddlebags the size of pony express riders' satchels on their backs trotted along blithely towards me one morning. They weren't tied to each other, but the couple who owned them had a sheep dog to keep them rounded up and headed out. He took his duties seriously and wasn't keen to let them stop for me to take a picture. He carried his own saddlebags too, which left Porgy and his wife free to walk along with only hip pouches and sticks. The whole deal looked pretty cute and, after talking for a while, Porgy offered me a job building houses in Jackson Hole, Wyoming and then gave me a message to deliver to Loring Woodman at the Darwin Ranch in the next valley. I said I'd pass it on if I could and left them in the care of their pets.

Mid-afternoon that day, I met a hunter and his wife riding out to the road to meet friends who were joining them the next day. Dwight and Glenda Schneider had already set up a fine tent camp a few miles up the trail, not far from where I was planning to stay the night. Glenda had shot an elk and it was hanging in a muslin bag behind their tent. They invited me to stay the night and keep an eye on the carcass in case hungry bears or greedy hunters found it. I was welcome to use their tent, horse pickets, lamps, stove and anything I desired. All that based on five minutes of pleasantries with a total stranger! I thanked them and said it sounded mighty fine and that I'd take care of their stuff overnight. Dwight explained how to find the camp and finished by offering me a job on a ranch if I ever made it to Wamsutter.

I set off up the trail and before an hour had gone by, Dwight came galloping back up the track to tell me to ignore the note he'd left pinned to the door of the tent. It was addressed to a mythical friend and was 'only there to fool elk thieves ya know'. With an apology for delaying me further he turned and galloped downhill to catch up with his wife. Now *that's* hospitality! Where else would you get someone riding hours out of their way just so you'd feel at home in their camp?

I found the tent and read the note ('Bill, make yourself at home, Me and the boys will be back real soon, we've just gone to collect the guns'), picketed Spice in a meadow in front of the tent, which was in a copse of trees, and checked the elk for signs of pilfering. All looked well, so I undressed in the heavenly luxury of a tent tall enough to stand up in, basked in the glow of a tilly lamp and finally retired to my cosy bed after carefully putting my hatchet within easy reach in case peckish bears came looking for foodles in the nightle.

I was woken by a loud whinny from Spice in the middle of my sleep. It was his distress call, so I grabbed my Maglite from out of my boot where I kept it for emergencies and sprang to the doors of the tent. There was a moment's pause while I wrestled with the unfamiliar double zips, when Spice let out another urgent protesting call. I heard a thud as he stamped the ground, and finally I burst forth, hatchet in hand and torch shining feebly forth. I saw before me a BEARISH SHADOW rising up TO EAT ME! I yelled and I swung the hatchet savagely at the centre of the shape! A sharp CRACK, a gasp, and I stared down the beam of my torch. I'd killed a small pine tree.

I'd forgotten it was just outside the tent, and, imagination working overtime, when the edge of my light had swept past it, the shadow it cast on the white background looked like seven feet of red slavering teeth and shining white claw. Sort of. I pulled my little axe out of the tree and examined the stumpy shrub. It didn't look a bit like a grizzly at all when I shone my feeble light on it properly. Another call from Spice made me look up in alarm, and then I realised the real reason for the fuss. It was snowing heavily, and the old fool was tangled in his picket rope.

I dashed barefoot on tiptoe across the snow and unwound him. There was no wind and it wasn't particularly cold so I nipped back to the shelter of the tent and dug out his high-line. I set him up on it at the edge of the trees where their boughs kept the snow off him and where he could find shelter if the wind came up. On frozen feet I raced back to bed and contemplated the unexpected turn of events until I nodded off again.

The accidental death of one small pine-tree bear was concealed by heavy snow.

Dawn broke without any more fuss than the silent falling of five inches of snow the night before. It was mid-September and I hadn't been expecting a fall so soon. My plans were to head east into the Wind River Range. That is some of the most vertiginous country in the lower 48 and most of it was higher than where I was then. There were no roads through it and it

A 'Cattle in the Glen' sort of day.

was prone to severe weather conditions at any time of the year. Not the place to be with limited food and no cold-weather clothing. I decided that it was foolhardy to enter the mountains without better equipment and advice at the least but more realistically, I thought the snow probably spelt the end of my plans to stay in the mountains any longer.

Thanking the Schneiders mentally and in writing for the enormous comfort of a proper camp on the only night that I really needed it, I set about packing up. I could have stayed, but I needed to leave eventually, and since it had briefly stopped snowing, and since I was only a mile from the last pass I needed to cross before I could drop down into the huge valley of the Green River, I decided to set off immediately.

Spice was pleased to be moving too. So with me wearing all the clothing I had, we cracked on the pace and started climbing towards the pass. Large herds of cattle were pastured on the mountain for the summer and hadn't yet been collected. Their tracks obscured the path I was following and the snow, which began to fall heavily again, blotted it out even more. Eventually, I simply aimed for the highest point I could see and planned to ease over the saddle whenever I saw it through the snowy clouds I was in. Shadowy steaming groups of cattle appeared and disappeared through the gloom as the morning wore on. They looked like a third-rate painting of Scottish cattle standing knee-deep in a misty glen. It was a pleasant feeling to be warm and dry in the face of such unfamiliar conditions and I was helped by my knowledge that there was no real danger. I was surrounded by hunters and to get out of the snow, I was sure that all I had to do was turn and walk downhill for a day.

By midday, I was high on a rocky snow-covered peak. I crouched down behind the rim and turned my back to the gusts of wind that tried to whip my hat away. The change from shirtsleeves and sweat to numb nose and icy beard had taken just 18 hours. The air was so cold and clean that it drove all memories of the balmy start to the previous morning away with the tattered remains of Spice's orange ribbons as I tried to plan a route down to the river.

I retraced my steps in search of the pass, but after an hour of finding only dead-ends, I finally decided not to bother, and simply plunged off the edge of the peak. Spice was keen to follow and so we both gingerly picked our way down from the icy winds of Mt Darwin into the valley below. Eventually, as the way became too steep and the snow too deep to avoid twisting an ankle on the unseen boulders, I turned Spice loose and followed his tracks. By 4 pm we were safely down and the snow was turning to sleet and rain. On the tops, a thousand feet higher, puffs of wind-borne snow were spiralling up against the occasional blue patches of sky — rips in the white canvas of the clouds torn by the freezing blasts of wind.

I finally came out of the snowline and started to cross small streams that marked the edge of the old Darwin homestead. Wet and cold, I wasn't looking forward to spending a night camping in steady rain, so I pushed on to the ranch house to deliver my message to the owner — Loring Woodman.

After telling him that Porgy couldn't meet him as planned, I discovered that the ranch was actually a dude ranch that entertained rich easterners on riding holidays. Ah ha. I stood there with my horse and tried to look cold and pitiful. Spice grabbed the essentials of the situation as soon as he saw the barn and smelt the hay, and so aided and abetted by a ham acting horse with hunched shoulders and shivering ears turned down lower than a Basset hound, I was invited to stay the night in one of the guest bungalows. When I put Spice in the barn to groom and feed him, he was smirking and chortling shamelessly. I chuckled along with him.

After feeding my fellow conspirator, I joined the guests for dinner with Loring and his extremely sharp wife, Melody. We talked over dinner and then I helped the staff to polish off their meal and did the dishes with them while the horse wrangler recited an epic poem about a man who drank too much and drove a four-wheel-drive Mustang. I guess you had to be there, but it was a nice change to have something to talk about other than riding and hunting. Eventually, a maid (!!!), a pretty, 18-year-old Irish maid (!!!) no less, turned down my bed and drew me a hot bath. Hopefully I asked her if she had been kidnapped by Indians at an early age and was she in need of rescuing? She said no and so I fired up the pot-belly stove and we swapped addresses and stories of how we each came to be so far from home. I thought about unleashing all my seductive charms on the girl, but luckily refrained. I had entered the general area of Pinedale, though I didn't know until later, and this meant I was in an area as famous for its abundance of attractive single ladies as Tibet is for surf beaches. As I was to discover, any single woman within 75 miles of Pinedale was being actively chased by more men than it took to free Kuwait. This one was no exception, but at least I had a real bed to sleep in for the first time since Great Falls Hospital, and I went to sleep to the sound of rain on the roof and the smell of damp clothes singeing in front of a wood fire.

After making my farewells, I headed down the dirt road towards the Green River. As the road dropped further and further down, the amount of traffic increased and eventually, the road turned to 'oil' or tar-seal. Along the way I spied a cowboy shifting cattle from one part of the valley to another. He was alone on his horse, but his pick-up and trailer were nearby. He rounded up the cattle by quietly trotting around behind each one and pushing it towards the group. It meant he had to ride a lot and I wondered why he didn't use a dog.

Later I would discover why, but for the moment I stayed out

Hard going for short cattle dogs.

of his way and considered whether I'd be able to do a job like that if I had to. After the storm, I was starting to consider options for completing the trip the next year, other than simply selling Spice and starting again the following spring. Boarding him while I played at being a cowboy looked like being fun.

The next two days were fairly routine as the trail broke out on to the road and then headed down into the ranching land of the Upper Green River. The sun came out with a vengeance and commenced (although I didn't know it at the time) a fabulous Indian summer that lasted far past the time I would have needed to get through the Wind River Range.

My arrival in the next town, Pinedale, was fortuitous as it was not only the only town for miles in any direction with a store, but it was also the last town for 100 miles where I'd have any hope of either finding a home for Spice until the next year, or of selling him outright.

As I followed the road down the 25 miles to town, I became aware of a grass lane fenced in on both sides that lay between the highway and the pasture beyond. It was about the same width as a two-lane road and it followed the highway for an indefinite distance. 'What is it Spice?' I asked. He didn't know, but it was ideal for us, so we let ourselves into it at a convenient spot and followed it down. It looked as if it was purpose-built for letting animals walk down it without having to worry about them getting run over, or wandering off into the hills, but I was damned if I could see who'd spend all that money on such a device for so little return. I mean, how many animals walked up and down this way by themselves each year? Why would they do that? Who wanted them to? It was all very puzzling and we hadn't figured any of it out by the time it came to leave it and head for town.

When I got to camp in a small public fishing ground on the edge of the New Fork River, I'd decided that I'd have to either find a buyer for Spice who'd agree to sell him back to me the following year or else I'd have to board him on a ranch. This would allow me to head back to the UK and earn enough to return and finish the ride the following summer. The last and least likely option was to find a ranch to board on for the winter as long as the VISA people played the game and gave me extra time to pay off my credit card.

At a respectable hour the next day I saddled up Spice and rode into the capital city of Sublette County. It took me three hours to ride all the way through, but that's only because I spent an hour each in three separate places. If I'd ridden straight through, I'd have been outside the town in under ten minutes. Sublette County (area 5000 sq miles) has about 3300 citizens and a third of them live in Pinedale. Another 530 odd live in Big Piney, the second city of the region located about 30 miles south-west. With around 100 apiece in the towns of Bondurant, Boulder, Cora, Daniel, Farson, Marbleton and Merna, that left the remaining 1000 or so to inhabit an area the size of Wales. That puts them ahead of Antarctica, but way behind Siberia in terms of population density. I've been arrested by more people than live in some of these towns. As a matter of fact, when 25,000 New Age Travellers-cum-hippies camped in the woods at the back of Dan Budd's ranch for a month, they became not just the biggest town in the county by a factor of 25, but they were briefly the third largest city in the state of Wyoming! In all that space, there are about six single women, which makes them more rare and endangered than the Sublettes' Swoop Eagle or a Fremont Lake Drift Fish.

Chapter 11

ALL THE CIVILISATION YOU NEED

Lots of states have little mottoes on their car licence plates, most of which are predictable like 'New Jersey — The Garden State', but some are cool like 'New Hampshire — Live Free or Die', and some are just weird like 'Idaho — State of Great Potatoes'! Wyoming has a picture of a cowboy on a bucking horse called 'Steamboat' who threw riders from a dozen states at rodeos in the early 1900s. Wyoming more than any other state is real cowboy country. They still do things the way they did in 1890, whereas in Texas and Colorado and New Mexico, things are a little more modern.

Pinedale is in the western part of Wyoming about 50 miles over the line from Idaho. On the road at the western edge of town is a sign that welcomes you. It announces that Pinedale has a population of 1000. It doesn't make any little jokes like 'and growing' although it

'Head 'em up, move 'em out and no double parking.' Pushing stock through Pinedale.

is. It leaves that for you to figure out, which is completely in keeping with the local way of doing anything. The next thing is that it casually announces its elevation — 7100 feet.

That, of course, doesn't really register at first. You have to stop and think about it to realise that Denver, the 'Mile High City' or Mt Ruapehu's Top O' the Bruce ski field are both a third of a mile *lower* and that, therefore, the growing season in that part of the state is about 60 days and there are only 30 frost-free days a year. And that is in the river valley. The mountains stand another 7000 feet higher!

The sky above is invariably either IBM blue or snowing. It's rare for it to stay overcast without snow. Rain comes in brief violent thunderstorms that are blown south-east in minutes. In summer, there are no clouds to speak of for weeks at a time and in winter, when it's not snowing, it has a fabulous frigid blue sky that blinds you with light reflected off the snow and dazzles you with the leaping sparkling points of moisture frozen in the air, but too light to fall to the ground.

After the signs for gas, food and lodgings at the far end of the four-lane wide street, is a single sign that sums up the town as well as anything. It says: 'Welcome to Pinedale — All the civilisation you need.'

It's absolutely true too. Pinedale has a sheriff, a doctor, a vet, a good newspaper, a feed store, three bars, a masonic lodge and a veterans' lodge, a grade school and a high school, a huge supermarket selling everything from handguns to pickled pigs' feet, a sporting-goods store, four or five cafés, the best little restaurant in the west, a courthouse, two lawyers, several churches, a big library and a terrific museum. Pretty good for a town of 1000.

Above the sign at the east end of town is a high hill with the clinic, the museum and a baseball diamond on top along with some of the newer houses. The road up to them turns and winds north towards Fremont Lake and the foothills of the Wind River Range.

The range dominates the town. To the left is the fabulous vista of the Wind Rivers. Jagged peaks form a solid wall 14,000 feet high that runs for 100 miles. That is Pinedale's own Manhattan skyline. Steep slopes, shining summits, snow covered nearly all year round, with permanent glaciers feeding streams and rivers that irrigate the valley fields before flowing into the New Fork or the Green. Dozens of lakes store water for irrigation as well as countless beaver dams. Pines, willows and 'quakers' are the foliage that colour its slopes and hide the deer, bears, birds and occasional buffalo or mountain lion.

Closer to the road are five-strand barbed-wire fences with barbs on each wire. This isn't sheep country, this is beef territory and smooth wire wouldn't keep the cattle in when the wind begins to blow, and sometimes, when the snow starts to drive them before the storm, even a fence won't hold them. The cattle are mainly Hereford, either pure or crossed with red or black Angus to produce a red or black baldy. These beasts are hardy, smart and a lot wilder than cattle in New Zealand. They usually show a bit of respect for a man on a horse, but if roused, they'll have a go at anything. They'll fight off coyotes, cougars and bears as well as surviving winters that last for seven months of the year. They won't do a thing for a man on foot and even dogs have a hard time moving them if they're feeling stubborn.

The fields by the time I arrived were dry and brown, and thousands of tons of hay had been cut and baled into one-ton round bales or small 60-

Hay fields ready for the cattle to come home from the mountains for winter.

pound square bales. Irrigated all summer, a single cut is all that's possible in the time available to mow and bale before winter. Few cattle were back from the mountains yet, and the edges of the fields where the swathers couldn't reach were ready for their hungry tenants. By the first snowfall in October, the pasture would be cropped to a crewcut instead of the mohawk that betrays each irrigation ditch.

Every mile or two is a ranch house, either modern or old, usually with a couple of trailer houses clinging to it. These are the long narrow portable houses that are like railway carriages that have put down roots.

An economical shopping basket for the little woman.

This area was settled just a century ago by Mormons and other Christians, heathens and Democrats. They came after the trappers, the loggers, the Oregon trail immigrants and the railroaders. Next the ranchers arrived in the 1890s and after them came the oilmen and the tourists.

The traffic on the road is light but steady and consists mainly of semi-trailers or pick-up trucks. The pick-ups are huge six- or seven-litre 4WDs that are useful to get from the house to the snow-ploughed highway in winter. In summer, they bounce across the mesa, haul wood from the mountains, collect supplies from town and, above all, haul horse trailers. Occasionally they crash, but it's hard to hurt yourself at 20 miles an hour inside a steel box as heavy as three Hondas. They have the aerodynamic qualities of a block of flats and get gas mileage the Queen Mary would be ashamed of. Six or eight horses at a time is not an uncommon load and at half a ton per animal, those trucks pull up to five tons across all kinds of terrain without protest.

Buildings are made of wood or breeze blocks, which are called cinder blocks. Everything is insulated and heated heated to stop the –40° temperatures from freezing the water as it leaves the ground to enter the house. Tin roofs or shingles are common and so are log cabins. Satellite dishes are in most yards along with a cord or two of logs for winter and a snowmobile, frequently partially disemboweled. Whoops, I meant 'under repair'. Everyone (women and babies too) wears a Stetson or a baseball cap in summer, and an Elmer Fudd hat complete with pom-pom in winter.

The rodeos and the re-enactment of the 'Green River Trappers Rendezvous' from 1826 to 1838 are the big calendar events each summer. Read Michener's *Centennial* (the chapter on 'The Yellow Apron') which tells the story of the rendezvous. Ranchers still drive cattle through town and even guys like me get to ride their horse on the sidewalk once in a while. The gas station is open 24 hours a day and sells 41 varieties of beef jerky but no bottled water.

Pinedale is small-town America and people want less taxes, less government, less drugs, less crime and less welfare. They don't ask for more of anything much. If they want more of something, they're happy to get it themselves.

I knew none of that when I arrived leading a skinny grey horse to the feed store on the edge of town on a bright sunny September morning. It was at the feed store that I started talking to Ruth Schaeffer about finding a buyer or a temporary home for Spice over the winter. She said she knew just the person. Her friend Kay McGill was looking for a biddable sort of horse so she could go riding and hunting with her husband Dave. I could find her down at the Wrangler Café at the other end of town, opposite Faler's store. That sounded good to me since I could buy food at Falers, then get a breakfast at the café and talk to Kay at the same time. Ruth said there was even a grass lot for Spice to graze while I was busy inside.

First though, I went shopping for grub. The grocery store is owned by the Faler family who were keen hunters judging by the trophy heads of elk, deer, moose, mountain goat, bighorn sheep, and smaller game that were lined up in ranks along the 300-foot front wall. It's not often you see a bear tacked to the wall of your supermarket and it makes you think twice about shoplifting. The store was enormous — as big as any major supermarket and it was stocked with everything from hardware and fishing licences to food and books.

I had already peeked into the second biggest store — The Cowboy Shop owned by the Bing family. They stocked everything a working cowboy needs (sometimes locally pronounced 'ca*boy*') as well as tourist toys. That's where you got tack, boots, jeans, shirts, quilted coats, slickers and Stetsons. Anything they didn't have, Tom the saddler opposite them would make up for you. Leather chaps (pronounced 'shaps'), hand-made saddles, spurs and boot repairs kept Tom flat out all the time. His work is top quality and it was cheap too.

Mixed among the shops were the six or seven motels that catered to the hunters, campers and fishermen. For around $25 a day you could get a comfortable room and if you helped out with a few chores like I did when I got there, you might get a few dollars knocked off the bill. I made enquiries as I worked my way down to Falers where I loaded up on baked beans, Cheez Whiz and salami.

I paid my bill and crossed the road to the Wrangler Café where Kay was busy waitressing so I pulled up a stool at the breakfast bar and settled in to kill time by eating a bushel of pancakes, sausages, bacon, ham, toast, tomatoes, hash browns and coffee. After half an hour she was still busy so I ordered a repeat. That one took me 45 minutes and she was still too busy to talk. I went out back to check on Spice and he was fine. The walk raised my appetite so I ordered orange juice, coffee, hot cakes (fluffy scones) and a sundae. By the time I'd hacked my way through that, Kay was able to spare a few minutes to say that she would like to see the horse with her husband and that she had a friend just out of town who looked after their horses and who would let me put up there until they could take a look at Spice. I got directions to the ranch and she phoned ahead to let them know I was coming. By then it was lunchtime so I ordered a hamburger with fries, coffee and a milkshake. Soon after 1 pm I headed out of town feeling a little unwell and sloshing slightly while Spice followed me warily. I think he was afraid I would explode in a cloud of cholesterol, caffeine and saturated fats. In my defence, I must point out that I was three stone lighter than my normal weight, so I had every reason to binge.

Within a couple of hours I had left Spice on the ranch, dumped tack in the barn and had cadged a lift back to town. Kay said it would take a couple of days for her and Dave to make up their minds about buying Spice and I planned to spend the time looking for work and eating. I checked into a little motel for $20 a night and then headed for the Wrangler Café at best speed. After a quick snack of toasted ham and cheese sandwiches and a half gallon of Mountain Dew, I gathered a pile of quarters and set off for a bar.

The three main bars each had quite a different character. The Stockman's was at the top of the market with a nice big restaurant, rooms above, and a medium-sized bar with a big screen TV, dance floor and live music each week. People who own ranches drink there.

Across the road was The Cowboy Bar — 'Pinedale's Thinking Service'. No rooms and no food, just a pool table, dance floor and live music each week. Behind the bar a sign said: 'Fishing equipment sold here by the case, bottle or can'. People who work on ranches drink there.

Further down the road was the last of the big three. Its sign said it was 'The World Famous Corral Bar'. A neon cowboy twirled a rope. It had a good pizza-type restaurant, a dance floor and a juke box with plenty of heavy metal music. Occasionally a Harley hog or two would be found parked there while Motley Crue hammered away. Young people, tourists who didn't know any better, and people who wished they lived on a ranch drank there.

On a busy Saturday night in summer, people cross between all three bars like New Orleans tourists carrying their beers back and forth in search of friends, better music or something rarer than rocking-horse shit — a single woman under 40 and 150. That's years and pounds.

I took my stomach for a walk to the Cowboy Bar to spend the afternoon with a beer and a phone book listing all the ranches in the county. After an unproductive couple of hours I decided it was time to investigate dinner and I lashed out on a French Dip with fries followed by olalieberry pie. That night I watched TV for the first time in weeks and happily channel-surfed through sitcoms, sports shows and news hours while munching on Carolina bars, beef jerky, tootsie rolls and Pringle's potato chips washed down with cherry colas and beer. Ahh, great times, great times.

The next morning I resolved to do something about the cast on my arm. I figured I'd do better with more than one working arm so I headed down to the café to get breakfast and directions to the local doctor. After ordering another ham steak breakfast with pancakes in syrup, coffee and a root beer float, I settled down to read the newspaper. Sitting across the counter from me were a couple of characters of a distinctly agricultural bent. Both had cowboy boots well worn and scuffed, blue jeans faded and neatly patched, thin check cotton shirts and ancient baseball caps with ranch supply logos on them. Typical ranchers. One was about 70 and smoked roll-your-own cigarettes. His face was tanned and deeply lined like corrugated cardboard. The other was about 50 and sported a big moustache, not quite a handlebar, but not far off. The younger one looked across and asked me where I was from.

I was used to this as the Kiwi accent is sufficiently rarely heard in these parts as to confuse most folks. They judge you to be either English, Canadian or Australian and so I was used to the surprised look on their faces when I said where I was from. That was followed by the usual six questions, but the younger of the two guys seemed to be on talking terms with everyone who came in the door and passed the breakfast bar, and so squeezing my replies into the gaps left in his greetings to old friends and acquaintances took me the whole of my breakfast as well as two cups of coffee from the bottomless coffee pot. (American cafés, by the way, have achieved a level of perfection that no others even approach, typified by the bottomless coffee cup and the free newspapers. Add service and chat from the waitresses and you have all the ingredients of the Cheers bar crossed with the store at Petticoat Junction. Just as the English are the only people who can run a country pub without it looking like a Hollywood set, so the Americans are the only people who can serve proper, fast, home-cooked food in a setting like the Walton Family kitchen, as opposed to the rest of the world, where cafés resemble the dining hall on Devil's Island.) Every café has its regulars like the two I was talking to, and I decided to pump them a bit for information as to who might be boarding tramps. Their advice seemed to be to keep doing what I was already, but it took a while to get it. The younger one had plenty to say and it was interesting to listen to him. From them and others, I got a couple of names of places to try. I finished up by asking how to get to a doctor to get my arm seen to and they pointed me up the hill to the clinic.

The walk up to the clinic and back perked up my appetite and so with my mended arm feeling oddly weak and thin, I decided that as I'd lost at least four pounds since the doctor removed the cast, I was overdue for another shot at the Wranglers' menu.

I ordered a hamburger with bread and butter on the side as well as more coffee and some cherry pie for dessert. By now I'd eaten nearly $100 worth of food since getting to town and I still had a huge recurring craving for greasy food. I think that I'd finally exhausted all my body's reserves of fat during the weeks of walking and riding and I was trying to put it all back in the space of two days. It was a real delight to know that I could pig out with no fear that I'd get fat, and at the same time, Spice would be able to eat all he wanted to as well. Once again, I loaded up with quarters and headed off to the bar to make my phone calls. Prudently, I took some snacks to prevent hunger pangs from distracting me from my work.

By the third beer and the second bag of Licorice Bridge Mix, I was up to the Ms in the phone book. When I rang the Murdock Cattle Company the voice that answered was familiar to me. I explained what I was looking for and the voice introduced himself as Stan Murdock. He said that he knew me and that he'd talked to me in the café that morning. He said, 'Yep, I think I might have room for you if you want to wait a day or two while I get a few things sorted out.' That suited me down to the ground, so we agreed a price to include Spice's board for the winter and then I asked if I could try my hand at cowboying. Stan asked if I had worked on a farm, lived in the country, could drive a tractor or could rope a cow. My answer to all those was an honest 'Nossir'! Kindly he said, 'That's OK, son. If you've ridden from Canada on that horse alone then you'll make out all right.'

Stan said he'd come out and pick me up in a day or two. That gave me time to meet Kay again and explain that now I didn't think I'd be able to sell Spice after all. Two days later, Stan came to collect me in his pick-up towing a six-horse trailer. I loaded up my horse and gear. On the three-mile drive from town I mysteriously became an amateur cowboy.

Chapter 12

I BECOME ACQUAINTED WITH THE TRICKS OF CATCHING HORSES, ROPING COWS FOR TV AND RIDING THE DRIFT

I resolved to lend a hand around the place as an aid to rehabilitating my hand so the first thing I tackled was the simple task of pulling down old stackyards. They are the barbed-wire pens used to store the hay in the fields. Since there is so little rain in those parts, the bales are stacked in the hay fields and fenced off to prevent moose from breaking in during the winter. Round bales are stacked in pyramids of six bales, and are lined up in rows of 20 or so. That's about 120 tons per stack with usually two stacks per pen. Each cow will eat a ton or more over the winter. Bales are stacked and taken down using a forklift-type attachment on a tractor or a purpose-built machine called a Drube, after its inventor. Feeding out is by a rotary unit towed behind a tractor.

Small bales are cut and baled the same as in New Zealand, but are stacked using a baler that piles the bales up in a brick containing several dozen bales at a time. Inexpert operators create leaning towers that have to be propped up using odd timbers. That is a source of mild cowboy shame. Likewise, round bale stacks are also informally graded for their level appearance by haystack connoisseurs.

Loose hay is still put up using tractors or horse teams as sweeps to push the hay up a steep slide. The hay then drops on to the top of the pile, which then settles to form a rain-resistant loaf of hay that will last 25 years in the open and, when fed out, will deliver hay as tasty and fresh as the day it was cut. Horse teams are also used to feed out loose hay. Teams of horses are in widespread use as they're a very cheap alternative to several hundred thousand dollars' worth of mechanical feeding equipment, and in deep snow, a hay sled carrying a ton or two of hay, pulled by a team of two experienced horses, is often more reliable than the expensive machinery.

Working alone in the blazing Indian summer sun with a Country and Western station for company, I discovered that my right wrist was healing up well, but as soon as I tried hammering, the jarring made my hand go numb. Once when I was twisting staples out of a post, I swear I heard the bones creak. Each night, I'd wake up two or three times and shake the pins and needles out of my fingers.

The other job that occupied those first few weeks was repairing and tightening the fences around the 6000-acre ranch. Each year, moose as well as cattle battered the fences and, before bringing the cattle back down from the mountains in the fall, all the ranchers spent time tidying up their fences. In particular, it was vital to have the hay securely locked up, as cattle caught in a snowstorm or those that are simply hungry will pile up against a fence and, if there is the slightest slackness in it, they'll be eating their way through the stack in no time at all.

At the time I was pottering away, the other two cowboys on the ranch were also fencing as well as putting away haymaking equipment and getting ready for the fall drift. Ian was the full-time regular help on the ranch and he lived alone in the larger of the two houses for the hands. He was a taciturn sort of a guy with a short temper and strong opinions on how things ought to be done. I never got on with him very well but that was true for everyone who knew him. He was a pretty fair cowboy though and could turn his hand to nearly anything.

Patience wasn't his long suit and I recall one morning following him out to the corrals to catch my horse during the fall drift. It was pitch black at 4 am and the horses we were going to use that day were penned in a corral about twice the size of a tennis court. As usual, most of the horses would let you walk up to them and catch them, but two or three would always try and fool with you a bit by pretending to run away. To stop all that nonsense, the trick was to edge them into a corner and then wait while they feinted left and right to get away. As long as you were reasonably nimble and were in a mood to play the game, all you had to do was make a couple of false starts when they feinted and as soon as they saw you were just as quick as they were, they quit fooling around and let you quietly walk up and catch them. If you were grumpy or half asleep and didn't make a fast three-step dash to head them off each time, then they made a run for real and all you would see was clods of dirt flying back at you as they thundered past into the darkness. If that happened twice, then they knew you were beaten and the whole herd would set off galloping around and around the corral. Then the only solution was to run them into ever smaller pens until you could catch them.

That morning, Ian was after a particularly ornery horse that beat him on the first go. It took off with the herd and for a couple of minutes they tore around the corrals. Eventually they settled down and I walked up and caught my horse. Ian tried again and for the second time his horse beat him. He couldn't be bothered playing the feinting game and was damned if he'd admit defeat by herding them into a smaller corral. Instead, he took off in pursuit on foot, cursing and stumbling over the uneven surface. Running in high-heeled boots, long johns, skintight jeans and chaps is like running in a dream. Enormous effort for virtually no gain, and in half a minute he was gasping like a goldfish and swearing violently with all his spare breath. As the herd passed him for the fourth or fifth time he tripped over a pile of frozen shit and fell full length in the dirt. 'Sonuvabitch!' he roared.

I was watching from through a crack in the barn door as he got to his feet scarlet with anger. 'You cocksucker!' he bellowed. 'You better fucking well stop!' I knew that this was no time to offer to help and, sure enough, the next time the horses circled him he hurled the halter and lead rope at them. As he let go, the end of the knotted rope somehow caught him in the face and he fired a volley of oaths into the darkness. The horses were having a great old time by then and so was I as I watched him bend down and snatch clods of dirt and dung, which he proceeded to hurl into the mob as he chased them into the darkness. Periodically they reappeared in the dim misty light of the barn parading past him in a shower of dirt and a cloud of profanity. He wasn't a bad shot, and as lumps of manure bounced off the heads of the horses, I stole silently away to finish saddling up, leaving Ian standing in the middle of the corral, winded, gasping threats and weakly flinging rocks at the delighted herd.

I shared a house with the other hand, Warren, who was hired just for the haying work and the fall drift. He was an outgoing friendly guy who competed in rodeo events as a roper and as a bronco and bull rider. Soon after I arrived I got him to show me how to throw a rope at a dummy calf, but as with everything else, my wrist wasn't up to the strain and it took several weeks before I was able to hit the dummy consistently.

A roping dummy consists of a plastic calf's head shoved into a bale of hay. The cowboy stands two yards behind and slightly to the left of the bale and practises throwing at the dummy. I spent a lot of time roping my own head as well as pretty much everything in a radius of 15 feet from the dummy. If you want to see how hard roping is, then try spinning a plate on a stick with one hand while stroking the cat with the other. Now jog. Not impossible, but it takes a while to get the knack.

Bonnie doing all the thinking while I daydream.

On about the third day I was there, an Australian TV crew turned up in town to film a documentary about the return of wolves to Yellowstone National Park. I met them in the Cowboy Shop and they explained that they wanted to interview a rancher and get some shots of cowboys at work for their documentary. Stan's name was mentioned and so later that day, the crew turned up to film us moving a bunch of 60 or so cattle across the high plateau to the east of the ranch house. Ian,

Warren, three or four neighbours and I were all decked out in our best cowboy gear, which for them included big hats, chaps, spurs and ropes. Stan was interviewed on camera and acquitted himself well, while the rest of us loitered in the background. To get the shots of cowboys hard at work it was decided that we'd move the bunch of cattle alongside a dirt road while the film crew would drive alongside filming. It took several attempts to get the required footage, but eventually we did it and then they asked us if we had anything else they could film.

Coincidentally, one of the cows in the bunch was limping and needed doctoring. Since it was a full-grown beast and therefore couldn't run or dodge as well as a half-grown steer, and since Warren was there and he was judged to be a helluva guy with a rope, it was decided that Warren would rope the animal and then they'd throw it and doctor its foot.

The film crew edged into position and Warren stalked the cow which was near the edge of the herd. He was riding a fairly small but fast horse called Bonnie that he hadn't roped from before. He began the catch by trotting up alongside the cow and throwing a loop deftly at the head of the cow. And missed. We couldn't believe it! An absolute sitter. He coiled his rope and began again, but by now the cow was wise to his moves and she took off as soon as the rope was swung. Instead of racing for clear ground, she headed back into the herd at top speed with Warren right behind. The herd scattered and a minor stampede began with all the cowboys on the outside struggling to hold the herd together. In the middle of the herd, Bonnie got confused and tried to chase the wrong cow. While Warren wrestled with the reins, the cow vanished into the scrum. Ding ding. End of the round.

There was a long pause while Warren gathered up his horse and we settled the herd down. Round Two. Once again, Warren roared into the midst of the herd, rope whirling, hooves pounding and hat flying away behind him. This time, Bonnie latched on to the cow and followed it as it turned and plunged through the ruck of nervous cattle. At the critical moment, Warren threw the rope and a perfect loop slapped the side of the cow and slipped neatly over her head. All that remained was for Warren to dally the rope around the horn of his saddle and the cow was caught.

The most amazing thing happened. Warren apparently forgot to do anything. That was understandable as in rodeo roping, the rope is pre-tied to the horn and, after throwing the loop, all the cowboy has to do is jump off and run out to throw the calf or steer. Real life is different and in the next second, 1200 pounds of beef jerked the rope and for a sizzling second, Warren tried to hold the burning nylon in his ungloved hand. The knot at the end caught in his fingers and for an instant, it looked as though he would be jerked out of the saddle. He finally let go and the cow took off into the milling herd trailing 30 feet of rope. From Stan came an astonished 'Jesus Christ!'

The cow was away and Warren had no rope to catch her with. If such a thing happened to a lone cowboy on the range it was worse than not catching the cow at all, since the trailing rope could easily catch on something and choke it. This was worse though. This could end up on TV!

Returning the cast of thousands to their field.

In and out of the herd we went, hats flying, cows bursting out of the mob, their little legs going like

pistons, tails straight out and heads down, only to be hunted down and chased back by sweating and embarrassed cowboys. Warren bemoaned the lack of a rope and Stan dolefully observed all his high-paid help doing their best to run six months of fat grazing off the herd in a single afternoon. We looked like the Keystone Kowboys. The film crew was delighted by the spectacle and seemed confident they could edit out such phrases as 'Beautiful horse-friend!' if only a finale would arrive before the light faded.

At one point, his mind completely addled by the appalling pageant, Warren resorted to chasing the cow on foot in the hope that he could grab the trailing rope. What he planned to do after that had all of us beat, since we had visions of the cow, the rope, Warren and the film crew all in line astern, disappearing into the sunset.

Eventually, the exhausted cow slowed down to a walking pace and was blowing and panting like a consumptive steam train when Ian got a rope over her head. What remained was for another cowboy to rope the hind legs and pull the rope tight. That would cause the cow to drop down — just the same as tying someone's shoelaces together. Incredibly, all the assembled talent was unable to throw a single loop that would do the trick, and finally, when the film crew were signalling that they were nearly out of film and when the cow looked fit to have a coronary, Ian and one of the neighbours dismounted and grabbed hold of her tail and pulled her over like furniture movers working a sofa through a door. As we expected from the turn of speed she'd shown us when we were trying to catch her, there wasn't a whole lot wrong with her foot, so she was given an injection of LA200 and set free. There was no talking on the way home and after that Warren quit giving me lessons in roping. To be honest, the standard of roping was normally much higher and I never again saw such a spectacle. It must have been stagefright.

Our houses were across the yard from where Stan lived with his wife, Madeleine, a teacher at the local grade school, and their 13-year-old son Scott. Stan had grown up on the ranch, which had been in the family since the land was settled and there wasn't much he couldn't tell me about the ranch, the town and the county. Stan enjoyed a good conversation and his ability to debate local issues got him the nickname of the Mayor of Sublette County.

Madeleine originally hailed from Scotland. She had a lively sense of humour and had an interest in all sorts of artistic and cultural pursuits, some of which she was able to rope Stan and Scott into supporting. Generally though, Stan's social calendar was fully filled with his attendance on a myriad of local committees and clubs as well as his regular visit to the Wrangler Café. Scott kept a low profile around the ranch, but for the fall drift and other busy times, he was allowed to abandon his homework to lend a hand.

Madeleine and Stan.

As soon as the stackyards were down, it was time to begin the real work of the season. This was the fall drift, where the cattle were brought out of the mountains and collected at the drift fence three miles away. The actual drift fence wasn't a snow fence at all. It was a large fenced field that served as an arena for rounding up and cutting out cattle. The 'drift' word comes from the fact that if left alone for long enough, all the cattle would eventually drift up against it in search of better grazing, just as they drifted against the fences on the mountain ranges during summer.

At the Pinedale drift fence, they were split up into the various ranches' own herds and trucked or walked back to their home pastures. To get from the mountains where they spent the summer grazing, while hay was growing on their home ground, they walked down the 30 miles of driveway that Spice and I had followed. The fenced-in runway was built so that cowboys didn't have to spend weeks chasing the cattle down the highway to the drift fence near the edge of town where the separating took place. When the weather or the grazing dictated, the gates at the bottom of the mountain valley were opened and gradually the cattle would trickle down from the high country into the river valley and out into the driveway, which ran from the mountains past Pinedale and on south for a further 40 miles. About half the cattle lived on those southern ranches and, after they were cut out from the groups of cattle that belonged around Pinedale, they were pushed back into the driveway to head south.

Mad and the horse's ass himself.

The driveway actually was not a continuous highway, but every few miles it ended in a huge pasture with water and some sparse grazing. That allowed the cattle to rest, feed and water themselves each day as they plodded south. When they reached the cutting ground near Pinedale (which was called the drift fence), they were gathered into a corner of the pasture by all the available cowboys from the ten or so Pinedale ranches. Each day those cowboys then split them up into groups belonging to individual ranches.

The whole process can take as much as five weeks or as little as five days, depending on the weather. If it's fine and sunny, then the cattle are in no hurry to leave the mountains and, if not forced, will form small groups and dawdle along for up to a week in the driveway. If it storms and snows, however, they all leave the mountains together in a great wad and march quickly down the driveway, hardly stopping at all. Then it's possible to go out to the drift fence ready for a morning's cutting and find 2000 cattle huddled in a corner, bawling and blinking in the snow and rain, demanding to be let out of the gates so that they can walk back to their ranches.

The older cattle that have made this trip six or seven times

Drifting along.

know which gate to go to and, if let out, would find their own way back to the right ranch in hours. The problem is that, in their hurry to reach their pasture, they often tend to leave their calves behind, and also, the cattle would be a hopeles mix of steers, bulls, pairs and strays.

That's the way things work in theory. In practice, cattle refuse to leave the mountains, and have to be pushed out. Some get confused and stray north over the top of the ranges and end up near Dubois, over 100 miles from their own ranch and have to be trucked back home. Some are sick, lame, injured or have calves with problems such as brisket (similar to altitude sickness), who are short-winded and can't travel. Many bulls are reluctant to leave and will break back again and again, wearing out cowboys and horses until finally a cursing cowboy emerges from the dust or the trees on a sweating horse with a chastened animal on his rope. Occasionally a bull will fight the rope so hard that it chokes itself down and dies. In that event, the animal still comes down out of the mountain — in the shape of steaks and hamburger.

Once the cattle are pushed out of the hills by 30 or 40 cowboys from the ten or so Pinedale ranches, they have to be pushed down the valley and into the start of the driveway. This is straightforward trail driving with dust, yelling, swearing and laughter. Once in the driveway, they are left to walk at their own speed, but if they are lagging too much, or if the weather is closing in, cowboys are dispatched to gather the resting fields and water gaps and shove them back into the driveway again. Meanwhile, the majority of cowboys are arriving at the cutting ground each day at 5 am to gather in the previous day's arrivals and separate them into their proper groups. That is done by having five or ten cowboys holding the herd of 500 to 1000 cattle in a corner, while the best cowboys on their best cutting horses ride quietly into the herd reading the brands. That unholy congregation looks totally disorganised. As one friend put it: 'It's a regular clusterfuck!'

But there is both rhyme and reason to the way it is done.

Cow/calf pairs are handled gently. It's important that all the calves be correctly paired up with their mothers as without their care, they will suffer over the start of winter. Calves stick to their mothers well, but not if the herd is stirred up by too much racing around. Many calves have indistinguishable brands, or were born too late to be branded and are clean skinned. By quietly riding into the herd and watching a pair to ensure that the calf is sticking to a cow, it's possible to be right 99% of the time when cutting out a pair. To try to do the same thing by running cattle through a stockyard would be a disaster, and for this reason, the cutting is performed just as it was 100 years ago.

Having identified a beast or a pair, the cowboy uses his horse to gently ease the animal to the edge of the herd. The cowboys holding the big herd move aside to let the animal see its way past them to the smaller herd that it belongs in. The cutter, perhaps with help from another of the four or five cowboys working the herd, then edges the

Cutting cattle.

animal out of the big herd. Once it is in with its own small herd (called the 'cut') it is the job of another cowboy to keep that cut separate from the other groups. That involves a lot of riding around to keep cattle from breaking back to the big herd or from joining another cut.

By ten or eleven o'clock the ground is populated by six or seven cuts belonging to the separate ranches. The southern cattle have been released through the southern gate to continue their walk down river. Each herd remaining then has to be worked over by its own cowboys and further divided into bulls, heifers, steers and cow/calf pairs. As soon as the pairs are separated from the rest by working them in a corner of the field, the pairs are then walked off to the ranch. The remainder of the cut is put into the corrals and worked on foot until the bulls, steers, heifers and strays are penned separately. These are usually loaded on to small stock trucks or horse trailers and delivered to their own pastures.

The cowboys who trailed home the pairs then ride the herd to check for sick animals and, if necessary, they rope and doctor any that need treating. By mid-afternoon the whole job is done for the day and, unless the foreman has decided that cowboys are needed to push cattle off the mountains or down the driveway, everyone returns to their own ranches to tidy up and get ready for the next day. Having risen at 3.30 am to breakfast and saddle up and drive to the cutting ground, it's a relief to get out of the saddle after ten hours and sit down to lunch.

Chapter 13

I OBSERVE THE EDUCATION OF A CALF, JOIN IN A MARVELLOUS THREE-PARTY COLLISION AND I AM BULLIED BY BULLS

The first day of the fall drift was much like all the ones that followed. Up at 3.30 am to tumble out of bed and into the shower. No lights for that as it took a while for my eyes to get used to the idea of having to work in the middle of the night, so I'd dress and eat in darkness broken only by the dull glow of the light on the porch. The central-heating duct underneath the towel rail warmed both the towel and my clothing. Each night the temperature dropped below freezing and it was a pleasure to pull on the warm socks, long johns, T-shirt, shirt, jersey and scarf forming the inner layer of clothing that cocooned me from the icy wind that rose each day at dawn. A quick look outside to see if it had rained or snowed and to check that a cosy yellow light was shining out the kitchen windows of the other two houses. Breakfast of cornflakes, toast and coffee and then it was 4 am and time to bundle up in a heavy coat, woolly hat, boots, over-boots and gloves. I'd shove some tobacco, beef jerky and peppermints in my inside pockets and then step outside into the sudden chill of the frosty night.

Bud checking Travis's boots are on the right feet. (At 4.30 am it's not impossible they aren't.)

The barn from my porch.

I'd follow Warren across the yard to the huge white wooden barn that dwarfed the houses. The weak light inside gave the impression of greater warmth, but the major relief was to get out of the faint but icy breeze that drifted in from the west. The 220-foot walk across the yard was usually sufficient to start my nose running and to condense my breath in my moustache. On one particularly chilly day, I had icicles in my beard in the time it took me to walk from the house to the barn. That day it dropped to –30°F and the air was bright with the intense sparkling of moisture frozen and floating in the sunlight. On days like this the air is so still and so clear that distance judging is difficult and mountains 50 miles away look as if they are only a tenth of that distance. The brightness hurts your eyes, and ears and nose ache with the cold. On a day like that, you check your friend's face for the whiteness that signals frostbite. It's all the more dangerous for the fact that it can happen in your own backyard.

That day, though, I collected my halter and caught Spice in the corral. I rode him alternately with Bonnie to try and keep him fit without tiring him out. The shadowy shapes of the other horses, disturbed from their sleep beneath the roof of the calving barn, watched with steamy breaths as I quietly led Spice into the cheery light of the huge Dutch barn, built in the

1930s to house teams of work horses. Each stall was big enough for two Clydesdales and left plenty of room for one small Arab and his rider. The ceiling formed the floor of the hay loft above, which then held only a few dozen small square bales for sick animals and horses.

Tying Spice to the stall I would deposit a gallon of grain in his feed box for him to eat while I brushed and saddled him. We'd start up the stock truck and the pick-up and then we'd load up the horses into the trailer and drive out of the yard down to the road and then turn west for the highway and the drift fence.

About a mile north of the drift fence, Stan would stop and let out his two and a half cowboys plus any hangers-on and we'd mount up and ride into the driveway fields to begin pushing the cattle down to the cutting ground. Often it was a struggle to swing into the saddle since my too-tight jeans and long johns meant I could hardly bend my legs at all. After shoving a plug of chewing tobacco in my mouth I'd pull my scarf up and my hat down to cover as much of my neck and ears as I could from the cold. Working alone in the darkness, turning to half light, we'd seek out the cattle, and with subdued yips and whistles and much slapping of hands on thighs, we'd turn them south and start them walking for the underpass that led into the cutting ground. It was a relief to see shadows and hear the same noises being made by other sleepy cowboys off on the flanks as I rode across frosty scented sage and thin grass. Gradually, the light would increase and with it the volume of the rider's yells. As the dozen or so riders converged on the underpass pushing perhaps 200 head before them, the familiar faces appeared.

From the ranch opposite Stan came Dusty and Robert, both smoking and slouching in their saddles. Every day the same greeting from Dusty :

'Wwwell how's Lee today then?'

'I'm a box of fluffy ducks thanks Dusty, mornin' Robert.'

'Mornin' Lee.'

From the left came Warren and Ian talking quietly with Tommy from the ranch a mile south of Stan. 'Mornin' Tommy.'

A huge grin from him and a cheery, 'Hello Lee. How've you bin?'

'Flat out, like a lizard drinking.'

A couple more figures rode up and the group paused while a bunch of stragglers were pushed up by riders from further afield instantly recognisable by their horses, their hats or their greetings. As the last cow was pushed into the underpass that led beneath the highway, the group rode through and emerged on the cutting ground. The wind that comes up each day at that time now cut through the five layers of clothing and penetrated to the toes through rubber, leather and wool. For the next two hours, until the sun heated the air, eyes watered, noses ran and horses tried to tuck their tails in and turn away from the wind. At no time did it rise above four or five miles per hour but it could chill and disable hands that tried to roll a cigarette. Yorkshiremen call it a 'lazy' wind; too lazy to blow around you so it blows straight through instead. I have a different word for it, but it's too short to put here.

Already the big herd was forming in the far corner where more cattle were pushed in from the south-west as other riders cleared their own areas. By then the cattle had started the ceaseless bellowing and milling that is the chief impression of those days. As mothers called to lost calves and as bulls tussled and chased the hot cows, a ring of cowboys started to form around 500 or so cattle. Breath condensed in clouds above the herd and mixed with the first clouds of dust rising from warm places where cattle had slept. As soon as the cattle arrived, the first cowboys on the scene were already cutting out the easy pairs and singles that knew where the ranch cuts are meant to form. Those early groups form the nucleus of the cuts and if the cowboys are lucky, they will quickly settle down into a peaceful stationary mass that will attract other cattle to them. If not, then they will mill and bellow and constantly try to break out of the cut and join others or return to the main herd. The least experienced cowboys are assigned to hold the cut as it is the simplest job, and so that is what I was entrusted with.

Broadly speaking, my job was decidedly cold and extremely static for 90% of the time and rather too hot and lively for the rest. The other cuts were harder to hold than mine as I had the advantage of having a fence to push mine

Holding the cut separate from the herd.

against. The next nearest cut was 100 yards away in the open with several more beyond that. A block of salt for the cattle to lick was placed in the centre of each cut to encourage the cows to linger and it often worked well.

Periodically a cowboy or two would steer a pair towards me and when they were within 50 yards I'd ride down and get behind them and push them into the herd. Then it was back to the uphill end to watch for breakouts and to prevent the group from drifting over the top of the hill and out of sight of the main herd. If they did, then the cattle being brought out of the herd would be unable to see a group of cattle to join and would run all over the place, twisting and turning back and generally causing havoc instead of trotting peacefully into the cut.

Occasionally a cow would be as blind as a bat and would be so intent on what was going on behind her that she'd never even look in front to see the herd and would take off, legs pumping, for another cut miles away. That would send cowboys off at full tilt in pursuit of the ignorant old tart while all around the ground, those holding the cuts would nervously watch the chase and pray that their own herds didn't choose that moment to join in.

It was a constant worry for me when those little chases went on, as even if the wayward traveller was turned and pointed in the right direction, often she would charge straight at the cut and blast into the centre of the herd like a hairy cue ball. The result was always the same. Chaos. Cowboys arrived to help from the main herd as the panic-stricken cattle took off in all directions. Horses thundered up and down trying to turn cows away from other cuts and the main herd also tried to get in on the act with cattle breaking out to join in the excitement. After a few desperate charges from one end of the cut to the other, some semblance of control would be established and the cattle would gradually settle down again into a circlejerk formation. Once all the escapees were chased back into the cut the help would depart leaving me nervously waiting for the next eruption.

As the day was as dry as the preceding month, it wasn't long before the sun was shining through a huge cloud of dust that hung over the ground like a pall of smoke. Out of the fog would appear a cowboy or two dogging a steer or pair into a cut and then they'd disappear again into the churning mass of cattle. On one occasion, Dusty appeared three times in quick succession with the same calf that obstinately refused to join its mother on the short walk to my cut. Despite plenty of help from the other cowboys, the calf beat him again and again. Too small for the horse to push around, the calf would simply run between the legs of the horse or else would stop and turn back in a fraction of the time it took a cowboy to spin his horse. Within ten minutes, nearly everyone had had a go at the little monster, but after the third time the calf disappeared into the herd, some language floated up to me that blued the air and I saw Dusty shaking out a loop of his rope. The end was in sight.

For the fourth and last time, the calf rocketed out of the herd with Dusty in full flight behind him. The chase was short and as soon as the loop flew out towards the calf, Dusty threw out a healthy handful of slack rope to give time for his horse to come completely to a stop and lean away from the calf. The rope snapped taut, and like a tetherball, the calf's head swung around on the end of the rope to face the horse so fast that its little legs shot out from under it. Dusty's horse had already turned and was trotting back to the cut before the calf hit the ground with a WHUMP! Dragging along behind the horse for 100 yards seemed to be a learning experience, as when Dusty dismounted to release it, the calf seemed to be much older and wiser. It lay ominously still until Dusty gave it a medicinal boot in the ribs, at which point it slowly got to its feet and obediently made its way into the cut. Educating calves can be hard work, but the alternatives were worse.

It's worth noting at this point that none of the cowboys carried guns. This was for a variety of reasons, but chief amongst them I feel was the certainty that they would have been used to relieve the frustration and anger caused by the mule-headed stupidity of the cattle. It didn't take a great imagination to visualise cattle being shot by enraged cowboys. Every day I was working cattle, I'd want to kill at least one so badly that if the means had been conveniently available, I'd gladly have done so and paid for the cow later. Since each cow cost about ten days of a cowboy's wages, it doesn't take a great brain to see that for a hobby, cowboying with a gun rates up there with yachting and Formula One racing as far as expenses go.

Even years of work with cattle didn't ease the pain and frustration of seeing a herd or even a single stubborn retard turn back on you after perhaps hours of hot sweaty work to get them to a gate or a crossing. While a hundred cattle would plod faithfully along in any direction you aimed them, there was always 5% that would balk at rocks or sage bushes, leave the group at the drop of a hat, turn back at a glimpse of the corrals or else lag behind so disgracefully that cowboys would even dismount and rush at the stragglers in the faint hope of catching them out and being able to land a slap or a kick. On the mesa or in the mountains once in a while, from a hollow or valley out of sight of the rest of the cowboys, the most appalling curses would come rolling up on the breeze. White-haired old timers, raised to call men 'Sir' and women 'Ma'am' would use language that could boil water and glaze rocks when cattle would stubbornly refuse to enter corrals or cross rivers, or lie down with the rest of the herd. Occasionally a cowboy would dismount and fill his pockets with pebbles to hurl at them. If trees were handy, then a branch might be obtained and used to hurry them up, but all the cattle had an amazing sort of radar in the tail that told them when a cowboy was within striking range. You can quite easily ride a horse to within all but a half inch of kicking distance of a cow, but only once in a thousand times will you get close enough to unholster your boot from the stirrup and drive your toe into their behinds. On the rare occasions that you do it, it's like the relief of sneezing after a dozen failed attempts — a truly memorable moment.

It's worth noting that in the Pinedale area, there are a few ranches owned by extremely wealthy dudes as toys or tax write-offs. With all the money those folk have at their disposal, I don't understand why they don't simply massacre their herds in difficult times. Clearly they can afford it. Perhaps the very rich aren't prone to the same rages that we peasants are.

By mid-morning I'd finished my sweets and cigarettes and was stiff with the cold. Spice was bored with the whole affair, except for the brief moments when we had to chase cattle and then he'd take off without the faintest clue as to what was going on. Long after the cattle had turned, Spice was still accelerating in a mad dash towards God knows what. He was not a 'cowy' horse.

Just as some cowboys are reluctant and others are keen, so too are the horses. Some catch on to the idea of driving cattle in a herd, but not of cutting pairs out of it. Others get their greatest thrill from roping and as soon as the rope is uncoiled, will perk up their ears and begin to prance. These horses are highly prized and can cost five or ten times as much as another sound horse with no special abilities.

All horses have peculiarities of gait and manner that distinguish them from their peers. Spice's delight was a full-speed run with no turns. To hold him to a jog or a lope was almost cruelty. Horses that I rode later were lazier and would freely trot or canter but hated to be pushed into a gallop. For working cattle, a quick-turning horse was better than a fast one and a horse that could predict a cow's movements accurately was best of all. That type of horse was usually used for cutting out and seemed to take pride in steering a pair out of one herd and into another. With their heads almost on the behinds of the cattle they would trot briskly behind the cow, turning like a semi-trailer as the cow twisted and dodged all the way to the cut. As soon as the pair were in the cut the horse would relax and bring her head up to look around for the next job. Riding a horse like that is pure pleasure. The feeling of satisfaction gained by having a true working partnership with an intelligent friend from another species is something that few people are able to enjoy these days and some even deny such mutual delight exists.

Once in a while though, even the best partnership isn't enough to beat the wilful stupidity of the most obnoxious cattle. On the ranch, and later the feedlot, I saw plenty of occasions when sterner methods were needed. Once when Steve (who replaced Ian) and I were trying to turn a cow and calf out of the calving field, the calf caught on to the idea immediately and obediently trotted out the gate. Somehow, the mother didn't see that and took off at a run back up the field to where we had started from in search of her offspring. The two-day-old calf waited patiently on wobbly legs just outside the gate while we trotted back up the field and got in behind the cow again. As we approached the gate again, the cow tried to turn back once more and after several attempts she dodged past us and ran back up the field to look for her baby who was bawling feebly at her retreating behind.

With very little patience for such a hopeless mother, we turned and galloped up to head her off. She beat us both and made it to the far end of the field before we were able to turn her and drive her back towards the gate. By then we were cursing her loudly and with sweating horses we ran her at speed directly at the gate. Twisting and turning at every step, the lead-headed old nail turned and doubled back past us at the last instant.

At that point her calf trotted back into the field and tried to follow her. While Steve tried to turn the calf, I ran the cow to a halt against the fence and forced her to turn around. She turned back, I got ahead of her, she turned inside me, I ran her into the fence again, she ducked past me and took off with the wide-eyed, mindless unstoppability of a 1000-pound chicken.

Steve finally caught the calf on foot and dumped it outside the fence a small distance away from the gate, where it stood and bawled. Normally the call of her calf would be enough to bring a cow running from hundreds of yards away, but by this time the cow had left both instinct and reason behind in her stubborn determination not to go through the gate. With Steve and me both yelling vile abuse at her, we ran her at top speed down the length of the field towards the gate. With one of us on each side, slightly to the rear, we felt that at last we had her beaten.

As before, she waited until the last second, and then as the gate loomed tantalisingly close, she dug in her feet and skidded to a stop. Before we could turn she had spun around and for the sixth time, took off up the field. Steve and I were apoplectic. Half an hour wasted out of a very busy day on a chore that should have taken us two minutes. The cow's panic-stricken confusion and terrified flight would have undoubtedly been cause for sympathy in any observer, but for us they were the final proof of her totally predictable bovine stupidity. At moments such as those, when we lacked a gun and were not riding rope horses, we prayed for divine intervention. A lightning bolt between the horns for instance. No flash of light was forthcoming, but instead we got something almost as good and that's why what followed is still among the sweetest moments I ever had aboard a horse.

For the last time, we turned and trotted up the field to get around the cow. Promising each other that if this didn't work we'd rope her down and drag her out with a tractor, we turned her and pointed her down field. She turned and twisted at every chance, but we ran her alongside the fence with Steve behind her and me on the open side. Seeing she was beaten, she galloped ahead and veered away from the fence towards the open gate in the middle of the fence that ran at right angles to our approach. Steve moved up to the righthand side and I did the same on the left. The cow was moving at full clip between us when at the last instant before thundering through the gate she pulled her favourite trick and slid to a stop and turned on the spot. Head down and legs pounding she accelerated up the field. This time, instead of turning inwards, since we were travelling so fast, Steve and I both turned outwards and at full gallop we raced to head her off. As we caught up to her we angled in towards her head, aiming to cut her off. Neither one of us had eyes for the other as we thundered towards each other at an acute angle. By the time we realised that both of us were trying to head her off at the same time it was too late to prevent a collision. Instead of trying to rein in, I simply turned inwards more tightly and aimed to go behind Steve and the cow. Sadly, Steve did the same. We both saw the unavoidable collision in the making as we were within two paces of the fleeing beast. At that moment God revealed himself to the cow and instructed her to stop. Between us. Hallelujah!

Like two torpedoes fired from slightly astern, we struck that cow amidships on each side with about 1500 pounds of flesh travelling at 20 miles an hour apiece. Simultaneously she took a horse in the ribs on each side and let out an almighty PHWAAARGH! As she deflated like an airbag, her legs buckled, Steve's horse stumbled and they did a forward roll right across her, driving her into the ground under half a ton of horrified horse and rider. My moke hurdled the wreckage and slid to a halt next to the fence. As Steve's horse lurched to its feet with a stunned Steve still in the saddle I turned to look at the cow. Eyes popping, winded and shell-shocked, she reeled up the field like a drunken sailor.

As Steve and I walked slowly up the field and turned her around she finally heard her calf call, and tottered through the gate to meet it. Steve and I looked at each other and smiled. It's not often you get to sack the quarterback from both sides.

Moving bulls is a different story completely. Whenever we had to bring the 30 or so bulls together, there was a good chance that they would fight. Left to themselves, they would spread out and lead separate lives either alone or in small groups of similar-sized animals. As soon as we bunched them together, the pecking order was upset and challenges were made. Those fights were impressive as well as dangerous to animals and men alike. A big bull weighing over a ton can inflict a huge amount of damage on whatever it hits even when it is not charging. An unexpected flick of its

Mr Greedy flipped the hay feeder on to himself and found he couldn't reach the water trough. We let him out the next day after he had calmed down.

hindquarters can knock a horse down if a rider strays too close to a quickly turning animal. To be struck head on by an angry bull is certain to be fatal to horses and men, and occasionally to bulls as well.

Once in a while a bull may be ambushed by a challenger and be hit in the flank. At times like that, death can occur instantly. Broken legs from fights where a bull has not parried a charge are not uncommon and usually result in a trip to the baloney factory for the unfortunate cripple. When bulls fight, it's best to stay well back.

In corrals it isn't wise to keep aggressive animals penned closely for longer than a few minutes, as, without their being able to retreat from a challenge, an unnatural tension results in fighting that can destroy fences in seconds. Nothing except three-inch steel pipe fences set in concrete will slow a bull down and even those can be bent in a collision. Regular wooden pole corrals are respected by bulls, as are barbed-wire fences and wooden gates, but in a crisis a bull will crash through them without even slowing down. For that reason, the safest place to be around bulls is on a horse. Those cowboys who ride herd buffalo have my utmost respect as I wouldn't try to move a herd of buffalo except by train. Nudging them along in a pick-up truck would just aggravate them.

On only one occasion did I have to dash out of the way of brawling beef and on that day the fight spilled through a fence and out on to the road. Eventually the younger bull retired at speed and the herd settled down as we drove them to the dipping vat.

If driving bulls is fun then dipping them is a real laugh. Make no mistake, cattle have good memories and the annual swim through the dip is well remembered. First problem is to get them into the chute leading to the 30-foot-long concrete trench filled to a depth of ten feet with foul-smelling lice dip. The chute is fashioned like a film set. It looks robust from a distance, but up close you can see it's a sham. Ancient, withered and desiccated timbers are held loosely together with rusting nails, tangles of fuse wire and odd bits of string. Once in the chute, which somehow survives each year with only a few more half-hearted repairs, the bulls have to be encouraged to swim down the trench and, as they do that, two cowboys use a long pole to push their massive necks and heads under for a ducking. The best way to nudge them in is to use a bull behind to push them on. By using a hotshot or a stick, most can be driven to push the one in front of them into the trench, but the last one in each group has to be driven in by manpower. By edging him forward and putting a bar behind him at each step, the bull can be penned on the edge and with a final electric prod usually takes the plunge.

Because of the design of the chute with its low, overhead cross braces, there is no room for a rider to push the bulls up the chute using a horse. Lots of feedlots use this method to load cattle on to trucks. That probably saves several lives a year in the industry, as if the cattle turn back and run over the horse, the cowboy just grabs the nearest high crossbar and swings up out of the saddle while the scrum boils beneath him. The horses usually back out OK, where a man afoot would be trampled.

On one memorable day, I was on foot pushing stubborn bulls into the chute, when one at the front of the pen refused to enter. I walked along the top of the fence to give him a swat on the back with a stick when he finally stepped forward. I leapt into the pen to swat the others on and as I landed I turned slightly. I dropped to the ground like I'd been shot as my knee gave way. At that point, the bulls started to back up towards me. I yelled out to Billy to open the gate and with my arms churning like a surf rescue canoeist I clawed myself along the ground at top speed. Fortunately, fear and frantic activity were sufficient to get me through the gate in time for Billy to drag it closed before the bulls trampled me. Clutching my twisted knee, I looked up at the only barrier between me and the irritable bulls. The ancient gate was hinged with wire, secured with string and was braced and repaired with innumerable fragments of other broken gates from previous ages. It had all the stopping power of a lace curtain. This feeble construction was regarded with apprehension by the bulls. I could tell what they were thinking.

'Right, mate, you might've made it this time, but if we ever catch you in our pen again . . .'

Stan observed me writhing on the ground in pain and remarked casually, 'Hurts don't it? Did that once myself. 'Bout pissed a bootful.'

Chapter 14

How I am made privy to 'Tall tales and true from the legendary past'

By now, I was starting to become familiar with a few people around town, mainly those who I rode the drift fence with. I was in the Cowboy Bar one Saturday evening with a group of friends when I first heard of snipe hunting Pinedale style. I am a reasonably keen hunter of certain animals, but I've never hunted birds, and certainly not the way they did it there. In Pinedale, in the quiet times after the fall drift, it's customary to hunt snipe in time for the Thanksgiving Day dinner.

Snipe are small birds that live in a variety of habitats. Agile fliers, they are distinguished by a curious whistling sound when they dive. It is called winnowing or wittering or something, and they do it as they hunt insects. I didn't know any of that till I looked it up in one of Scott's encyclopaedias a couple of days after we started hunting preparations.

It was in the Cowboy Bar that the argument over hunting techniques began. Initially it was a dispute between Dusty and Robert, but soon it spread to include everyone in the bar. Later, I mentioned it to two friends, who were not at the bar that day, Dave Goulette and Travis Bing, and they said that I was a fool to hunt snipe any way at all except using the Indian method. Its advantage, they said, was that you didn't actually have to be in

Bing and Goulette — phenomenal liars, feeding me false information as usual.

the woods to get your snipe, but could set a trap and come back later to collect them. The down-side was all the preparation work. It was slower than just shooting them, but it was more fun. There was still two weeks left before Thanksgiving so they said they'd show me how it was done.

The first step was to make the poison bait. To do this, we took a trip in Travis's truck up to Fremont Lake early one evening. He'd loaded up a small canoe and Dave provided the nets on poles. I had a couple of lanterns of Stan's and a flashlight. We began by squeezing into the canoe, only to discover that three adults don't fit into a single two-child canoe. A wet reappraisal suggested that, instead of fishing around the inlets to the lake, we would have to content ourselves with having me operate the lights from the edge of the dam while Dave and Travis worked the nets.

The plan worked well enough, and within half an hour, a small driftfish had risen to the surface, attracted by the light. I don't know whether the fish gets its name from the time of year when it is hunted most (just after the fall drift riding) or whether it is because it is a bottom feeder that kind of drifts around the inlets and outlet of the lake in search of food stirred up by the currents. Opinion in town differed and nobody much seemed to care.

Either way, the actual fish is small and flat and ugly, but its major feature is its poisonous skin. Strictly speaking, I don't think the skin is poisonous, but maybe it has glands that can release a kind of toxin that affects predators' nervous systems if they bite it and break the skin. It's harmless to humans on contact, but you shouldn't swallow any or wipe your lips with your hand after skinning a fish. It wouldn't kill you but it would make you sick.

We were pretty pleased to get one so quickly but, though we spent another three hours paddling and shining lights, we never saw another fish. Drinking beer didn't help attract them and neither did peeing in the lake, so after frying a few sausages and making hot dogs, we packed up and returned home with our single fish.

The object of that expedition was to get a skin, which was then to be turned into paste and used as the active ingredient in the bait for the birds. That night, we carefully skinned the fish and froze it to keep it fresh until we had a chance to find some pine sap.

Work overtook us and it was a week later before we had time to get together for the next step. No one had found time to collect pine sap to mix with the paste, so Travis borrowed some pine-scented toilet deodoriser from Madeleine, which he swore was just as good if not better than the real thing, and crunched a few granules into a bowl. Snipe are attracted to the soft shoots of the pine trees in summer, and in winter, a strong pine scent will bring them in from miles around. The Indians used to gather sap and mix it with teepee tar and the pounded-up skin to make the paste. We had two of the ingredients but none of the third.

Teepee tar is a naturally occurring oil-based goo that oozes out of the gaps between rocks all over the west, especially in oil-rich Wyoming. Trappers called it tar because of its similarity to the tar used to help caulk ships, and in fact the Indians used to use it to seal seams on teepees. It can still be found quite easily wherever roadworks have exposed new rocks. The streaky marks it makes on the side of road cuttings are a sign that this sticky goop is present. We couldn't be bothered driving into the hills to find any that day, and since it was required only for its stickiness, we decided to raid the workshop.

A wide selection of silicon sealants, glues and greases were available, and so we took a dab of this and some of that until we had a ferociously sticky compound that didn't look like it would harden too quickly. We pounded up the driftfish skin with a bit of water and the pine scent and, using a stick, we smeared it over the sticky mess. I was concerned that we had strayed too far from the original recipe, but Travis pointed out that the Indians probably only used tar and sap because they didn't have access to a Selleys Home Handyman bar or Pine-O-Kleen crystals. It looked and smelled OK, said Dave and Travis, so we bagged it and loaded up the truck with post-hole diggers and a handful of steel pegs.

We drove up to the edge of the forest and set off on foot to a small clearing near the remains of an old bridge. Here we used a post-hole digger to make a narrow shaft about four feet deep. On top of that we put the steel pegs in a wide grid and weighted down the ends with rocks from the stream. Lastly, we took some of the bait from the bag and spread it liberally on the grill. It took about half an hour to build the trap and we still had plenty of time left so we went about a half mile further into the wood and repeated the process. We planned to return the next day to check our traps as the poison bait doesn't work for very long.

The theory behind the trap is that the birds eat a little of the poison. To give it time to act, the poison has to be on a sticky surface. While the bird either eats more or unsticks itself or just cleans the goo off its beak, the poison works away and in a short time, it falls unconscious through the grill. If it doesn't die from the poison or the fall, which is usually the case, then when you return to check your trap, you have a live bird in the bottom of the trap. The shaft is too narrow for the bird to fly up and the grill at the top is smaller than their wingspan, so unless another predator digs the bird out, each trap should yield at least one bird and possibly more.

We got lucky with the first trap and found two birds in the bottom when we returned. A quick tap on the head and then we were off to check the other trap. One bird was in that, and, since we had no more fresh bait, we filled in the holes and returned home. The birds were then put in the porch to hang, out of reach of the cats.

The plan to cook them was to bake them in clay, in an open fire, feathers and all, and then when they were judged to be cooked, the hard clay would be broken open and the now-plucked birds would be ready to be eaten. Small clay moulds can still be found here and there around Pinedale — some of great antiquity. It was optional as to whether they were stuffed, but as the snipe is a small bird, that seemed a bit unnecessary. Eventually the birds were served roasted like chicken, with a sauce made from a sage and onion soup base. Delicious too, with the advantage of not having to worry about accidentally breaking a tooth on a shotgun pellet. I guess the Indians knew a thing or two about hunting snipe, though I'd like to have tried calling them into a gunnysack by whistling.

This was Billy's favoured method. Apparently, you take the reed from the carburettor of a motorbike and put it in the throat of a one-pint Pennzoil bottle. If you cut a hole in the bottom of the bottle and blow carefully through the neck, it makes exactly the same sound as a bird does when it dives. The hunter then sets up a comfortable position on a cushion at the bottom of a tree with a shooting blanket over his legs for warmth. This also helps change the shape of the body so that to a snipe, it doesn't look like an upright human any more. (The bird, like some of the hunters, cannot be considered to possess a first-class brain.) If you keep still and hold a gunnysack open and whistle with this contraption, the snipe will land a short distance away and, after looking around a bit, it will ignore you and walk right into the bag in search of the intruder on to its territory. The drawback to this method is that it gets damn cold sitting up against a tree in the snow with nothing to do but blow on an oil bottle. Naturally, this is the reason why a few warming tots of whisky are required, and this in turn is why you see quite a few snipe hunters return from the woods with a gunnysack that clinks, absolutely smashed out of their heads.

That was the only hunting I ever did on the ranch and I don't regret it at all. Even though Stan allowed townies to hunt on the ranch, he didn't hunt himself. I think that was because, like so many ranchers, he could see the

Mule deer exploit the 'Pax Magdalena'.

diminishing habitat of the wilder animals, and he sympathised with them. Ranching the old way, as it is practised in Pinedale, is on the endangered list as well.

Meanwhile, though, moose, deer and antelope all enjoyed the comforts of grazing in willow swamps, haystacks and fields. A half-tame herd of mule deer lived near the houses on the ranch and each fall it was not uncommon to see them grazing in the backyard, just a foot from the windows of the house. They wandered freely but nervously across the yard from the safety of the willow thickets on each side in groups of six or more. They were under Madeleine's protection and for a couple of months a year they repaid the compliment by showing off their tiny spindly legged fawns as they slowly matured. In the soft evening light the silent procession of a family of those delicate creatures as they tripped across the lawns was a pretty thing and lent an air of peaceful contentment to the end of the day.

Fawn about to discover that the pax does not include the vegetable garden.

As the night gathered and the light faded, the high-pitched yipping and howling of the coyotes grew. Those elusive but numerous animals gather in family groups to chatter and to hunt and their cries make a weird chorus to wake to in the middle of the night. Their voices, though, lack the awful spine-tingling chill of a wolf, and a coyote's call will not alarm horse or man. The cattle are also unafraid of them, but if the calves are newborn, the sight or sound of either a dog or a coyote will send the mother cows into overdrive. In the case of coyotes or dogs, cows will not hesitate to charge the intruder and will combine forces to chase them well away from the herd. At calving time, a dog can trigger a riot with angry cows chasing them right through the herd while calves shelter behind their mothers' legs. In spite of this, calves are vulnerable to attack by coyotes although sheep suffer more.

Just after birth, the tiny defenceless calves have to be left alone at times while their mother grazes and for the first few weeks will be nudged and nuzzled into a hollow and pushed to lie down. There they will stay, asleep or awake until their mother returns. Like a fawn playing dead, they will lie without stirring, even allowing a man to walk right up to them and handle them. Their bodies are limp and feeble and often are mistakenly diagnosed as sick. They will often stay in this trance-like state bordering between shock and unconsciousness despite all the attentions of a concerned cowboy. Left alone, however, they will spring to their feet as soon as their mother returns and begin butting her to let down her milk. The transformation is hard to credit.

As they grow older, this method is replaced by the crèche. A group of up to 20 calves may be left in the care of just two or three cows while all the other parents graze over a wide range, or, in dry lands, make the journey to water. I have no idea how this duty is rostered, but somehow the mothers get together and arrange it so that all of them get to drink at least every two days. The calves meanwhile enjoy the company of their friends and play happily in their small circle. All these habits are far removed from the somnolent routine of dairy cattle and farm-raised beef cows.

Because of the aggression that some cattle show towards dogs, much work that would be done by cattle dogs in New Zealand is done by cowboys. There are other reasons too. Terrain is a factor. Knee-high sage brush is a big handicap for a dog that has trouble seeing over it, let alone running through it. Distances to gather cattle play a part as well. A walk of three to ten miles just to get to the herd is tiring for a dog, on top of the work of gathering and pushing. The commotion that a dog can cause is a reason why they are not used to hold or push large numbers of cattle held in by fences. A cow is quite capable of chasing a dog through a fence or a nearby cut and this would cause a stampede in most circumstances. Lastly, training a dog is time-consuming and many cowboys would rather spend the time training a horse.

Proof of the strength of the maternal instinct was shown by one calf that was attacked by a bear up in the mountains. At the start of the drift, we had ridden up into the mountains to gather and push cattle down towards the driveway. One pair was nearly impossible to move. The mother fought every attempt to be moved. Her calf stuck to her like glue in spite of his injury. At some point he had been attacked by a bear, which had taken a mighty swipe at his back, tearing a chunk of meat out that nearly exposed his spine. The huge wound was now flyblown and gaped open. The mother had obviously driven off the bear and now was violently opposed to any more interference. By mobbing her we eventually got them loaded into the horse trailer and shipped them back to the ranch. The next day, after the vet's advice was sought, I went down to the corral to separate the pair so that the calf could be treated. The mother was still wild and angry and as soon as she realised what my plan was, she fought her way out of the corner I had backed her into and ran through the fence. As she crashed through the willows and disappeared behind the house, Ian heard what happened and, without rebuking me for being stupid, looked at the calf standing in the corner with a stubborn set to his jaw. 'Well, I guess he's weaned now,' was all he said.

We were able to get a halter on the calf so that each day he could be caught and the wound could be cleaned with disinfectant and then dressed with an antiseptic cream and fly repellent. We never tried to gather up the mother and left her to crash through fences around the corral until she rejoined the herd as it was brought in from the drift fence. The calf gradually settled down and eventually recovered enough to return from a winter on the feedlot and go back up on the mountain, indistinguishable from the rest.

By then I was riding Bonnie regularly and Spice was getting plenty of rest. It was common policy to ride a horse only three or four times a week, and to saddle a fresh horse each day from the 30 or so that lived on the ranch. No particular effort was made to check that a saddle fitted the new horse. Just as any backpack will fit any human more or less comfortably, so it was with the horses. I only once saw a saddle gall a horse, and that cowboy immediately went and traded it in for a new one that cost $350 more. Compared to Britain, where each horse has its own saddle and blanket and bit, it was like the difference between owning a car and collecting them. The British treat their horses like vintage cars: they are petted and primped and fussed over. No doubt they enjoy it. Western horses are treated more like a pick-up truck. Hop on them and turn the key. If they don't go, then grab another one and call the vet. They aren't neglected but they aren't babied either. All ranch horses spend the winter outside with no more shelter than a clump of willows and, apart from eating a ton of hay each, they just grow a thicker coat and thrive in the knee-deep snow. They don't wear New Zealand covers or get any hot mash and the sole concession to the icy weather is to remove their horseshoes for the winter. A surprising number are kept for sentimental reasons long after they are too old or slow to be ridden. Other less-favoured animals are sent to Europe for sausage making, which was Spice's fate until I intervened.

Of the 30 horses on the ranch, some were pensioners, four were work horses, several were unbroken or too much for me to handle, so that left about a dozen horses split between four full-time riders as well as Madeleine, Scott and visitors. It was quite common to see friends of the family helping out at the fall drift as it is undoubtedly a fantastic day out for a townie, particularly if you don't have any responsibility for the success or failure of your job. Townies were absolved from blame if they screwed up, but not the paid help. The amazing thing was that no one but Stan ever corrected me, and I can't honestly recall him doing it except in the most measured and friendly of tones. I think that 40 years of yelling at cattle had made him sympathetic to even the most hopeless help like me.

The stereotype of cowboys as taciturn loners more at ease in the company of their horse than a human has plenty of exceptions, and in the late twentieth century has become watered down from the original picture, but in general, cowboys are still gregarious only on home ground and view suburbanites with suspicion. There is a treasury of tales hoarded about the people and the place. Outsiders aren't offered it until they've established their credentials. I was still working on mine, but occasionally a titbit popped up in conversation. More often than not though, I had to just study things until the pieces fell into place. Keeping your mouth shut and your eyes and ears open is better regarded than firing off a barrage of questions. As in most small towns, everyone tended to know everything about each other, but folks were careful not to let slip too often. There were several feuds quietly maturing in the county — some had ancient origins, others were based on recent grievances. Everybody needs a little soap opera in their lives and, in the absence of wife swapping or insider trading, they gave the breakfast conversations at the Wrangler Café some spice. If something big happened, then you could bet that all the town would know within days and you'd be able to read about it in the *Pinedale Roundup* on Thursday.

As in all American towns, there is a little gunplay from time to time and the odd person becomes shot, but those are routine tragedies typical of any small town in the world. Guns are not a feature of daily life any more than sheep are for most New Zealanders even though both are supposed to be national icons. Actual feuds tend to be fought with higher technology. That's why there are two lawyers in town. Probably if there was only one, he would starve, but two can make a packet.

Chapter 15

In which I learn more about cows than most Christians

As the days passed and the nights grew colder and longer, it became obvious that there was not a lot to do on the ranch over winter. Warren left for work in Arizona as soon as the drift was over and I started to consider a trip away at the same time. Once the cattle were all back on the ranch, the work slowed down and consisted mainly of shipping calves to feedlots for the winter and steers to meatpackers for slaughter. Other jobs such as re-decking a truck or getting ready for winter didn't take much time. With reluctance I began planning to return to the UK to find work for the rest of the winter, while I boarded Spice on the ranch.

It was after explaining this to Stan that he suggested that I should not be in too much of a hurry to go. A couple of weeks passed and I started to get concerned about overstaying my permit. Finally I said that I'd have to make a booking to fly to London at the end of November and a day or two after that Stan came and asked me if I wanted to stay on a feedlot owned by a friend of his over the winter. I got in contact with the Immigration Service and explained things and in due course they approved an additional stay of six months for me and that opened the door to visiting Gerry in Nebraska.

I was delighted at the thought that I would be able to continue to be a kind of cowboy, even though a feedlot is quite different from a ranch. The economics of the US agricultural system are complicated, but in general, you can say that in certain climates, it's easier to raise corn than cattle and that, as a result, ranches find it economic to send their cattle to the feedlets, often hundreds of miles away, for a midwinter holiday to gain weight while their home ranch is two feet deep in snow. From the feedlot, most animals are sent to slaughter, but a fair proportion are returned to a ranch to fatten up or to become breeding stock.

Up to 100,000 cattle may be housed in groups of 200 per lot, with each half-acre lot next to another in rows of five or ten. There are alleys down the middle of each double row of pens to move cattle in and out and the whole feedlot resembles a grid of streets with pens for semi-urban cattle.

The cattle are fed from concrete troughs on the outer edge by a feed truck that spreads a mixture of chopped hay, silage, beet pulp, molasses, tonic and cracked corn. Different diets are fed out depending on the age and desired weight gain of the animals. Animals can be fed to gain up to a pound a day or kept at a little better than maintenance weight if necessary.

Driving the feed truck and mixing the feed loads is a full-time job, as each pen is fed twice daily and to feed quickly and accurately requires concentration. The feed is loaded into the truck with a payloader from 100-ton piles. A slip of the hand can easily drop a few hundred pounds too much of any ingredient and it is impossible to retrieve it from the hopper as it is immediately mixed in with the rest by the augers. It's like mixing and delivering different types of concrete 30 or 40 times daily. Frequently, the afternoon feeding is finished at night after starting at 6 am.

Any interruption to their feeding schedule can upset the cattle enough to cause illness. Even the way the feed is spread in the troughs is critical. All the cattle in the pens have a pecking order, and after the first few days, they each have their own place at the trough to eat from. If food isn't put directly in front of them then they have to challenge another animal to get their place at the table. Low-ranking animals can't do this effectively so they simply miss out. If the driver makes that mistake three or four meals in a row, then an animal will fall sick through hunger.

While the feed driver is doing all this, the cowboys are riding the dozens of pens looking for sick cattle. When they are identified they have to be quietly cut out and pushed through the gate of their pen into the alley without letting any healthy ones escape into the growing collection of sick cattle from other pens listlessly waiting outside. By mid-morning all the alleys are checked and the cattle are then walked to the hospital for treatment. There the crush is used to catch their heads and if necessary it can also squeeze them gently to immobilise them while their temperature is taken with an electronic thermometer. From observation of that and other obvious symptoms, a diagnosis is made. Treatment is administered and then they are discharged into a sick pen. From there they will be brought back for two more treatments on successive days and then, if cured, they will be returned to their home pen. If they don't recover, then they are usually not treated much more, but are put in a chronic pen and left to fight for themselves.

Most animals recover quickly on this three-day treatment programme and so every day after treating the first-, second- and third-day patients, the last bunch are split up into alley groups and are then escorted back into their pens. The process and the doctoring takes up most of the rest of the day and by three or four o'clock the cowboys are ready to begin checking the free-range cattle.

Most feedlots are also ranches raising their own free-range cattle as well as arable feed crops. Calves from the ranch are raised normally until weaning, but then are put together and fed outside in the stubble of the corn fields. The sparse grazing provided by the stubble is augmented by feed delivered to portable feed troughs. These little critters have to be checked as well, but as the hospital is too far away to drive them to it for treatment, they are roped in the field and doctored on the spot. Once this is done, it's time to unsaddle, feed and water the horses and other odd animals such as pet sheep and cattle dogs, before heading home in the dark for tea. Any spare moments during the day are spent cleaning the hospital, scrubbing water troughs, fixing fences, shovelling manure out of alleys and pens or any of the other routine ranch jobs.

It's the mess in the pens that makes the job so unappealing. Hundreds of cattle kept in close quarters deposit tons of manure in the pens and payloader crews work nearly constantly to load manure-spreader trucks that haul it off to fertilise fields. A separate crew of contracters often does this job but, usually, riding the pens means stumbling across a frozen lunar landscape of deeply pugged muck or else slopping through greasy mud later in the day. If the weather is dry, then a fine dust can be raised that chokes and blinds. It's a far cry from trotting across newly mown hay or through sunny mountain meadows. Everyone agrees that feedlot work is a dirty job.

The environment is not really like battery farming and a lot of work has been done to ensure that cattle are well fed and cared for. Stress affects weight gain so feedlots take this into account with the design of the lots as well as the policies on how cattle are handled. I went along with the cowboys to a lecture delivered by an animal behaviourist who advised feedlot owners and staff how to handle cattle efficiently without having to yell and prod and swat them all the time. Simple things like changing the ground surface from dirt to concrete causes cattle to bottle up while each one examines the new surface before trusting their weight to it. This slows down the movement of cattle through corrals and sheds and causes frustration and lavish use of the prod. A change of floor surface coinciding with a gate or a roof causes even more delay so the correct layout of facilities makes a huge difference to the job and can reduce staff numbers and take hours off the working day as well as making cattle less afraid of entering corrals. These and dozens of other tips (don't hang your hat on a gatepost — cows will stop to look at it) were offered and many were trialled on the feedlot. They worked too.

Medical treatment keeps losses down to about 1% which is better than a ranch could ever achieve. Nevertheless, the difference in behaviour between ranch and feedlot cattle is plain to see. When cattle are let out of their pen to be weighed it's like the last day of term. They race up and down the streets like children at playtime, throwing their heads around and kicking up their heels. They make mock charges at each other and buck and jump for no reason at all. Groups will race back and forth for the sheer pleasure of running. Back in the pen they resume the weary indifference of old lags. Bored rigid by their daily grind of eating and sleeping, their only activity comes at feeding time, though any new activity in or near their pen will rouse their curiosity.

On many occasions I stepped into a pen to scrub a tank and the entire herd raced around in confusion. That was one of the few times they had seen a man on foot and while they had no fear of me, they weren't in the least bit hostile either. Usually after a couple of minutes they would crowd around the tank in a circle exactly like children, the ones at the back pushing those at the front forward in their curiosity to see what was going on. Often I'd be so busy bending over the tank that the stealthy approach of 100 yearlings to within a couple of inches of me was only heralded by hot breath on the back of my neck as a shaggy face peered into the tank with me. I'd look up and see the circle of cattle watching intently with eyes wide at the spectacle of me swilling water around with a stiff broom. Riveting stuff.

Touching and funny as those moments were, they had to reflect a level of boredom bordering on neurosis. I wished I'd had a ball to throw into a pen. I'm sure they'd have enjoyed butting it around. Horses do that if the opportunity exists and catalogues sell 'balls' with handles designed to be gripped by horse teeth for horses to play with. Cattle are probably smart enough to enjoy that as well. Ranch cattle have far more scope for amusement and much more to see and do so the same level of desperate curiosity doesn't exist amongst them.

Matt — approximately normal.

I arrived at Gerry's ranch in Nebraska right after Thanksgiving, and moved into a tidy little bungalow cabin near the main ranch house. Around it were the houses occupied by the other two seasonal cowboys and another housing Gerry's mother and father. The cowboys, Matt and Ron, were college students taking time off to earn another year's worth of tuition fees. Matt drove the feed truck and Ron worked with me. Together, with an experienced Mexican cowboy called Ignacio we were the semi-skilled labour. I say semi-skilled because although Nacho had two first-class degrees from the two best universities in Mexico, they were in civil engineering and town planning and weren't much use in his present job. When I asked why he worked as a common cowboy, he said that in Mexico it wasn't what you know or even who you know, it was who you can afford to bribe. Here, he said, he could earn more money.

Ron — will probably die laughing.

Above us was Bernard, with a couple of degrees in animal physiology. He was our veterinary advisor. Above him was Ambrosio. He had no degrees, but what he didn't know about cattle hadn't been found out yet. Occasionally, other people would help out when we got overrun with work, but we were the core of the cowboys. Also on the ranch were the farmers. They were the men who kept the millions of dollars of machinery working, and raising thousands of bushels of corn, making the hundreds of tons of hay and processing the thousands of tons of feed that was bought in from neighbouring ranches and farms, for Matt to mix and feed out. Working around all this talent was an education for me.

Ambrosio and Nacho watch Bernard trying to act cool.

Each day began for me by getting up at 5.30 am to pack a lunch and drive to the feedlot in one of the ranch pick-ups. I think they had about seven or eight but they never sat still long enough for me to get a good count. Mine was an old Ford that used to belong to Gerry's father. It was a seven-litre automatic that had the best accelerrrrrrration of any car I've ever driven from 0 to 100. After wrapping up in a heavy coat I'd meet the other cowboys and saddle my horse. Together we'd set off to ride the pens. One to each pen we'd check for ailing animals.

For the first three weeks, I accompanied Ambrosio until I'd got the hang of spotting sick cattle. It wasn't easy to see all the cattle as they meandered around, but by weaving in and out long enough it was possible to get a fairly thorough look. The easiest to spot were also the most seriously ill. Those were the 'bloat' cattle. Bloated cattle can die in minutes once they get to a certain point. Running them around can both kill and cure them. Occasionally it will cause them to let out the excess gas but the strain on the heart can also turn them tits up. The best way was to quietly get them to the hospital and doctor them. Fortunately, the enormous bulge in their left side made them stand out. The worst cases looked exactly as if they'd swallowed a basketball. Unfortunately, a lot of perfectly healthy cattle also had suspiciously large bulges in that area but, when in doubt, I took everything that looked like a zeppelin and, as a result, I never lost a cow to bloat. Plenty of them, however, got an unwelcome dose of mineral oil that they didn't need. The treatment for bloat was to put a one-inch diameter rubber pipe down the throat into the stomach and then to use a sort of bicycle pump to lubricate them with a half gallon of oil. As soon as the pipe was carefully pushed into the first stomach chamber, a foul methane gas was usually released and at the same time the basketball deflated. If that didn't work, then the crush was used to give them a gentle squeeze. That often worked and the cow would let out a sibilant burp. The last option was not used when I was there, but would have been to stab the stomach with a knife to release the gas before the build-up squashed the heart and lungs. The oil only worked like a laxative to encourage things to keep moving. The first time I tubed a cow I was worried that I'd get it in the lungs instead of the stomach, but the fizzing gas rushing out the pipe was a giveaway that I'd hit the right spot. Drowning a cow with medicine was frowned upon.

Next most serious was pneumonia. The symptoms were a lowered head, droopy ears, a hunched back, coughing, an empty belly and a reluctance to move. Droopy ears on a calf or cow was a dead giveaway that they were sick, as was a reluctance to walk. In some cases the reluctance extended to lying on their sides with their legs out. That was an advanced case of pneumonia known as death. All forms of cold, bronchial upsets and coughing were typecast as pneumonia and the treatment in most cases was the same — a dose of LA 200 or Tylan in a cocktail injected under the skin or into the muscle. Extremely bad cases sometimes had a husky cough that called for a special injection of a solution that we mixed up only when needed as it had a very short life in suspension. Those very sick animals reacted spectacularly well to that antibiotic and were often bouncing around inside a week if they didn't die.

Another ailment was pinkeye, which if left untreated would blind the cow. Powder was dusted into the eye for that and was fairly successful. To help the eye heal, a patch cut from an old pair of jeans was glued over the cow's eye until it fell off after a week or two. Abscesses were not uncommon, and they were usually lanced, cleaned out and then squirted with penicillin or iodine. I always enjoyed treating them as it was possible to see the relief in the patient's face as soon as those horrible bulges were drained. Added to all those were the odd ailments like lameness, tumours or early pregnancies. There was almost no fighting between animals so injuries like broken legs and such happened only when overkeen cowboys tangled with aggressive cows. Even sick animals showed surprising health at times and plenty of cows resented being taken to the hospital for treatment. Most of the handling was done on horseback, but on the rare occasion that we worked them on foot, such as when we sorted them into or out of their sick pens, some cattle seized the chance to work us over.

One breed of cow was notorious for bad temper and aggression and since they were also the biggest breed we handled, we took care to stay away from the Charolais on foot. From the moment we entered the pens, we stayed on horseback, opening and closing gates almost at a trot by reaching down from the saddle and using the horse to swing the gate open or shut. Once we had the cows in the alley we would herd them all the way into the hospital on horseback. There we dismounted and tied the horses until we had finished doctoring. First we pushed the cattle from the corral into a steel-walled circular pen that had a heavy gate on a pivot. This was pushed around and used to crowd the cattle into the start of the chute that led to the crush. There was a rubber brake on it that stopped it from swinging back if the cattle leaned on it. Standing behind the gate it was possible to prod and shout and slap freely, without any chance of a cow turning and leaping over it or of kicking your knees to bits. I had a lot of confidence in the gate, but I took it too far.

I was leaning on the gate one day poking idly at a cow that wouldn't walk up when suddenly she lashed out with a hind foot. It struck the gate so hard that it snapped back over the brake and jammed. The speed and force necessary to do that to a 300-pound gate was amazing. All I can compare it to is the kind of finger-crushing force that you could achieve if you slammed a car door as hard as you could on your hand. Even though the gate only moved back about four inches before the brake jammed, the impact threw me flat on my back in the muck. It was a long time before I relied on just jeans to save me from a cow's foot again.

The power that a 1000-pound animal can get into a hind-leg drive is scary. It can shatter knees and shins quite easily, but often there is no practical alternative to slapping a cow on the backside and simply hoping that she doesn't kick hard and accurately. To be honest, most cows kick as lazily as they flick their tails at flies, and of all the kicks I've had, none have broken bones.

It was hard to feel sympathy for some cattle though. One particular cow (a Charolais naturally) fought and fought not to be taken from her lot to be treated for a minor ailment. All the way to the hospital she twisted and turned in the alley until we reached the corral. Here, she raced round and round and refused to enter the circular pen. After all the other cattle were in the pen she still refused. Every day was a race against time to get the doctoring done in time to ride the cornstalks looking for sick calves before last light, and on this occasion we had missed out doing it the previous day so we were in a hurry to catch up this day. None of us were in a mood to deal kindly with an obstreperous witch like this. Plus, we all hated Charolais on sight. Just outside the hospital chute was a pit the size of a swimming pool that contained a noxious slurry that was hosed out from the hospital each week. When this noisome pit was filled it was scooped out by a payloader and used to fertilise a far distant field. On that day, it was iced over with a good solid three-inch crust at the edge. Dust had blown across it and the surface looked very much the same as the rest of the corral. Usually the cattle never went near it because it was right next to the wall of the hospital and cattle don't usually head for buildings, preferring to keep closer to the fences or gates. Finally, after Ron, Bernard and I had all been unable to cut off her attempts to turn back on us and had resorted to trying to chase her round the corral and then cut her into the pen at speed, the inevitable happened. The cow ran into the uphill corner of the corral and we had her boxed in.

The only way out was to edge past the pit. I dismounted to do that and got behind her by climbing the fence in the corner. The mad beast took off and leapt from the hill down on to the ice-covered pit. It held for the first step but the second was one too many and she disappeared into the reeking depths head first. Like a porpoise she burst out on the other side covered in liquid shit and ice. Unfortunately, she had dived at such an angle that she hit the bottom chin first and had torn her bottom lip away from her jaw. Bleeding from this wound she was wide-eyed and shocked. The combination of icy water, darkness and impact followed by pain and stench was too much and she was really on the fight when we penned her at last. The wound couldn't be treated so she was shipped off to the slaughterhouse. The only cow I ever saw get her just desserts.

Naturally it was a Charolais that gave me my closest call while working cattle on foot. We were sorting the third-day patients before returning them to their lots when a group from a Charolais pen broke the gate and rejoined the rest of the unsorted mob. We straightened them out and had them penned when it happened again. That time one had jumped the fence, which led the others to try until they had knocked the temporary pen down. For the third time we sorted them, but one obstinate cow refused to join her two companions. Her give-a-shit fuse had blown and she was even pawing the ground like a bull. I charged at her, yelling and swinging my stick. She refused to turn and run into the pen and so I retreated. She followed up and I fended her off by smacking her in the face with my stick. What I needed was a baseball bat, but Gerry didn't issue those. My little stick was making no impression at all, chips were flying off the end as it whittled itself away. Soon I would be reduced to wielding a toothpick so I retreated sharply. It quickly developed into a straight sprint for the end of the alley. Halfway up, floundering in my long johns and overboots, I saw I'd never make it and opted for the fence at the side. I leapt for the top of the steel pipe fence and got one leg over before she got her head underneath me and tossed me up in the air. I landed in a muddy puddle on the far side of the fence while she tried to climb in after me. I bolted for the barn and left her victorious on the field. If she had been a second earlier or if she had had horns, I'd have been a candidate for hospital. Shaken, I watched her race up and down the alley, snorting and blowing. The other cattle cowered in a corner while all this went on. Later, I came back on a horse and chased her all the way to her lot at a gallop.

Big Dave weighs 250 pounds. The calf weighs 150 pounds. Dave ain't winning by much.

Occasionally, one of the cowboys would take advantage of a cow in the crush for a little entertainment. This involved telling Ron or me to go and open a gate for the cow while she was being treated in the crush. When we were halfway down the alley, Bernard would release the cow from the crush. If he was sporting, he'd yell a warning, otherwise the first we'd know about it was an angry snort and the sound of pounding hooves behind us. We were always quick enough to get over a fence in time, and there was no doubt that such athletics warmed us up better than any amount of coffee on a cold day.

Teaching calves to yodel with a branding iron.

Learning how to doctor cattle in the crush each day was a slow process. Bernard or Ambrosio made all the decisions about treatment, but we helped out by diagnosing the problem. Often only the cowboy who had brought the animal into the alley knew the reason why the beast was brought out. Treatment was swift and sure and delays in diagnosis were not welcomed, so I got good at remembering which cattle I picked and why. Once a decision was made, often Ron or I gave the injection. Almost all ailments were treated at least partly with a syringe and I got quite good at intravenous injections as well as subcutaneous and intramuscular ones. We also castrated the occasional steer that had escaped the cowboys at branding time, and the products of this were saved for breakfast by Nacho and Ambrosio and Bernard. I would rather have gargled sand.

In spite of all the care that we took, accidents happened and cattle died as a result. One steer was being unloaded from a horse trailer, and as it ran out the back, it kicked up its hind legs as many cattle did when passing through a gate. That time though, one of its feet caught in the top of the gate about six feet off the ground. Feeling painfully trapped, the steer began to kick to free itself. There was nothing we could do as we watched the horrifying spectacle. It kicked its leg off. By the time the foot twisted free, the steer had broken its thigh bone and the leg was dangling by a small piece of skin and flesh. The shattered bone showed through the wound. The animal was wild with pain and anger and was attacking everything in sight. In the end, it was lured back into the trailer by Ron, who was delegated to show himself to the animal, which inevitably charged him. A three-legged cow can still outrun a cowboy and Ron's instructions were to make for the trailer, run up to the far end of it and exit by the small side door which I held for him. It was a close run thing and if Ron had slipped I think he'd have been badly hurt if not killed by the maddened steer. Once in the trailer, the steer was raced away to be slaughtered. Things like that tended to keep you on your toes around the animals, but in spite of that I was careless, and nearly paid a heavy price.

We were weighing a test herd at the time. That was a herd of many different types of cattle from different ranches that were all fed on the same trial diet to compare growth rates. That meant that they had to be weighed individually each month and the results logged. As we were sorting them out and letting them on to the scales, I turned my head and looked behind me. Just as I did this a cow kicked back and struck me on the side of my head. Amazingly, she must have been just at the limit of her reach and instead of my brains flying out my ear, I just felt as if I'd been sucker punched. I had a strange buzzing in the back of my head for an hour but apart from that I was unscathed. I never saw the cow responsible and I didn't even feel angry at the anonymous assailant. I was just rather grateful that I was still walking so I got on with the work while everyone who saw it obviously concluded that I had no brains to risk.

Chapter 16

I witness the most daring and amazing acrobatics

If working cattle on foot was risky, then the danger was at least equalled when we rode forth to rope the calves in the corn fields. That was usually the high point of the day and we looked forward to it as some of the finest entertainment the ranch could offer. It had everything. A huge stage, a cast of hundreds, a keen audience and the ever-present danger of a fatal wreck. It was like going to a Demolition Derby and being invited to drive.

As I was the junior dude, I was delegated to carry the medicine and do the doctoring. I kept that job until it was taken from me by Shelly, a veterinary student who couldn't rope. Until then, I only got to try roping if I was particularly handily placed or if everyone else had failed. I carried a pouch with a couple of bottles of LA200 and Tylan, three or four syringes and needles, some marker paint, eye powder, glue and patches. All that was hung off the horn in a small bag wrapped in a woolly hat for safety. All the cowboys would cinch their saddles up tight and unsling their ropes. Furry cotton roping gloves were donned and big hats were discarded in favour of baseball caps. Riding out into the 640-acre fields in the cool golden late-afternoon light we felt like cavalry going out to do battle, and sometimes that was closer to the truth than we preferred.

Poor rope horses were sometimes exchanged for better ones but, in general, we took whatever we'd used that morning for pen riding and made the best of it. Most of the horses on the ranch were simply rank or idle. I always rode with spurs when roping, but never at any other time. Without them, some horses just wouldn't run at full speed and that meant that we had to chase calves for far too long.

The procedure for roping on the feedlot was different to the way I'd seen a single person do it on the ranch. First, we roped in pairs, and secondly, we had another person to do the doctoring. As soon as a sick animal was spotted, one rider would throw a loop over its neck and the second rider would throw a loop and catch its hind legs. As soon as the beast was down, the first rider would dismount and remove the head rope and hold a foreleg back so that the patient couldn't stand up and jump around while I put in the injection. Once the calf was marked with a paint stripe on the forehead, it was allowed to stand up and step out of the loop on its back legs. By then, the head roper and the doctor were mounted up and looking for the next one to treat. That was the theory anyway.

In practice, Bernard or Nacho were the best ropers, followed by Ambrosio, Ron and Bruce (who helped out regularly) and then there was nothing. After nothing, there was me. The top ropers would begin by riding quietly up to the ailing one and, lazily turning their loop, would cast it quickly at the calf. Unless they were lucky and the animal was very sick, it would usually take fright at the sight and sound of the twirling loop and would bolt. None of these boys could throw a Houlihan loop, which is a quiet backwards flick of the wrist that neatly sends a loop out over the head without any preliminary rotations. As a result, 90% of the time, the first throw failed and the chase was on.

Gathering your rope while galloping in pursuit of the calf was not too difficult and shaking out a loop ready to throw was possible too, but in the intervening half minute, one of the other ropers usually got on to the tail of the calf and threw. Typically that also would fail to catch the calf and the first rider would then get a second throw.

To get into position for a perfect throw required a bit of skill. Steering the horse as it galloped across corn stubble, furrows, puddles, mud and ice was hard enough while swinging the rope. Avoiding the overhead sprinkler system was another trick as well. Some horses took fright at its shadow and started bucking under it, which was exciting in a deadly sort of way. It was low enough so that you could quite easily hit your head on the sprinkler arms that poked down, or else you might catch your rope on part of the hugely expensive structure. That didn't bear thinking about. All in all, it was better to avoid it completely, but as it was a quarter of a mile long, and pivoted about the centre of the field, this was not always possible.

If the chase was prolonged, then one of us would join in on the other side of the calf and haze the target in a straight line so the roper could edge up just behind the calf on the left-hand side. Naturally the calves would seek refuge in the small herds that made up the 350-odd head in each field.The result, when viewed from a vantage point, was not unlike tenpin bowling, with the threesome blasting into the frame like a bowling ball. It wasn't uncommon for calves or horses to completely forget about the frail electric fence that circled the field on two sides and a sharp TWANG! as the fence parted was followed by the customary observation of, *'Oh shit shit shit!'* No lasting damage was done to man or beast by these accidents unless a herd happened to be loitering near the fence. Those calves could be relied upon to go AWOL immediately, and in the chase to round up the escapees before they left the county, the original patient usually escaped.

Bernard applies traction while Shelley makes it all better.

Assuming, though, that the pursuer avoided trees, streams, fences, feeding troughs, sprinklers and so on, then the instant the loop left the cowboy's hand, the horse was supposed to turn slightly away from the calf and slow down. That allowed it to take the strain of several hundred pounds suddenly wrenching on the saddle. To 'dally' is to quickly tie off the rope to the saddle horn by wrapping it around the horn two or three times. Great care had to be taken not to do this with the thumb of the hand pointing downwards as many a cowboy has had a thumb amputated when the rope jerked tight with his thumb inside it.

To stop the stiff nylon or manila rope from slipping around the horn and coming undone, a length of inner-tube rubber is wrapped around the horn to protect it and provide something for the rope to bite into. This rubber leaves black marks on the rope about six feet from the end in the case of good fast ropers and all the way up to the end in the case of bad ones. Real slow ones don't have any black marks at all. Mine had black marks. Eventually.

The speed at which all this happens is the speed at which a baseball is pitched and hit. There is no time for thinking, only practice and instinct allow the right movements to be made in time. One of the worst sinking feelings is to see a calf disappear with your rope trailing behind it as that means that, after five or ten minutes of frustrated spectating, the rope will be handed to you by a fellow cowboy, dripping sincerity and saying things like, 'Say feller, this wouldn't be YOUR rope would it now?'

When the rope tightens, the saddle will slip unless it is very tightly cinched. Since normal riding doesn't demand that, plenty of cowboys have been caught out when they've had to unexpectedly make a catch or take over the rope from someone else, and have forgotten to lace up tightly. If that happens, the saddle spins round, depositing the surprised rider beneath the flashing hooves of his bucking horse. That is a novel adventure that I can admit to having experienced once or twice. The first occasion sent my horse into such a fit that, after I was dumped, he bucked himself all the way to a far corner of the field, dragging the thunderstruck steer with him for a surprising distance before the dallies unwrapped. If morale is low on the ranch, I can guarantee that such a happening will raise it considerably. The first time I did it, Ron laughed so hard he got hiccups.

On another occasion, after a lot of riding, the saddle pads slipped backwards and the front of the saddle was unsupported. As soon as the strain hit the saddle, the front edge bit down and pinched the shoulder blades of my horse.

The second cinch strap stops the saddle from tipping forward too far and sending the rider over the horse's head, but the system relies on having adequate padding under the front when the pressure is on. That time, the horse reacted as all horses do in an emergency; he jumped up in the air. When he landed the saddle bit him again and so up he went a second time. Being as dense as most of the ranch horses, he continued in this pattern like a record locked in a groove. For a while it was like riding an especially lively rocking horse. The calf, however, was starting to look a bit poorly after all the jerking, so for its benefit more than mine I reined the horse in.

Once the calf is caught, it faces back at the horse, bawling and bucking and pulling backwards as hard as it can. It tends to circle sideways around the horse, which turns to face the calf so as not to get slapped on the butt by the rope (which would cause a panic attack) and to avoid getting the rope tangled around its legs. If it did, then the whole cat's cradle of rider, rope, horse and calf would crash to the ground. That kind of thing would give Ron convulsions.

By then, the second rider should have arrived to rope the back legs. That requires him to ride up behind the struggling calf and throw a loop that lands on the ground under the calf's belly. The calf will (will?) then step into the loop, which is instantly jerked tight, snaring the legs. Sure. Since many horses don't even want to ride up within 20 feet of the whole bawling tantrum, it can be a struggle just to get close enough to throw a loop. Much encouragement is applied to the horse's ribs to accomplish that.

Doctoring. The ambulance horse arrives with Shelley wielding the syringe.

As soon as the foot, or feet, are snared, the rope is tightened and the calf should topple over on its side. If not, then the doctor runs up and leans across it, grabs it under the neck and belly, lifts it up and throws it down, which can be quite a chore with a 200-

pound calf. But by using your knees as a fulcrum and risking nothing more than a fatal rupture, it can be done quite handily.

The doctoring is quickly done and then the cowboys step back and mount up. The calf stands up and it kicks out of the slack hind loop. It's important to be out of the way when it gets up as the odd calf is still full of fight and will attack its physician. Horses left alone while the doctoring is done also tend to wander off and, if an angry calf attacks them, they may bolt back to the barn instead of staying ground hitched. That is called being barn-sour and there are few cures for it once it has been indulged. About the only time I was left with a really long walk back to the barn in pursuit, I collected the horse and walked him backwards all the way back to the place he'd wandered off from. This was supposed to be a sovereign remedy for such misbehaviour, but it did no good and the next time he did it I chased him throwing clods of dirt at him and calling him names. It didn't do me any good but Ron appreciated it.

As the weather grew colder, the risks increased as the horses slipped and slid on the icy ground. Nebraska doesn't get a lot of snow or rain, but the freezing winds that whip across the prairies lower the temperature dramatically. We had only two heavy snowfalls, but one dropped about two feet of snow that drifted in places to four feet deep. An icy wind accompanied us as we rode out one day to check on the calves for the first time in three days.

The heavy snowfall with the firm dry surface beneath was safe to gallop over so we looked forward to plenty of roping after the bad weather. In due course a sick calf was spotted and Nacho set off in pursuit. He failed and his hazer, Bruce, took over for the second throw. As it was the first catch of the day, Ron, Bernard, Ambrosio and I were all free to watch the most spectacular horseback wreck I've ever seen.

It started out normally enough with Bruce running up at full speed behind the calf after Nacho peeled off. As soon as he got within striking distance though, the calf burst into life and quickly stretched out into a flat sprint up an almost imperceptible rise. Bruce followed hot on its heels.

The problem that was about to manifest itself lay in that tiny

Above: *Cattle trying to beat the wind chill.*
Inset: *Twenty-four hours from dust bowl to snow drifts but the 'Ronmobile' thrives on it.*

slope. All hills have to end sooner or later and in Nebraska after two days of strong wind, all those little slopes and hills have snow drifts behind them. Deep ones.

As a native Nebraskan, Bruce was well aware of that and his idiot horse certainly should have remembered, but the thrill of the chase was in them and all thoughts of caution were cast aside. If there is such a thing as a 'Prudence Scale' with say, 'Belts and Braces' at one end, and 'Fighting a Land War in Asia' at the other, then metaphorically speaking, Bruce was charging at the Great Wall Of China.

The calf was first to vanish. It simply disappeared off the end of the low ridge into a shallow valley of snow four feet deep, coming to an instant and thoroughly unfortunate halt. Bruce, being only two paces behind, had no time to stop as his horse plunged off the crest into the snowbank. The bottom half of the horse stopped dead. It was a great pity that the top half couldn't. The excess momentum was transferred upwards and afflicted the rider most curiously. By gripping fiercely with his knees, Bruce was able to stay in the saddle as he rocketed over the horse's head. To fly over the handlebars is nothing unusual, but to have the horse follow you over is something else. Aided by Bruce's death grip on the saddle, the horse turned a violent somersault. At the same time, the horse's chest struck the rear of the calf, pile-driving it into the ground. As Bruce and the horse completed their awful rotation, the horse's legs somehow got tangled up with the recumbent calf and it was flung into the air like a soft toy from a cot. As Bruce dived head first into the snow, the horse was upside-down above him, the calf, which had first been buried, was now exhumed and scribed a gentle arc in the frosty air.

Incredibly, Bruce was still in the saddle after a complete somersault that at one point had him in the saddle beneath the full weight of a very surprised pony. His unstoppable forward motion, now that he was right-side-up again, threw up the final theatrical touch — a fabulous rooster-tail of snow that arched up behind the horse as it slid on its chest for a further 50 feet, legs splayed apart like a baby giraffe.

The calf descended from the cloudless sky and vanished into the snow for the second time with a gentle PHLUMP!

As fine snow drifted to the ground, Bruce, who was by now completely white, finally lurched out of the saddle as his horse rose to its feet, shaking snow from every crevice. Bernard announced that there was nothing we could do for the calf and we agreed that it was a miracle cure too. We left it to wobble off in search of its peers. The snow had saved everyone from injury except Ron who nearly had a heart attack laughing. We paced out the skid marks from the point where the calf vanished and it was 70 feet as best we could judge. That was the longest, most complicated and most cinematically impressive wreck that any of us had ever seen, and in that spirit, we applauded Bruce and commended him for his skill in staying aboard his delinquent horse. Naturally we asked him why he hadn't simply baled off when his horse plunged off the ridge and he shook his head and said slowly, 'If I coulda thought that fast, I wuddn'ta ridden off the fucken ridge in the first place.'

Chapter 17

I EARN MY SPURS AS A ROPER AND MIDWIFE

My first attempts to rope were pitiful. I couldn't swing the rope without knocking my hat off or slapping the horse's neck with it. I was unable to concentrate on steering the horse and frequently couldn't get within range of the calf for long enough to throw. All my throws missed by a mile and I didn't yet know that I had to retain hold of the rope with my right hand as well as my left in order to dally.

The trick to dallying was to let the rope slide through your throwing hand until it was time to dally and then your hand was in position with the rope correctly held for wrapping around the horn. I just opened my hand at first and let the whole mess fly out. At the same time, I was supposed to be steering with my left hand which held the balance of the rope in a coil. Finally, Ambrosio put me right, but while I concentrated on dallying, my twirling, pitching and riding got worse. I worked hard on the roping dummy but, though I could catch it 50 times in a row, I could not catch calves. I got frustrated and blamed the horse, I swore, I practised at night, I tried other ropes, I swore some more, I watched the others and asked for advice. I practised more. Finally I was able to twirl the rope instinctively and was able to concentrate on riding and throwing.

On the rare occasion that I hit a calf, I was too slow dallying and the calf shook off the loop or else ran right through it. It took weeks of trying before I started to show a little improvement and was able to dally while the calf was at least still in the same county as my empty loop. Each failure hurt my pride and day after day I dreaded the nod from Bernard that said it was my turn to try. The audience was silently sympathetic but they still expected me to pull my weight and wanted me to master the art as much as I did. I felt as if I was under a high ball at Eden Park each time I tried.

Sheer persistence finally paid off and one day, to my intense pleasure, I got everything right and before I could blink, I had a calf plunging and pulling on my rope. I hastily put another few wraps on the horn, determined not to lose my first catch while the others rode up and began to try and catch its hind legs. Ron dismounted and took the medicine from me as Bernard caught the hind legs. I sat back in my saddle and revelled in the comfort of it all. As I watched Ron wrestle with the calf I basked in the feeling of having done my job properly and looked forward to not having to spend all my afternoons climbing up and down from my horse, scrabbling around in the dirt getting butted and kicked, and forever having to race to pack up my medicines and gallop across to the next calf.

Ron removed the loop from the neck and I had all the time in the world to coil it up and then shake out a loop ready for another calf. I watched from my throne as Ron gave the injection and waves of contentment washed over me while he packed up the medicine and handed it to me like a squire to a knight. There is an enormous superiority that any mounted man has when he looks down on a pedestrian and on this occasion I was revelling in that as well as the warm glow of approval that came from the other guys. In typical cowboy fashion, not a word was said about the catch and they treated me with the same nonchalance that greeted all my previous failures. The only sign they gave that I had done well was that at the next calf, Bernard gave me the nod to try before he had thrown himself. I missed it, of course, but from then on, my tally of catches grew in proportion to my attempts. By late January I was getting nearly half my calves and I finally felt I could rib the others a little about their missed throws.

As the winter continued I decided that I was overdue for some shopping. Up until that point, I had only taken the pick-up as far as Scottsbluff for my monthly grocery shopping. Banner County, where the feedlot was located, was underpopulated. It couldn't even support a bar or a gas station. It had a school and a post office but for anything else it was a 50-mile round trip to the nearest town of any size.

Scottsbluff had about 15,000 people and had all the big chain shops like Corral West Ranchwear and Walmart. It was there that I bought my Drizabone-style oilskin slicker for $170 as well as my Wrangler jeans for $7 a pair. (Out west, no true cowboy wears Levis. It's Wranglers or nothing.) I also bought my silk bandanna for $25. That flimsy rag was a godsend on days when the freezing prairie wind came up to howl. It doesn't seem possible that such an insubstantial cloth could save so much body heat, but it was almost as good as a hat when it came to conserving heat. I think it was because it provided insulation to the neck where gallons of blood flow close to the surface instead of deep within the body's core. For the amount of weight and space it occupied it made more sense to carry it than a hat.

Scottsbluff, however, was not the home of Cabelas's. That western and outdoor sporting-goods shop is the biggest in the west and probably the world. It incorporates elements of a museum and zoo as well as acres of neat stuff to buy. It is located next to Interstate 80 at Sydney, Nebraska, about 60 miles from the feedlot. I took a day off and headed out to do some serious shopping. The selection of goods covers every conceivable fishing and shooting doodad as well as cowboy wear. Stuffed animals and fish decorate the walls, period furniture displays modern stock, the gun racks could equip a battalion at least and the bow hunting section would give Rambo fits. Vegetarians be warned, this is a store for carnivores. I had previously spent many an envious hour leafing through its mail-order catalogues and now I had the whole store to browse through. I was like a dog with two dicks.

After spending a full three hours examining everything of interest I began shopping for a hat and a pair of boots. I selected a plain, dark brown, low-crowned, flat-brimmed hat and a pair of Goretex lined, plain brown, low-heeled cowboy boots. I indulged a Mac attack that had been building for four months and then drove 60 miles back to the lot.

I'd spent about $200 but I'd got exactly what I wanted. My old hat was battered and squeezed out of shape and was made from a thinner felt than the new one. I hadn't handled the old one properly; I'd pulled it down by tugging on the brim and I'd lifted it by pinching the crown. It was in a sad shape and I was glad I'd replaced it. The only part of the new hat that I didn't like was the cheap hat band. That was solved when I walked into the barn one morning and noticed that all the horses had suspiciously short tails and manes. Ambrosio had trimmed them to collect hair to plait hatbands with. He wanted to earn a little small change to buy his daughter a swing set and so he'd decided to make some horsehair hatbands. He'd seen some at the Denver stock show for $60 a piece and after examining them he decided that he could do just as well. After washing and combing the hair he set to work to make the tiny intricate plaits that made each band. They were secured with thin nylon thread and then he tied the slip knots that were used to pull the band tight on the hat. Finally he added the tassels to the knots and announced after all this work that they were for sale for $25 each. I was happy to pay that and the final appearance of my hat was breathtakingly debonair. My horse, however, looked moth-eaten for weeks.

Handsome headgear and practical too.

Fine working boots.

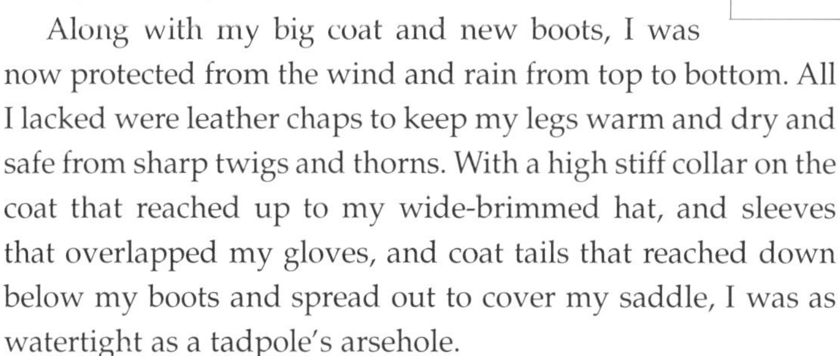

Along with my big coat and new boots, I was now protected from the wind and rain from top to bottom. All I lacked were leather chaps to keep my legs warm and dry and safe from sharp twigs and thorns. With a high stiff collar on the coat that reached up to my wide-brimmed hat, and sleeves that overlapped my gloves, and coat tails that reached down below my boots and spread out to cover my saddle, I was as watertight as a tadpole's arsehole.

I was glad to have kitted myself out with all the items of clothing and tack that I lacked when I began the trip. As winter wound down and the first calves were born to the permanent herd, I started to make plans for the second half of the ride. By now I was driving the feed truck regularly, which was warmer, but I was looking forward to finishing that and resuming riding full time. By mid-March the weather had cheered up enough that I thought I might be able to risk an early start to the trip. That would allow me to ride at a more leisurely pace and still make it to the Mexican border by 30 June. I had rescheduled my flight by phone and booked it for a year after I bought it, which was the last date it was valid for. In due course, the last day at the feedlot arrived and with it, the best roping catch I ever made.

We were checking the second herd of calves in the field across the road from the lot and had just finished and had turned to head back across to the ranch at about 5:30 in the evening of a cold clear day. Far away in a corner, Ron noticed a steer that looked to be moving oddly. We debated leaving it as it was a half mile away, but we had a new girl riding with us, and I didn't think it would look too good on her first day, so I turned and unslung my rope. I knew what the others were thinking, since I often didn't make a catch on my first attempt, and that day I hadn't made any at all. Nevertheless, I took off at a trot and as I got closer I could see that the steer was big and brawny but was also moving slowly and seemed to have some kind of pneumonia. As I got to within 100 yards, I spurred my horse to a gallop and soon the furrows and broken corn stalks were blurring beneath me as we descended the gentle slope towards the line of cattle trailing alongside the boundary fence. The cold air rushed past as I stood up in the stirrups and began to swing the loop. We came up so fast that the little herd hardly had time to begin running before we were upon them. I leant forward and pointed my horse at the steer who was halfway up the line of cattle. Before the horse even knew which animal we were chasing, I had swung the loop three times and fired it at the steer. It struck perfectly. He jumped forward and even as my horse braced and leaned back, the loop tightened around his shoulders and my hand had finished the dally. The rope snapped tight and my horse turned to face the steer who was jerked to a halt at the end of a vibrating rope. A perfect catch.

Like aceing a serve, it was nothing special by world standards, but it had all the precision, economy of effort and baffling speed that stuns the spectators. It may have had a few faults to a purist, but to me it was the best thing I'd ever done as a cowboy and to do it in front of an audience on my last day was a great way to exit the stage. It was a sweet moment to equal the skill of all those born and bred cowboys just once.

The next day I thanked my hosts, gave them a book about New Zealand landscapes and boarded a bus for Pinedale and settled down to plan my route to Mexico. I updated my diary with a brief summary of events over the past five months. Very brief. One page actually. By the time I got to Rock Springs I began to see that I might have begun the trip too soon. Even there, 100 miles south and 2000 feet lower, the spring grass hadn't come through yet. As the bus to Pinedale took me north again I could see that I was about a month ahead of the grass. As I expected, I met Stan at the Wrangler café and on the way out to the ranch he agreed that there was no feed for Spice between here and Colorado, but, fortunately, he said I could stay on the ranch until it was time to leave. Since he was knee-deep in calving work, I thought I'd help out.

Nothing much had changed, although Ian had left and been replaced by Steve. Together, we took care of calving during the day and Stan made the rounds at night. Each morning a new calf or two would be there to greet us in the barn and out in the calving lot, other arrivals would be stumbling around on the frosty grass, blinking in the bright sunlight as their mothers watched us suspiciously.

Each new calf was ear-tagged and logged in the herd records, and after a day or two was turned out with its mother into the large adjacent horse pasture along with the other first- and second-time mothers. All the younger cows were kept in the two large grassy lots close to the barn. They were checked several times each day and night and if they looked to be having difficulty, they were walked to the barn to be helped.

Usually this meant pulling the calf out if it was a big one or straightening it out if it was all jumbled up inside. Once everything was in position, two soft straps were looped over its front feet and the other end of the straps were attached to the hook on the puller. That device was a long pole with the hook and a crank in the middle. By turning the handle the straps around the legs of the calf were pulled steadily backwards and the calf was eased out. The other end of the pole split into a 'Y' shape with a wide strap across the open end. That strap pressed against the cow's back end and provided resistance for the pulling operation. It was a very simple system and worked very well. It was essential to do something to help smallish, unwilling or exhausted cows to deliver largish calves. Although care was taken to breed first-time mothers to smaller bulls, some calves were just too big or else some bulls jumped the fence.

Fishing around inside a cow looking for the front legs of a slippery calf is engrossing work and the rewards of seeing a healthy calf were worth the effort many times over. These calves weighed 50 to 90 pounds at birth. The mothers and babies were kept in smaller pens next to the barn for a day or two until they were well enough to join the herd in the lots or the horse pasture. We fed them sweet hay and kept an eye on them until we were sure that they had mothered up properly.

The other cows, which comprised the main herd, were quartered across the stream from the barn in the home field, a couple of hundred acres of good hay meadow bordered by the stream on one side along with the willow thickets that gave such good protection from the snow and wind and, on the other side, by the swampy bull paddock and a neighbour's field which contained two Goddamn llamas. Those damn things would whistle and snort and spit and race up and down the fence every time any activity occurred, upsetting cattle and cowboys and precipitating riots and rebellion. Once, one of them broke into the home field and started charging fully grown cows and was knocking them down like ninepins! Finally even Stan's patience snapped when the Goddamn llama (that is their correct scientific name around Pinedale) charged him, and his horse took to bucking. He unlimbered his rope and gave it a look that said quite clearly, 'I'm gonna settle your hash you pencil-necked prick.' Cowboys hastily intervened to drive the crazy animal back to its pasture before someone roped and broke its goofy giraffe neck.

The calves in the lots and in the home field had to be checked daily as well. Cows that looked to be having trouble

'Welcome to our world, little guy.' Auntie Moo watches while I make sure the newborn calf gets a drink.

were quietly driven to the barn and assisted, but most of those older mothers calved without fuss or bother. Their babies stayed with them in the home field so we had to dismount and catch them by hand to ear-tag them, though in rare cases I would rope them on foot or even on horseback if they were especially lively.

All calves had to be checked daily and it was not as easy as it looked in the home field, which had never been ploughed and had plenty of ancient tracks and buffalo wallows. Those hollows dated back to the time of the great buffalo migrations that followed the Green River Valley and were now used by cows to conceal their tiny defenceless calves. It was easy to miss seeing up to 30 head of calves that way. The thing we were looking for was scour, a vicious form of diarrhoea that would reduce them to skin and bone in a matter of days and kill them soon after. It was hard to recover from, but easy to treat early on by giving them a couple of pills. They were the size of half a stick of chalk and were administered by putting them in a plastic tube with a plunger in it. Once caught, the tube was pushed into the calf's throat and the pill was ejected. That was repeated for a couple of days until the diarrhoea stopped. By the second or third attempt to catch them, the calves were alive to all the tricks necessary to evade capture.

As soon as my horse appeared in the field, I'd notice beady little eyes peering at me from the edge of the willow trees. A silent retreat into the bushes was all the sign that the old hands gave that the hunt was on. Less-experienced ones ran to their mother's side. Most days I rode the calves alone, as I was about as good as Steve at roping after having so much extra practice on the feedlot. I was riding Zaydo, a handsome palomino that belonged to Bob Bing of the Cowboy Shop. He was a keen amateur roper and a pretty good one too. His horse was dynamite compared to the others I'd ridden. Despite his age and arthritis, Zaydo moved quickly up on the calves and never lost them in a crowd. He was worth thousands of dollars. His only fault was that as soon as the rope was uncoiled he'd get excited and start prancing and trying to trot and this would stir up the cows a bit. He was used to the arena where that was OK, so I didn't hold it against him. He just enjoyed his work and got fired up and that's no cause for complaint in man or beast, but it paid to keep the rope coiled and slung until an invalid was seen and diagnosed.

Only once did he and I come to grief. I'd roped a calf and had dismounted to throw it while Zaydo pulled back and kept the tension on the rope. The calf bucked and pulled away from me even though I had a hand on the rope as I walked up to him. I'd dropped the reins as I usually did when I got off, as Zaydo was too well trained to wander off in the middle of the job. On that occasion, the calf ran sideways in a circle away from me and headed behind Zaydo who didn't turn. The rope brushed him on his behind and Zaydo bolted. Instantly the calf was plucked through the air and crashed to the ground where it remained to be dragged twice around the field and down the road to the barn. As Zaydo took off I made a grab for the reins and again as he passed me after circling the field, but I missed and there was nothing left to do but take off after him on foot.

As I expected, he stopped a quarter-mile away at the cattle guard before the barn with the poor little calf still behind him. Incredibly, the dallies hadn't slipped and the wee tacker was half choked. I raced up and undid the dallies and then released the calf. I left him to tie up Zaydo and when I turned back the calf still hadn't moved. I was sure he wuz a'dyin but I detected faint signs of life so I headed off to find Stan and ask for advice. The calf was covered in cuts and bruises where he'd been dragged through bushes and branches and down the gravel road. There wasn't much I could do about that and I certainly wasn't going to try and shove a scour pill down his throat.

When I told Stan what had happened, he looked at me in disbelief and said, 'Why didn't you tie the reins to the rope?' I said, 'Umm, how do you do that?' He showed me and explained that you never leave a horse to tend a cow alone without tying the reins to the taut rope so that if the calf moves around, the rope drags the reins and the horse's head around to face it at all times. I'd never seen this done before by lone ropers, but then they probably knew their horses a lot better than I knew mine.

By the time we got back to the gate by the barn, the calf had vanished. Stan asked me how badly it was hurt and I said I thought it would die. He agreed but never once did he reproach me for my ignorance and instead he left me to get on with checking the rest of the calves.

It was weeks before I found out what had happened to that calf. Though I looked hard for him every day, he was never found until finally, one day when I was on a different horse, I rode around a clump of willows by a stream and there he was, in front of me. He looked up when he heard us, startled, and then when he saw it wasn't the palomino horse he looked away again. Something, though, made him glance back and this time he recognised me. In a flash he turned and sprinted straight into the centre of a willow thicket and turned to face out at me. As I rode in a circle around him he turned to face me all the time. There was no doubt that he knew who was responsible for his injury and, although he'd made a good recovery, he wasn't about to let it happen again. He never forgot and as long as I rode that herd I'd see him scurrying off to the safety of the willows. I pitied the next person to have to catch him. I'd sown a wind and they would undoubtedly rope a whirlwind.

Chapter 18

Spice and I enjoy the easy life

After five weeks of helping Stan and Steve with the calving, I started to look at the possibility of heading off on my ride. The last item of kit that I wanted to get was an improved saddle blanket. I designed one that extended back behind the saddle and down the sides beneath the pack and saddlebags. It stopped the chafing caused by the swinging bags as well as provided more padding on Spice's hindquarters. I took a trip into Tom's saddle shop and he agreed to make it up in a double layer of artificial fleece. Two weeks later, it was ready, which was a record for anything made by Tom, and I showed it to Spice. He wasn't impressed. I think it was because it was a creamy shade that bordered on pink. Spice was a primary colour sort of horse and none too fond of pastel cladding.

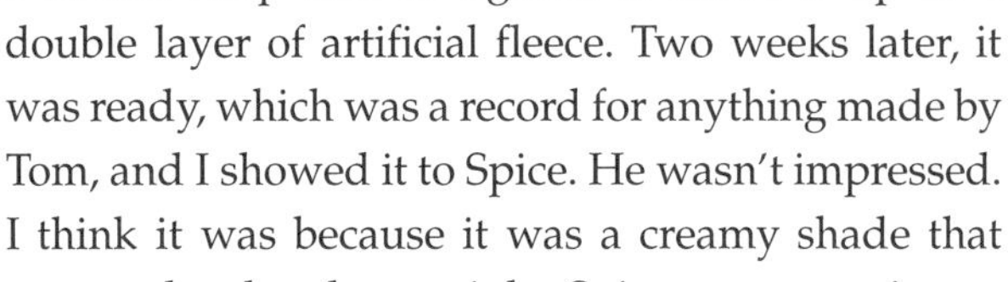

Saying goodbye to Stan at the start of the second half of the journey. Spice reluctantly displays his new saddle pad.

Stan had offered to give Spice and me a lift south to the Wyoming state line because there wasn't going to be any grazing on the mesa. We hoped that the grass would have begun to grow again in the warmer lower regions of Utah and Colorado. That turned out to be true and in Colorado they had even begun to cut hay by the time I got there. It would be a full five months before the last hay would be cut in Pinedale.

By the time Easter rolled around I was champing at the bit and I bulldozed Stan into taking me south on Easter Sunday. I loaded Spice up into the trailer and packed my gear into the pick-up. The trip took all morning but by noon we had made it into

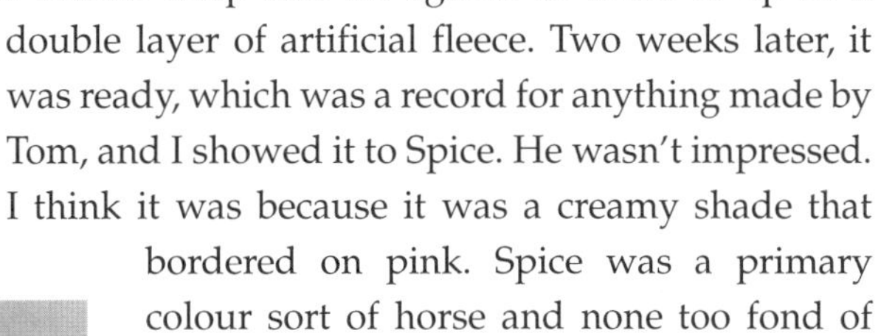

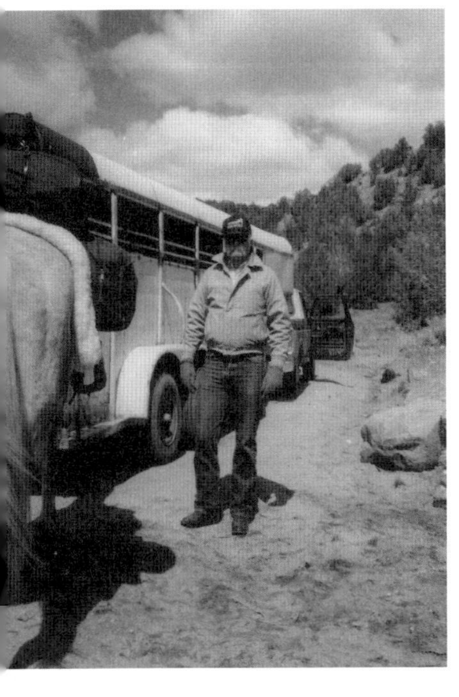

the Flaming Gorge National Park and I was unloading Spice on the banks of the Green River. We were just inside the Utah line about 30 miles west of Colorado near the entrance to the Dinosaur National Monument. I saddled up Spice and then I thanked Stan for all the things he had done to help me. Neither of us were keen on big farewells, so we took a photo each and then I turned and waved goodbye.

Spice and I were soon out of sight as we descended to the edge of the river and began to follow it east. My horse looked non-committal about the resumption of the trip, but there was no question that he knew what was happening. As soon as he felt the saddlebags on his back, he quit dancing around, let out a theatrical sigh, sunk down on his heels and settled in for a long day. I started telling him what the plan was for the next few weeks, about how we were going to walk 2000 miles south to Colorado, New Mexico and Texas, but he wasn't listening. He turned and looked at me as if to say, 'I thought we'd finished with all this last year?' We walked off in silence.

The temperature climbed each day from near freezing to something over 85°F. Each day I walked more than I rode, with the pack across the saddle for Spice's comfort. I wore only jeans, boots and hat until sunburn made me wear my sleeveless quilted vest. Surprisingly, it was cooler than my T-shirt as the air circulated better and it didn't cling so much. In spite of that, I drank 10 or 12 pints of tepid water each day and still felt giddy occasionally as the heat reflected off the white canyon walls in waves. In windless places I'm sure the temperature rose to over 100°F. I piled on the chapstick but I still developed dry lips and the salt oozed out of my boots leaving permanent white stains.

On the third day I started to get concerned as several water holes that I tried were dry and the tributaries of the Yampa River weren't flowing at all. I finally called in at a tiny ranch a couple of miles up a sandy draw and watered at their bore. On the way back out, I was escorted by two huge Angus bulls. They fell in beside us and walked us all the way to the gate. At one point they got ahead of us and when we turned the corner they were standing tail to tail like statues watching us with unblinking eyes. I nervously climbed on to Spice and then took a photo. We detoured around them and they followed us again up to the gate where they watched us until we were out of sight. It was eerie to say the least.

One night I had to water Spice from a ranch trough and then canter back to the whistle where we were camped. A 'whistle' is a small underpass that is fenced so as to funnel cattle into it. With a little bit of work it made an ideal small pasture for Spice to roam and graze freely in. Wherever possible I stopped in pastures and camped where Spice could spend the night off the high-line, but only if I got permission first. There were a few ranchers around that carried guns and wouldn't think twice about using them if you were found trespassing.

In addition to harmless fools like me they had to deal with cattle rustlers, pyromaniac hikers, poachers and incompetent hunters. It was worse for the ranches that were close to big cities — 4WD vehicles regularly tore up their pasture and fishermen left gates open. Apart from ranchers, there were security guards for gold mines, strange federal installations and people called 'Ole Doc' with shotguns, dogs and probably bear-traps too. I took care to remain unseen when trespassing and I never slept on private property without permission.

Eventually I came to the Little Snake River which was flowing and from then on I had no water troubles until we reached the Rio Grande. The desert now changed from glassy white sand to rock and wiry grass tufts, then rough pasture and finally hay fields. We had crossed into Colorado on the third day out and soon after that the road changed to tarmac. I now had a steady 120 miles to go to get back into the mountains. This was all side-of-the-road walking through a couple of small towns and two large ones — Craig (6000) and Steamboat Springs (10,000). The riding was easy and the grazing was plentiful. People would stop on their way and talk to us as we made our way through Sunbeam, Maybell and Hayden. Spice excelled himself with his good behaviour. I had no qualms about leaving him to graze the long acre while I chatted to motorists. Several stopped and offered us places to camp and some even drove out to find us the next day to chat some more. Spice didn't mind as it made an easy day for him.

Dry river bed, Utah–Colorado.

With the load comfortably across the saddle he carried only about 35 pounds and was having a very smooth time, but I wasn't yet footsore and I didn't mind walking.

I ran into a friend of Stan's by the name of Don Jensen in the town of Craig. I'd met him at the ranch when he was passing through on his way to Canada or the Arctic or somewhere. Anything was possible for Don as he was a dynamic guy and travelled all over the place at the drop of a hat. While we ate an ice cream in Burger King, Spice grazed the median strip in the parking lot and every so often would look up to see where I was. It was funny watching him through the dark windows as he couldn't see me but I could see him getting progressively more annoyed. Finally he got thoroughly cheesed off and started to whinny so I said goodbye to Don and dashed out to get him before he made a scene.

Not long after that, when I was camped by the river, Spice caught his fish, but soon after that, I was handed a pack of homemade cookies by a woman who'd seen me riding the day before and had actually gone searching for me that night with a complete dinner. She didn't find me so she was determined to give me afternoon tea the next day. Another woman stopped and handed me a couple of cold cokes and a guy tossed a cold beer at me while we were waiting at some road works. Obviously that was a happy hunting ground for us, but I was still keen to get back to the mountains.

All the advice I received said it was still too early in the season to expect the passes to be free of snow, so I changed my plan and decided to head down the valley of the Blue River until I reached the valleys around Vail. Instead of heading east from Steamboat Springs up into the Routt National Forest I turned south-east. First though, I had to climb from Steamboat up over Rabbit Ears Pass. Steamboat is a ski resort and from the town you can see the runs carved out of the forested slopes. I could also see the snow still on the tops.

As I left the town, ranchers on the outskirts were cutting hay and I waved to them as they sat in shorts and T-shirts on their tractors and swathers. I plodded along in front of Spice, shirtless and sweating in the roasting heat. The road wound steeply up the side of the mountain and when I got to a point where it turned out of view of the town I stopped and took a breather and a panorama of photos showing the green meadows, sparkling ponds and the hay crews working. I turned and stared glumly at the road as it wound higher and higher in front of me. Trucks coming down had the hot stink of burning brake pads and the emergency turn-outs showed signs of recent use. All afternoon I plodded up the road, and by three o'clock I was starting to see small patches of snow lying in the shade of steep road cuttings. By four o'clock we still hadn't reached the top and the snow was continuous. At five I tried to find a place to rest on the side of the road, but the snow was chest deep and Spice couldn't flounder through it. Finally, half an hour later, we broke out on to the top of the west summit and I stopped on the edge of a large car park by a scenic viewpoint. The snow ploughs had thrown a wall of snow up that was over ten feet tall. Beyond it snowmobiles raced back and forth across the flat top of the mountain. Overhead the sun blazed fiercely in the sapphire sky, but the deep snow on the ground chilled the air.

As soon as I stopped, I had to put on more clothing and, after talking to the snowmobilers, it was obvious that this stuff continued all the way to the east summit eight miles away. Not two miles away in a direct line, people in the valley were sunbathing. Here it was a glorious midwinter's day with thousands of acres of snowy forests and lakes extending north into Wyoming. The altitude difference was less than 3000 feet and the pass was only 9400 feet high.

Even though we were only eight miles from the pass, and the road was now fairly flat, it was too far for us to make it before nightfall. I decided to try and find a camp site, but at every attempt Spice balked at the four- or five-foot drifts and I was reluctant to pitch a tent in such inhospitable conditions. Eventually I saw a small clear patch of ground at the top of a cutting where the wind had swept the snow away. I scrambled up and examined it. Pine trees and snow drifts surrounded it on three sides and the steep drop back to the road was the other boundary reducing it to a strip about six feet wide and 40 feet long. As darkness was falling I had few choices so I bustled Spice up the near-vertical slope and tied him off to a high-line that ran the length of the strip. I pitched my tent at one end and filled Spice's nosebag with hay cubes, which were compressed alfalfa briquettes that seem to have a fairly high salt content. At least they tasted salty to me so I'd got them for him when we were sweating a lot in the low country. Later I carried a few lumps of salt for him but he wasn't keen on it. Apart from the hay cubes there was nothing but pine seedlings, which I knew he liked, so I gathered plenty of these and together we made the best meals we could. I even lit a small fire to cheer us up, but by eight o'clock we were both asleep. I rose a few times to check on Spice and watched him standing motionless in the bright moonlight, white and silent against the pine trees just like the snow on the ground.

The walk the next day was magical. We began by wrapping up for the march through the winter snowscape. Frozen lakes and half-buried fences dripping icicles from the wires, dark green branches bent with snow, tracks of hares and birds in the crisp white powder, frosted spider webs, and all around the absolute stillness that absorbed the sound. No wind, no traffic

Mid-winter snow just two miles from hay meadows.

and no noise from either of us as we floated through the cornflour snow. Fabulous.

Eventually we reached the pass and started to descend steeply into the valley. As the day wore on and the temperature climbed, I started to feel footsore for the first time and stopped to soak my feet in an icy stream. By two o'clock all memory of the snow had faded and I was wiping salty sweat out of my eyes. Looking at the map that night I counted up the high mountain passes I would have to cross in Colorado. There were four over 10,000 feet and many smaller ones. Each one required me to climb 3000 or 4000 feet in the morning and then descend at least half that again in order to reach adequate grazing before nightfall. The next day I'd have to slog another 25 miles and get ready to do it again. Generally it wasn't possible to stay on the tops and follow the trails as the snow was too deep except where the roads crossed the passes. This meant that I spent a much greater amount of time on the side of the road than when in Montana or Wyoming, but I also met more people and visited more towns.

Lake built by beavers.

The scenic beauty of central Colorado is spectacular and I wished that I'd been able to range further away from the roads, but, in spite of the restrictions, I saw a lot of the forests and lakes that adorn the mountains. Ghost towns and ski towns, ranches and mines, we saw it all in the weeks that it took to creep south, until finally we reached the lower hills near Pagosa and were able to cross Monarch Pass and head across fairly flat country towards Gunnison and Montrose.

By now it was necessary to get Spice re-shod, so I made enquiries and was directed to a shoer named Russell New. He was about 75 and was still fit enough to talk and fit shoes at the same time. That's no mean feat at any age and if you don't believe me then you ought to try it. Like shearing, you need a strong back. Russell had been doing it for 60 years as a sideline. He started riding when five years old. He stood on a box to mount a burro and rode four miles to school. There was another box at the school for kids to dismount on. He quit school at eight in the third grade because as he put it: 'I didn't have a teacher I liked and I wasn't too fond of the burro neither.' His family left Texas in the late '20s and moved to Colorado in what was generally considered to be the last authentic wagon train in America. An interesting gentleman indeed.

As I got closer to Montrose, I experienced again something that was fairly common on the trip. Misdirection. It took several forms. The most dangerous was the type perfected by the rangers in the National Parks and State Forests. They would cheerfully advise you that a certain route was clear and well marked and in every respect just the best damn trail in the lower 48. I'd set off and halfway along I'd discover that the only bridge across a chasm was down and had been for two or three years. (Something similar occurred when Spice got bogged and nearly drowned in Yellowstone Park after I tried to cross a stream near a bridge that had

Rain and hail brings out the Big Coat at a rest stop near Gunnison, Colorado.

been down for years. The ranger had assured me that all the bridges were fine, and even named the one that was down as being OK. He obviously had never ridden the trail in the last three years.) Alternatively, they would assure you that they had ridden a certain trail and it was fine. Halfway along it would turn to deadfall after a forest fire. Clearly the ranger hadn't ridden the whole length of it, just the start. That sort of stuff was aggravating if there was nowhere to camp come darkness because of delays caused by bad advice freely offered. The general opinion of most ranchers is that government employees like these couldn't find their ass with two hands and a map. I have to agree.

The other common fault was with civilians who couldn't judge distance or time. I was constantly advised that some worthy attraction or fabulous camp site was just five miles down the road. This meant nearly two hours' walking to get there and two more to get back. In a car it was only five minutes each way, and to people who had never walked ten miles at one time in their entire life, my explanation that it was too far was met with blank incomprehension. How could such a little detour, only ten minutes, be too far? Since I'd already walked 2000 miles, they couldn't understand what another ten miles meant and there was no point explaining that 20 miles was a good day's work for me. Perhaps if I looked them in the eye and suggested that there was a great camp site for them to use just 200 miles away and all they'd have to do was sit on their arse and drive there for four hours . . . Perhaps not.

Time was another failing point for many people. One nice woman who stopped on the road to talk told me that she was camped with two horses of her own at a camp site near Montrose. She was just about to set off on her annual horse-trek holiday. Like me she'd started out one day several years before with a single horse and no idea what she was doing. She figured it out in due course and now took off for a month each year on horseback. She invited me to stop overnight at her camp site and said that I'd easily make it to town by dark.

I had some doubts about that and after she left I checked my map and realised that the distance left to cover was about four hours' worth. Shrugging my shoulders I started walking and figured I'd camp as soon as I found a suitable spot as it was late in the afternoon. Like so many others (including me) she'd overestimated the speed of horseback travel, but in her case I felt a bit disappointed as she was so experienced, but especially since she was good looking and fun to talk to. Moaning and complaining to Spice, I was stunned to see a horse trailer suddenly appear in front of me and stop. Out popped the woman, who with great embarrassment, explained that before she was halfway to her camp, she realised I'd never make it in time, so she dashed back and hooked up a trailer to come and fetch us! I loaded up Spice and she drove me ten miles to her camp site. She was so mortified by her mistake that she helped me groom Spice down and apologised to him too. He strained to reach his nosebag, shifted his leg stiffly and generally made like an invalid but a brave one nonetheless. Instantly, tender and caring hands shifted his fodder closer and massaged his leg. After a moment or two he managed a weak but manful smile of gratitude. He was in his element. When it came to playing heart-strings, there was no question who was the first violin and who was merely second fiddle. Later that evening I met the woman's male companion when he showed up to deliver her some feed. Her fiancé in fact. Typical. That stuff never happened to Kevin Costner.

After several weeks of continuous travel, I was starting to get a little tired and I wanted a break from worrying about Spice. I decided that I'd take a few days off in Durango just before I left the mountains and headed into New Mexico. This seemed like a reasonable plan and I thought I would emerge from my rest refreshed and restored. No chance. I should have taken note of the warning signs. Durango is an open-air asylum.

Chapter 19

'Niagara' is my middle name

I was fooled by Ouray. This town, a few days north of Durango, had a genuine livery stable right on the main street and when I rode through I was so pleased at that fact that I decided to stay in town at a motel where I was able to do some essential laundry. Spice was comfortably quartered at the stables and I planned to have a few beers in a bar across the road. Well, it was one of those nights when everything was perfect, good food, witty conversation, a great group of people gathered at the bar and all in all a very pleasant time was had by me. That led me to believe that Durango might be the same. Uh uh.

The first thing I had to do was settle Spice somewhere. I enquired at ranches as I approached the town but there were no stables, which is not surprising as it is a thriving tourist town of 10,000 or more. Its major attraction is a cute little steam train that runs to Silverton and back through some spectacular mountain scenery.

Beautiful Ouray. (Livery barn on main street.)

Since horseback treks are a common recreation for tourists, there were plenty of dude ranches on the outskirts so I settled on one of these about four miles from the town and arranged to put Spice up for three days. After I turned him out in the field, I selected a few things I needed and prepared to walk into town. One of the hands there offered me a lift, but said he wouldn't be leaving for an hour or two. As it was only midday, I didn't mind waiting so I helped him and the other trail guide with a few chores. That turned into a six-hour work party, almost all of the time being spent listening to the older guide telling the most appalling lies about things that had happened to him in the past. By the time the younger guide and I finally got away, I had discovered that, although he was presently out of funds, he had several million dollars in a trust account that his ex-wife had tied up so he couldn't get to it, that he'd killed two CIA agents by mistake in the '70s and that there was a contract out on him, that when he was in the Special Forces during Vietnam, his good friend Bob McNamara (Secretary of Defense of course) had posted a four-star General to Greenland at his request because the General had upset him over his plans to coordinate the raid on Son Tay . . . and on . . . and on . . .

Clearly, he was in dire need of re-booting. According to Brett, the younger guide, he was a pretty fair hand with horses and got on well with the customers, because he didn't feel the need to take them into his confidence the way he did with me. Brett and I eventually loaded up my stuff and headed into town. I checked into the youth hostel and agreed to meet Brett later at a bar for a drink. It only seemed fair, since he had done me a favour and wanted to introduce me to some friends.

After cleaning up, I walked down to the bar and met up with Brett and his buddies. It was like the casting call for the Addams Family. They all looked seriously weird. One was about seven feet tall, another was dressed like a railroad engineer (stripy overalls etc), another was going through a punk phase and was heavily tricked out in leather and metal and another was a woman that looked and sounded like Lee Marvin. Curiously enough though, apart from having the dress sense of Bosnian refugees, they were all perfectly sane and sensible. In fact they were a riot once the alcohol kicked in and by ten o'clock I was struggling to keep up. Brett was feeding me Tequila slammers, which, along with vodka, is a drink I cannot stomach. I didn't want to appear to be a piker, so I ducked off to the toilet and with only a little extra effort, managed to heave up everything but a lung or two. Emptied and refreshed, I returned to the party. By then, things were really moving, outsiders were joining in our singing and dancing and in general we had taken over the whole place. At the implausibly early hour of 1 am the bar announced it was shutting. Along with all the others, I expressed sincere disappointment at this wowserish puritanism, but secretly I was delighted as I hadn't eaten anything since breakfast and the addition of 40 or so shots of mixed spirits since my trip to the men's room was having a remarkable effect on my normally placid digestion. I was sober enough to realise that any more alcohol might kill me and even the load I had on board might need more than two kidneys to wring out.

Fortunately, as we were leaving the bar to head off to another friend's place to continue, Brett got into an argument with a bouncer. I stepped into the breach and managed to turn it from a verbal to a physical dispute. Just as we were about to get the tar whacked out of us, the cavalry arrived and arrested Brett for underage drinking. I was allowed to go home and, with well-concealed relief at avoiding the forced consumption of another gallon of firewater, I stumbled away to bed while the paddy wagon took a large part of the gathering off to the drunk tank.

The next day dawned and I hailed it by chundering. Ten minutes later I was doing it again. And again. By the time the interval between yawns had grown to an hour, I was drier than Thatcher's cabinet. At ten o'clock, there was a kind of false crest. I actually felt well enough to venture more than 30 feet from the toilet. No food or drink was served in the hostel, so I trembled across the road to a café and balanced on a stool at the counter. The waitress took my order for a piece of bread and a glass of orange juice. At this point, I didn't think I was likkered as I was speaking clearly and walking in a straight line. In addition, I'd thrown up at least ten times since the start of the drinking, and I was not convinced that sufficient alcohol had stayed down long enough to reach my brain. All that was utterly wrong. I was as pissed as a fish.

Actually, according to what other guests at the hostel later said, I was talking like a recorded message, walking like Gumby and navigating by Braille. What I didn't know was that my brain had in fact melted under the onslaught of a tidal wave of tequila that had engulfed it the previous night. Specifically, all the booze I had chugged back at two bars, which I do not to this day remember visiting, with the Addams before they were all arrested. I only discovered this two days later when I met Brett and the whole story came out, but to prove how blotto I still was, I did something that amazes me even now. I ordered a glass of milk.

Now milk is wonderful stuff folks, but not on top of a stomach that was still capable of leaching enough alcohol to light up the second stage of the space shuttle. For an instant, as the milk passed over my scorched tonsils and slipped down my bruised and aching throat, I actually felt relief. However, as it passed my battered diaphragm it somehow metamorphosed into a lively form of liquid rubber. Perhaps it was latex not milk. It bounced off the bottom of my stomach and roared back up gathering velocity as it negotiated the corners, until it hit the roof of my mouth at warp speed.

By then I was sprinting for the toilet and arrived in time to spray a fine mist from between my clenched teeth and pinched nose all over the little room. Noisy and athletic convulsions followed for several painful moments. It sounded like Old Faithful in full cry or a pack of hounds underwater. After unloading the toast and juice and milk, I tidied up with the aid of several hundred squares of greaseproof toilet paper. Part-way through I had to stop to blow a crouton of bread out of my nose. As we can all testify, it's the nose that always gets the worst thrashing in these affairs. (Once before when I woke up feeling crook after a hard night, I moped around all day with an aching head and all the other symptoms of a bad case of the flu — sinus congestion, headache etc. Finally after about 14 hours of that I happened to be blowing my nose when a pea shot out. Encouraged, I repeated this with greater force and a piece of bacon flew out of the other side. In seconds, my headache disappeared, I could breathe properly and all was sweetness and light.)

After I'd straightened up and rinsed the froth off my face, I was ready to move back to the counter. My bread and juice were still waiting and, as I was feeling in control of things, I decided to finish them off. Big mistake. Seconds later, I was back in the toilet. I made it with time to spare but that time, I could feel that something terrible was about to happen. The spasm began at my ankles and gathered force as it travelled up my body. With seismic power, a tsunami exploded forth. A white jet blasted out of my head with the thin intensity, speed and concentrated power of a laser. By the grace of God I was back far enough from the bowl so that the rebounding geyser didn't batter me senseless. As it was, the recoil nearly blew me out of the room. I was concentrating on holding my head, as I was convinced that hydraulic pressure alone would blow my eyeballs out. Projectile vomiting usually has to be seen to be believed. Not that time. The wreckage that emerged from the toilet was evidence enough. The aftershocks alone would have killed a horse but, by then, having endured the most violent internal gymnastics possible without actually turning inside out, I was so shattered that, like a completely relaxed person who falls without breaking a bone, the follow-up waves simply flowed through me like oil through water. The torrent that poured forth stunned me. Where was it all coming from? Was I dissolving?

Kneeling there in that small place so far from home, I was alone and afraid. Only the fact that I hadn't eaten for 24 hours stopped me from gushing from every orifice, but for a moment there, I was a human fountain. Slumped on the floor I surveyed the flotsam. I realised that by a lucky chance I was in the women's toilet this time and the supply of paper was undisturbed and adequate to the task. After dabbing away forever, I waited a tense half-hour to prevent another mad dash and when I finally felt as if I was under control, I quivered my way to the counter. I asked for the check and was halfway through counting out change when I felt that first ominous salivation that warns of another attack. I gritted my teeth angrily. I was determined not to succumb again. I couldn't understand where the volume of liquid was coming from and started to feel really concerned. I contemplated asking for an ambulance but I wasn't game to open my mouth long enough to speak to the waitress. After a moment the nausea passed and I began to rise from my seat. Instantly it hit me again. I sat down. Five minutes later I tried again, but with the same result. It began to look as if I was marooned in that café. Every time I got up to leave, I sat down again. Finally, in an attempt to resolve things, I went to the toilet again without result. After that, I stayed upright and made it out the door. I headed for the hostel and made it just ahead of another bout of dry retching. I didn't move more than 20 steps from the toilet for the next four hours.

By mid-afternoon, I realised that I had to do something to control dehydration, starvation and my aching head, which now felt like a microwave. I could have fired bricks inside my skull.

I tottered out to the garden where a group of travellers had gathered over coffee to chat and write letters. They had seen and no doubt heard (passing aircraft had also probably heard) my anguished trips to the toilet and sympathy was larded all over me when I sat down.

Word processors, by the way, lack the right symbols to simulate the sound made by humans in many situations. '*$#!@' will serve to indicate foul language or extreme rage, but only pictograms or original Greek letters could indicate the sort of hopeless gushing/screaming/crying noises I had produced in the hostel toilet. They were heavy on sounds like CHI! MU! IOTA! and the like. Clearly, if French is the language of love, German the language of warfare and Japanese the language of bad banjo playing, then Greek is the language of bodily functions.

Several people looked at me with bashful curiosity and I felt that only their innate decency prevented them from openly photographing me. Feeling utterly washed out, I half-listened to the conversation, head throbbing, pale and wan. Eventually someone enquired whether I was OK and I said that I thought I needed to get something for my head as well as something for my stomach since I hadn't eaten for over 24 hours. This ploy worked and one of the more talkative types offered to take me on the back of his motorbike down to a drugstore. I accepted. Big mistake.

By the time we got downtown I realised that I'd met up with another headcase whose umbrella had well and truly turned inside out. This guy was barking. He told me all about how he had been on the design team for the original Corvette (he was about 40 and therefore would have only been a few years old at the time), about how Princess Di wrote to him, about his relations with major Hollywood stars, Madonna, Nancy Sinatra and Jimmy Carter. I wondered if I was imagining it all, but when we stopped at a Burger King and I got a coffee I was brought back to reality with another trip to the men's room. Five minutes later I'd finished talking to God for the ickypillionth time that day. The loony suggested that I needed vitamins so I let him talk me into buying a couple of those little packets that they sell in the Seven/Eleven stores. Capsules containing all kinds of bee pollen, seaweed extract, yeast pills, eye of newt, wing of bat and so on. On top of four Panadol and half a bottle of Rekamatol it surprised me by staying down. All the way back to the hostel I heard about his time in a rock band and as road manager for the Eagles. Wonderful stuff.

After I got back to the hostel he left to do some laundry and as soon as he was gone, the group of people in the garden asked me what I thought of him. I cautiously said I didn't think he had all of his oars in the water and that maybe he needed to go back to the screw factory to get re-threaded. They laughed and agreed. As I was feeling a little more lively, we started comparing notes about the flaky people we'd met in Durango, and it seemed as though we had all met more headcases there than in all the others we'd ever been to. By the time dinner rolled around, I was well enough to follow them out to a movie and the following day a group of us met for lunch as well. The next two days passed slowly and I gradually recovered my health. Brett was let out of jail along with the Addams Family and no great harm appeared to have been done to anyone. Apart from having to avoid the resident nutter's offers of herbal teas and an ear massage(!) I was left alone to restore my health with a sensible diet of McDonald's and pizza.

The only time I have felt as sick as in Durango, was when I returned to NZ from Australia on a frigate and we followed the path of a tropical cyclone. For three days we pitched up and down and in all that time, after losing the first meal, I ate only a single chocolate biscuit. That also rebounded so quickly that I don't think it even got wet. I lay in my bunk for nearly 72 hours feeling like one of those drinking ducks or the nodding dog that sits on the rear shelf of every second Mexican taxi. When we arrived back in Auckland I asked one of my NCOs how they found the trip. They said they'd had a wonderful time. I viewed this with deep suspicion but discovered it was true. Apparently, because of the restricted space on the homeward journey, they'd been quartered in the petty officers' mess lounge on sofa beds. In the corner, well within arms reach of the beds, was a small refrigerator that held the mess's supply of squirt. 'Squirt' is Navy issue rum and is best served when it is cold so that it is thick and gooey like treacle. At room temperature it probably explodes or melts through the glass or something. It looks like fuel oil and is well over 100 proof. It has a 'best by' date on it, but what it really needs is a 'Hazchem' rating. A bottle of that stuff is simply 40 fluid ounces of Grevious Bodily Harm. The fridge where it is stored is more properly described as a magazine. (The New Zealand navy is one of the last to still issue tots of rum. It is also the only one to have accidentally (?) shelled an Australian Post Office during anti-submarine exercises. These facts are probably not unrelated.) For three days the NCOs stayed in bed, so gibbering drunk that the storm passed unnoticed. They did not throw up. They may have been in danger of spontaneously combusting though. Benevolent sailors generously restocked the fridge each day from their immense reserve bunkers of unconsumed squirt. Wonderful chaps, sailors. Salt of the sea.

Chapter 20

ALL GOOD THINGS . . .

The ride from Durango to Santa Fe was livened up by the sort of crisis that I'd been lucky to escape until then. I was leading Spice past huge fields of lush alfalfa one morning when he began to behave oddly. He kept wanting to stop and seemed to be thirsty. I took him to water twice, but he wouldn't drink. Finally, he stopped, sat down and tried to roll over. I pulled him to his feet before he wrecked the saddle and as he stood there he tried to kick at his belly with his hind legs.

Up and down, up and down, up . . .

It was obvious that something was wrong but I didn't know what. I was at a loss to know what to do, but I figured that the weight of the pack and saddle wasn't going to do any good, so I started to take them off. As soon as they were off, he lay down and rolled over. At that point a penny dropped and I hauled him up again. I thought that if he kept rolling over, he'd twist himself up inside. I'd read a story by James Herriot, where that happened to a cow, which was cured by rolling her over in the opposite direction while grabbing hold of her from the inside! I wasn't up to that so instead I led Spice quickly down to the road and flagged down a car. They saw the problem and drove off to a ranch a mile away to get help. Shortly after, a pick-up stopped and a cowboy and a cowgirl hopped out and started to look Spice over.

They diagnosed colic, and as soon as they said it, I realised how obvious it was. The kicking, groaning, lying and rolling were all classic symptoms that I knew about. Fortunately, by stopping him from rolling and by keeping him walking, at least I hadn't added to his problems. We loaded my gear into the truck and I walked Spice to the ranch. There they were able to dose him with some oil to help him pass the offending alfalfa and they called the vet for a second opinion. It wasn't a bad case so after he was given a painkiller, he was left in a pen too narrow to roll over in and I watched him from where I was pitching my tent.

Jean Bell, the manager of the ranch, kindly let me stay for two days while Spice got over his colic. The cause was probably the sudden change from grass to an abundance of rich green alfalfa that grew along the roadside. Any abrupt change in diet like that can bring on colic attacks that can easily kill a horse in a matter of hours. I checked with a vet as to how to handle it in future and he advised me to carry a painkiller and muscle relaxant, which I did for the rest of the trip.

Thank heavens for people like Jean.

Jean was a super host and I was very grateful to her for helping Spice to get better. On the second day I set out to walk to the nearest town and she met me on the way and gave me a lift there to help me do some shopping and prop up the bar for a couple of hours. I met all her friends and had a great Sunday afternoon. When I left the next day, she gave me a silver spur on a key ring and offered Spice a retirement home on her folks' ranch down in Texas. She swore that he was the spitting image of her own horse who was retired down there as well, and in the photos I had to admit that her horse was a dead ringer for

mine. Jean said Spice even acted the same, which made me wonder why she'd want two of the old fools to look after.

The next week was pretty straightforward. I walked the whole way to Santa Fe to let Spice recover properly as he had another much milder bout of colic on the way. At the edge of the city, I was hoping for a lift through it but no one was available to trailer us across town. Finally, after I'd set out to walk it, in the middle of a rainstorm on the edge of the city, a horse trailer stopped and asked if I'd like a lift! I was delighted to accept and got dropped off near a racecourse on the southern edge of town. I boarded Spice at the stables for two days and once again I checked into the youth hostel.

Mud walls everywhere in Santa Fe.

Santa Fe is a beautiful-looking city, probably the most architecturally pleasing style I've ever seen, but it's too full of tourists and artists to be pleasant to live in. Like Jackson Hole, it's too much of a good thing. I enjoyed my stay, and I liked visiting with the trainers that ran the stable, but I was glad to saddle up and leave as well.

From Santa Fe to Albuquerque is only 50 miles or so, but the climate and terrain changed from coolish foothills to baking flat desert. Indian reservations flanked the main highway and camping sites were few. I pushed hard and by buying a lift at noon on the second day, I was safely south of the city by that afternoon.

The next day I saw the Rio Grande for the first time and crossed the river on a freeway bridge. That far north it is a big river, at least a quarter of a mile wide, but as I followed it south to El Paso it grew ever smaller until it formed the border with Mexico. At that point, because of the heavy demands that irrigation puts on it, it shrinks to just a few inches deep and a few metres wide. Wetback is the wrong word for illegal immigrants crossing here. Dampfoot maybe.

It was my plan to follow the river all the way to the border, but I discovered a bug or three in the ointment. Mosquitoes to be precise. They attacked Spice and me mercilessly. By day and by night they swarmed all over us. Repellent and fly-wipe worked only half as well as we needed and in the end we resorted to travelling as far from the river as possible without getting into the desert.

On one occasion, near Belen, the mozzies were so vicious that Spice and I turned away from the river and sought refuge in the strip of ranches and small holdings that surrounded the town about a mile from the river. Here we were lucky enough to strike the Gulas family, Tom, Becky and their two children, Jesse (8) and Heather (6). They owned a large house with stables and a pony in a field adjoining it. They let me camp the night there and I turned Spice out to play with Heather's pony, Shadow. The two horses got on famously and I spent a happy couple of hours chatting to Tom and Jesse and Heather. The little pony looked to have an ideal sort of a life, with plenty of space to run around in, a little stream and a big shade tree and some sensible and affectionate owners. Tom ran an auto shop in town and seemed like a solid citizen. That night, before I nodded off, I decided that unless a better option presented itself I'd found a home for Spice.

The next morning, I left early and, on the way through town, I met relatives of Becky's who had heard that I was staying with them. They seemed to be as agreeable as Tom's family and I was reassured by that as well, but most of all, I was impressed by Jesse and Heather. Despite being so young, they were both confident and outgoing and weren't the least intimidated by the ragged, bearded stranger who camped in their backyard. They seemed to me to be the product of a good family. I didn't say anything, but I was relieved to have found at least one place that I'd seen first hand that would provide a good home for Spice.

Wall-to-wall fuck-all.

The cultivated portion of the valley was only a thin strip that could be watered from the river, perhaps three miles wide on either side at the most. Beyond it was the fiercest desert in America. For centuries Spaniards travelled up and down the river, trading and prospecting along the Camino Real — the Royal Road that ran from Mexico City to Santa Fe. For hundreds of years, the missions and fortresses dotted the river banks at regular intervals to aid the travellers. In places, though, Indians and drought drove them out and in some areas, settlements were abandoned quickly to the winds and the sun.

One such place was the Jornada Del Muerto. When I reached the edge of it a week later, I saw how difficult it was to traverse. Even with a freeway running parallel to the river in case of an emergency, I didn't feel confident of making it through. There were several reasons.

First, it was hot. Over 90°F plus whatever reflected back off the white sands we walked over. Secondly, the only water I was sure of finding was in the river, which was flanked by mile-wide barriers of impenetrable thorn and mesquite bushes.

By the time I could fight my way to the river for water, find a bank not too steep to drink from and then get back out to continue walking, it was time to go to water again. Ridiculous. Thirdly, the mosquitoes kept me away from the river even if I could bash my way through the scrub to get to the water. Lastly, the name of that section of desert meant 'Journey of the Dead'.

In the mid-1500s, a party of 300 experienced Spanish soldiers attempted to cross the desert in summer. Their remains were found by searchers. They had died of thirst. They were found within a few miles of the river. A combination of heat, fatigue and inability to get to the water had killed them.

There is effectively no difference between horsemen of 400 years ago and those of today so I figured that if tough competent explorers (and the Spaniards of the New World were the hardiest I've ever heard of) could be beaten by the desert, then I'd have to take it very carefully indeed. I noted the many windmills that dotted the horizon, but a lot of them would be turned off for one reason or another and I didn't want to rely on them. It was High Chapparal cattle country, too dry to support even irrigated crops. To arrive at a windmill and to find it empty when the next nearest one might also be dry would be reckless.

Instead I decided to stay as close to the river as possible and then make a dash across the worst of the desert at night. The first time worked OK and I made it through Socorro safely to San Antonio, a town of a couple of hundred. I managed to get Spice shod there, again for free, and the following day I set out through the Bosque Del Apache National Wildlife Refuge and made it to the two-house town of San Marcial by night. I couldn't lie up here by day as there was simply no grass for Spice to eat so I watered him from a hose to his canvas bucket and then drank myself. We set off early the next morning for Elephant Butte Reservoir. By 2 pm, I had covered 30 miles, but I was unable to get down to the river. I took a photo of Spice standing in the middle of the Alamosa River. It was completely dry. That was during the wettest spring in New Mexico since

1945. I had to backtrack four miles to the freeway and follow it down almost to the town of Truth or Consequences. T or C as it's locally known was named after the TV show. They said they'd change the name of the town if the show was broadcast from it. In New Zealand it would be called 'It's in the Bag'. From T or C, I picked up the road to the dam and camped there that night. I stayed there for two days in a state camp ground swimming and reading while Spice wandered around making friends and generally getting in the way of everyone who visited us.

That was the hard part of the trip over with. From then on, there were small towns every ten miles, which meant there was plenty of access to the river each day. I tried not to drink too much of the water from the river or the irrigation ditches but on a hot day it was unavoidable. I was lucky that I never caught any bugs from the ditch water as a little further downstream, Mexicans in Juarez were dying from typhoid.

Each day I walked past huge fields of wheat, onions and other salad vegetables. Hundred-acre groves of pecan trees and orchards of all kinds provided some much-needed shade. I tried to set out early each day and finish before the heat of the afternoon overwhelmed us. When I got to Leasburg Dam, I found a state camp ground that abutted the ruins of an ancient Spanish fort. It was a mixture of desert, cacti and lizards, but down by the river there was an area of grass suitable for Spice so I got permission to camp there. We had arrived just after noon, having started very early that morning. After I had pitched my tent and turned Spice out to graze, we were both drowsing in the heat of the afternoon when a mysterious rumbling became audible beyond the bushes and trees flanking the river. As it got closer I could hear cries and yells and the sound of hooves bearing down on us. As quickly as it had arrived, it faded away. Some minutes later it happened again. Thoroughly intrigued, but unable to see through the trees, I decided to saddle up Spice and discover what it was.

As soon as I crossed the river just downstream from the camp ground I saw that it was a polo game being played on the field opposite us. I trotted Spice around to the side where all the spectators were watching. Snacks and cool drinks were in evidence as were a whole collection of booted and spurred

My noble steed and I mug for Marcie's camera.

'Rah rah Harvard' types. Delicate flowers flitted about in light pastel-coloured skirts shrilly cheering on their menfolk. All in all it was pretty far removed from the company of ranchers, labourers and the like which I'd been keeping up until then, and since I didn't know a soul, I kept myself to myself and settled down to watch the game from atop a hay bale. Spice had plebeian origins too so he joined me at the hay bale seat and commenced to eat the other end of it. While I sipped muddy water from my whisky bottle and Spice chomped away at the furniture the equestrians at the other end gobbled and slurped and ignored us with ease. Every now and then the play would move our way and as the rabble thundered past Spice would look up encouragingly at the ruck. He showed no inclination to join in and seemed to think that his job was to get as much of the seating inside him as he could before the whistle blew. After about an hour of interesting viewing, the players seemed to agree that someone had won and the game moved off the field to the backs of the vehicles where the grub was hoovered back at speed by these scions of the valley. I hitched up my pants and made a dignified withdrawal to the doubtful comfort of my baking tent.

The next major town was Las Cruces, where I put Spice up in the stables of a woman who wanted to interview me for a magazine article. I happily agreed to be taken to dinner by Marcie and allowed a few really staged photos to be taken of me sitting on Spice in my slicker and hat in the melting midday heat. I enjoyed the interview, though I doubt there was enough material to cobble together an article. Whenever I was asked about my motivation for doing the ride I always gave a reason that stayed well away from the 'personal growth/midlife crisis/get in touch with nature' stuff that most people thought had to be the real reason. As a result, I had no message to peddle, no lessons to be learnt and no advice to offer. That kind of killed most interviews. When really pushed for a reason I sometimes lied and like 'Doc' in *Cannery Row* said that it was a bet and I stood to win $100. That satisfied everyone.

Three days later I made it to Canutillo, on the outskirts of El Paso. I was now within a half-day's ride of the border and the trip was nearly finished. As soon as I got to town I found some riding stables that had been recommended to me by Marcie in Las Cruces, and got Spice bedded down. I then got a taxi to the nearest motel and called Tom Gulas in Belen and asked if he wanted a free horse for Jesse. He was surprised but sounded pleased and we agreed that he would come down in two days' time to pick him up.

What are they trying to say?

The old fool, not interested in the view of El Paso, searches for grass.

The next day I returned to the stables and saddled Spice up for the last time. I left the saddlebags off as I planned to ride quickly down to the border and return the same day.

The border is a dangerous place even by day and I didn't want to spend the night there with a horse to look after. At night ranchers don't answer knocks on the door and don't ask questions about shadowy figures and mysterious lights moving across their properties. The drug runners and wetback guides leave the stock alone and often close gates behind them and that's enough for

The horse's ass on Mt Cristo Rey.

the ranchers. To confront them at night is a sure way to become shot. For these reasons I never considered riding through Mexico, although I would love to see it on foot or in a car.

Even by day, armed robberies, muggings and murder are routine since few have legitimate business on the border. Signs, guidebooks, local lore and rumours all recommend that you stay in your car with the windows shut and the doors locked. Since I planned to ride up Mt Cristo Rey, the mountain that separates El Paso, Texas from Juarez, Mexico, I decided that I'd have to do it in daylight and then return to the stables before night.

I set off after breakfast and rode along the banks of the river on its long sweeping curve from south to east. The bend on the river is the start of El Paso, a typical modern American city of a million that is a stone's throw from Juarez, a typical third world city of about the same size. Mt Christo is an old Catholic shrine for pilgrims. The path up to the top is marked at intervals by carved stone plaques showing the stations of the cross. It also has ancient stone houses from Spanish days, but I was only interested in the fact that it represented the clearest and most dramatic view of the border, as well as being within the El Paso city limits, and therefore open to the public. Other areas of the border were not.

Becky, Tom, Heather and Jesse.

By noon I was climbing the steep rocky trail to the statue on the top. It took two hours, but it was worth it. I had a fabulous view of both cities, so close to each other and so completely different. Spice looked out at the river below while I took a few photos. He probably couldn't understand why on earth I had brought him to this desolate rocky lump that obviously didn't lead to any kind of pasture. He bore it all without protest and probably put it down to my well-known faulty judgement.

3500 miles down, 0 to go.

Time was passing and so I took a final photo of myself with the timer and then set off back down the trail to the river. Spice was full of energy when I started to head back north. In no time at all we were galloping along the broad grassy strand that forms the banks of the river. I wondered whether he was still pining for the fjords or whether he was just enjoying a chance to run without the pack on his back. I still don't know, but we made it back to Canutillo in under three hours.

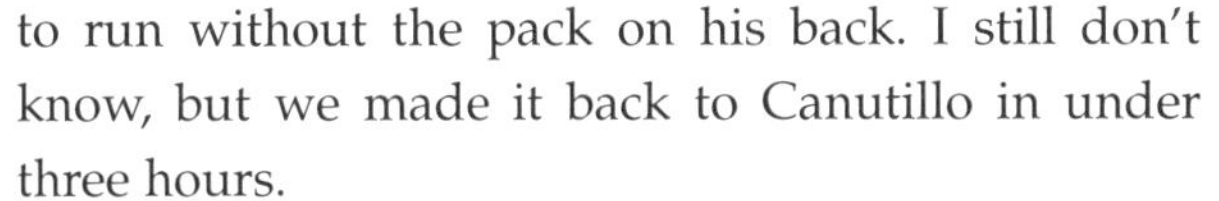

I waited until he had cooled down and then I washed him down with cold water and groomed him thoroughly for the last time. As we went through the familiar routine of brushing his coat, combing his mane and tail, wiping his nose and cleaning and oiling his hooves I was relieved and pleased that it was all over, as well as sad at the same time and for the same reason. I wasn't sure how either of us felt. After he finished eating I fitted his face mask to keep the flies out of his eyes and turned him loose to drink and talk to the other horses. I watched for a little while to make sure that the other horses accepted him and then set off for my motel to pack for the trip back to Britain.

The next day at noon, Tom and Jesse and the family arrived to collect him and take him back to Belen. I showed Jesse how he liked to be groomed and how his saddle should be fitted and how he would stand if you ordered him to, while you got on. I watched him ride around the corral and watched as he grimly tried to rein the old fool in. I gave Spice a few sharp words and told him to behave. Jesse was the only person other than me to ride Spice for nearly a year and I'm sure he knew what it signified. I could see that I was starting to drag things out, so I handed over the bag of tack and grooming gear to Becky and watched as Jesse led him into the trailer. I gave him a pat and they let me take a photo of them and Spice and then they closed the trailer door and that was the last I saw of him. He was Jesse's horse now. The long ride was over.

EPILOGUE

So what came out of that year? I saw the West, that's true. But then I'd already seen the West when I drove through it in my car. The difference was that then I was just another tourist entitled to nothing but the right to pay for ordinary pleasures. With Spice I was shown another world where people threw open houses and ferried us all around and rang friends to tell them we were coming and gave us gear and fed us and never asked for anything but the chance to talk to us and pamper us some more. Spice and I met the people you never normally meet as a tourist. In that respect Spice carried me to a special part of the West that I wouldn't have found on my own.

With him alongside I met cowboys and Indians, rode amongst bear and buffalo, crossed rivers and plains, deserts and mountains, met pretty girls and plenty more. It's true I never danced with wolves, but I didn't plan to. I was just looking for something to do on my summer holiday and I got so much more than I expected. Thanks, you old fool.

Spice is retired now. The last I heard, he was still with Jesse, Heather, Tom, Becky and Shadow at his home in Belen. He's probably under the shade tree now dreaming of snow and pine trees like an old dog dreams of hunting. Jesse writes regularly and sends photos of him. It is great to see him. He looks fine and I'm sure he will for a while yet. Not many others have done what he's done. Even when pioneers were riding the length and breadth of the United States, not many took one horse all the way without a packhorse or a spare saddle horse to help out. He's a credit to his breed. Whatever it is. And now, as they say, 'He's world famous . . . in New Zealand.'

I guess like me, he didn't know enough to quit. Still, we did it, and at the start, that's something no one would have bet on except me. I suppose that's the only thing you might learn from this story — if you want to try something, make the best plan you can, take advice from experts and then, whether you're ready or not, jump in and do it. That's all. Just do it.